BETRAYAL FROM THE EAST

BETRAYAL FROM THE EAST

The Inside Story of Japanese Spies in America

by ALAN HYND

NEW YORK

ROBERT M. McBRIDE & COMPANY

AMERICAN BOOK—STRATFORD PRESS, INC., NEW YORK

To My Mother and Father
And Walter Winchell
Three American Patriots

This is by way of expressing my appreciation for valuable assistance given to me in the preparation of this book by four critical ladies: Edythe Campbell, Evelyn Hynd, Lorna Popkin and Elizabeth Taber.

The author also wishes to express his appreciation to a long list of friends in official, semi-official and private life in the United States, Mexico, Panama, South America, the Hawaiian Islands and Japan for direct assistance, since 1937, in the preparation of this book. Among these is his friend, Stephen W. Birmingham, veteran investigator of the New York Police Department and of various committees of the Congress and, during the last world war, Special Agent in Charge of Field Agents in Military Intelligence, Washington.

Alan Hynd

New York City
September 1, 1943

Table of Contents

CHAPTER I

The Code in the Shop Window

LATE ONE AFTERNOON in the first week of December,
1932—nine years before the Japanese attack on Pearl
Harbor—two men, one of them a Japanese, stopped to
examine a window display of printing and stationery at
a small shop in the vicinity of the Hudson Terminal
Building at 30 Church Street, New York City. The proprietor of the establishment, an industrious man who
took pride in his work, was busy arranging some new
samples of letterheads and calling cards so as to make
the window display as eye-catching as possible, and was
therefore not aware of the presence of the Japanese
and his white companion until they entered.

"Do you change your displays quite often?" the white
man asked. The words were clipped and precise, but
were spoken with an unmistakable German accent.

The stationer looked up. "I make a new display every
couple of weeks or so," he replied. "People passing by
here don't stop to look at anything they've seen before,
and if they don't stop they don't buy."

"Permit me to introduce myself," said the man who
had asked the question. He reached into his wallet and
proffered a card bearing the name:

Count Hermann von Kietel

9

The stationer, impressed, saw that Count von Kietel's appearance was quite in keeping with his conception of a German nobleman. The Count, who was in his early forties, was tall and slim and of military bearing.

"How would you like to make up some personal stationery for me?" he asked. "Then you could display a sample of it and impress your customers."

"You mean you would give me permission to display a sample of work I did for you?" asked the proprietor. The Count turned to the Japanese and gave his companion what the stationer was one day to recall as a knowing glance.

"Most certainly you have my permission," said Count von Kietel. "And now let me see samples of the type you have."

The Japanese began to take an interest in what was going on when the stationer handed the Count a book showing the variety of type faces available to customers. He brought out a little notebook and made several jottings in it, obviously relating to the type faces. Then the Count placed an order for one hundred letterheads, bearing his name and his address, which was in the three-hundred block on Park Avenue.

The stationer said that the work would be completed three days hence, as a special favor to the Count, and asked if he wished the letterheads delivered to him. "Oh, no," said von Kietel, "I'll call for them. My offices are just around the corner."

The stationer concluded that the Count was very democratic, and he looked after the two men as they hurried off into the late afternoon crowds going toward Hudson Terminal—one of the busiest spots in the world. It occurred to him that they made an odd pair,

the German and the Japanese. The Count's Chester-
field hung on him like a garment in a tailor's window,
his derby was worn with an air, and the way he carried
his walking stick would have in itself set him apart. His
silent Japanese friend, by contrast, looked shoddy, not
because his clothes were cheap or not well cared for, but
because his squat body had thrown them out of shape.

Three days later, the Count appeared alone at the
stationery shop. He expressed satisfaction with the letterheads, and asked the stationer when he would next
be changing displays. "Not until Saturday morning,"
was the reply. This was Thursday.

"I would prefer it if you put up one of my letterheads
immediately," said von Kietel.

"Just as you say, Count." Von Kietel waited until the
letterhead was thumb-tacked in a prominent position in
the window.

The next morning, precisely at nine o'clock, a Japanese—not the same man who had appeared with Von
Kietel—stopped at the stationery shop and began to
study the samples on display. The stationer stepped outside and asked if there was anything he could do for
him, but the Japanese replied, "No, just looking." He
remained until his gaze came upon Count von Kietel's
letterhead. He studied it briefly, smiled to the stationer
and departed.

At one that afternoon, when the stationer came back
from lunch, an assistant who had taken care of business
for him during his absence remarked that two Japanese
had stopped by, within a few minutes of each other.
Each had been just looking, and each had seemed to be
interested in the Von Kietel letterhead.

Thousands of people, either arriving in lower Manhattan or departing for Jersey City and other northern New Jersey communities linked to New York by the Hudson River tubes, passed the stationery shop during rush hours. Every conceivable type of human being was to be found in the Hudson Terminal crowds, and it therefore did not occur to the stationer that there was anything unusual about three Japanese stopping to examine his samples within a space of four hours.

Exactly ten days after he had first appeared, Count von Kietel called at the shop again. He was accompanied this time by a dark-complexioned, striking-looking woman wearing a mink coat. "This is my wife, the Countess," he announced to the stationer. "She is thinking of having some stationery made up for her personal use. Would you be kind enough to show her your type book?"

While the Countess was examining the book and making notes on a little pad that she had taken from her purse, the Count decided that he wanted some calling cards. He selected for these the same style of type that he had chosen for his stationery, only in a smaller point. The selection made, he and his wife departed, the Countess having not seen any type faces that appealed to her.

When, four afternoons later, the Count called for his cards, he made certain that one of them was tacked up in the window for display. He insisted that the card be placed directly underneath the sample of his letterhead, and that the left edge of the card be in line with the left edge of the paper, despite the fact that the stationer recommended that a better effect would be achieved if the card was centered either at the bottom or the top of the paper.

The next day, between nine and one o'clock, four Japanese stopped briefly to study the stationery displays. The proprietor and his assistant couldn't be certain that any of these Japanese were the same as those who had stopped by eleven days previously, since all Japanese looked more or less alike to them.

The Count called again the very next afternoon. This time he ordered more stationery, only he selected a type face different from that he had chosen for the first letterheads. Once again he was insistent that the letterheads be completed within seventy-two hours.

It so happened that the letterheads were not ready when von Kietel called three days later, and he was quick to show his displeasure. He said that he would call again the following Monday, and added that if his order was not ready for delivery at that time that he would henceforth take his business elsewhere.

The following Monday—a morning on which the second letterhead would have been on display had the order been completed when the Count had wanted it— a Japanese appeared at the window of the stationery shop, glanced quickly at the display, and passed on. Two others appeared before noon and did the same thing. That afternoon, when von Kietel picked up his order, he waited while the stationer replaced the sample of the first letterhead with one of the second. While the change was being made, the Count said, "I believe you were right about where the card should go; I agree that it would look better above the letterhead, and in the middle." The arrangement was carried out in accordance with the Count's suggestion, and the next morning, between nine o'clock and noon, three Japanese stopped by and studied the arrangement.

By this time it had occurred to the proprietor that perhaps there was more to this patronage of the Count's than met the eye. The stationer, however, was too pressed by the routine of his life to devote much time to a possible analysis of the singular goings-on; but certainly he had no idea that the selection of type for the letterheads and the calling card and the display arrangements that the Count insisted on had any connection with a code system bearing on Japanese espionage in the United States of America.

In the three-hundred block on Park Avenue, at one of the most fashionable addresses in New York, Count and Countess von Kietel had, since leasing one of the best apartments in the building in the fall of 1932, become objects of considerable speculation to both tenants and employees. The Count had set aside one room of the apartment as a study. It soon became known among the building employees that neither of the two American maids whom the von Kietels employed was ever allowed in this study under any circumstances. A butler whom they had brought with them from Germany— a severe-looking bald-headed man of about fifty—always personally took care of keeping the Count's study in order. This aroused the suspicion of the maids—a suspicion they communicated to other domestics in the building—since the butler, whose name was Manfred, was something of a slave-driver and usually performed few chores that he could get anyone else to do.

The butler, in fact, was rapidly taking on the proportions of one of those sinister butlers you see in the movies. Obviously, there was more to Manfred than appeared on the surface. One night a curious maid in an apartment across the court from the German's quarters

looked into the von Kietel living room through a pair
of opera glasses, borrowed from her mistress, and saw
the Count, the Countess and the butler sitting around
quite informally, drinking and talking. Inasmuch as the
von Kietels went out of their way to impress neighbors
and building employees with the idea that they were
very superior people, it seemed hardly likely that they
would engage in informalities with anyone so far below
them socially as a mere butler.

Among employees and domestics in the Park Avenue
building, it was common gossip that Count von Kietel
never arose until early afternoon. One of the maids
usually served him breakfast in bed between one o'clock
and half-past one. After breakfast the Count glanced
through the morning newspapers and the early editions
of the afternoon newspapers. In addition, he was an
avid reader of a long list of magazines that he subscribed
to—mostly technical magazines. He always kept a large
pair of scissors—scissors that were quite distinctive in
that the handles were of eighteen-karat gold—on his
night table. It was his custom to clip items from the
newspapers and the magazines with these scissors.

It was only natural that the two American maids
eventually became curious about what the German was
clipping from the publications. But they were unable to
satisfy their curiosity, since the Count always removed
the clippings to the room from which the maids were
barred; and Manfred, the butler, habitually made it a
point personally to take charge of the disposal of any
magazine or newspaper from which the Count had
clipped something.

The two maids did not sleep in, as did Manfred; they
left each night after dinner. Dinner was usually served

promptly at eight and there were never guests. But frequently there were guests later in the evening—Japanese guests. Sometimes one or more Japanese would arrive between nine and ten o'clock, and not depart until almost dawn. It was obvious to building employees and to domestics in the apartment house who slept in that the Count and the Countess entertained their visitors for the most part in the Count's study, for during the occasions when the Germans had Japanese visitors the apartment was in darkness except for this one room, the windows of which faced the court. There were special blinds on the windows of the study—blinds similar to those which residents of the Atlantic seaboard and the Pacific coast were to use for blackout purposes some years later, after Pearl Harbor—but small chinks of light were nevertheless visible from certain points in the court and from certain other apartments.

Up until the middle of March, 1933, Count von Kietel continued to order stationery and calling cards at the shop near the Hudson Terminal. He continued to insist upon personally supervising the displays of samples of the work done for him. Japanese continued to stop at the display window, just looking.

In the middle of March, the Count told the stationer that he was moving to Washington. Accordingly, he had stationery and calling cards made up bearing the words:

Count Hermann von Kietel
Alban Towers
Washington, D.C.

When the new stationery and cards were completed, the Count made certain that samples of them were prominently displayed in the window and that all previous samples of work done for him were destroyed. The stationer, of course, had no way of knowing that the Count's new address in the nation's capital was the same as that of the private quarters of the Naval Attaché of the Japanese Embassy in Washington.

As a matter of fact (it was one day to be officially ascertained), the Count and Countess did not actually move to Washington. What happened was that von Kietel frequently took a midnight train for the capital, spent the day at fashionable Alban Towers on Massachusetts Avenue, visiting the luxurious fourth-floor apartment there of Commander Josiyuki Itimiya of the Japanese Navy, who was Naval Attaché of the Japanese Embassy, and then returned to New York on the midnight train. It wasn't until the following year—1934—that Commander Itimiya was to emerge as a figure of paramount importance to the United States Office of Naval Intelligence.

From the middle of March, 1933, until the middle of September of the same year, the stationer near the Hudson Terminal did not see von Kietel. When the Count did appear again after a six-month absence, he announced that he was changing his address again. He was, he said, moving to the Pacific Coast. Thus, a few days later, when Japanese in the Hudson Terminal crowds stopped briefly at the stationer's window, just looking, they saw on display there stationery and calling cards reading:

H. von Kietel
117½ Weller Street
Los Angeles

The Count explained to the stationer that he was dropping his title. "The use of a title isn't very democratic," were the words of explanation he actually used. The stationer thought very highly of this display of democracy on the part of the nobleman, not realizing that the Count's alteration of his own name meant that he was dropping deeper into the espionage shadows, all the better to accomplish what he had come to the United States for.

While the Count's activities in New York and in Washington were not to come to official light for some time, the Count himself walked right into the sights of the Federal Bureau of Investigation the moment he appeared at the newest address he had given to the New York stationer—117½ Weller Street, Los Angeles. This was a three-story house, over the double-entrance doors of which was the legend:

DR. FURUSAWA MEDICAL BUILDING

The medical building, or private hospital, had been under surveillance by the F.B.I. since the previous year, 1932, when a language student at the University of Southern California—one Takuya Torii—had been killed in a traffic accident at Gardena, California. When the body of the young man, who had supposedly been just another of the many Japanese studying the American language and customs in our universities, was removed to an undertaking parlor, pending investigation, things had begun to happen. At an hour when no word of the accident had yet appeared in either the San Francisco or Los Angeles papers, an avalanche of telephone calls began coming in to the undertaking parlor from important Japanese as far distant as San Francisco. The telephone callers hadn't seemed to be so concerned about the death of young Torii as they had been exercised as to whether or not he had been carrying a briefcase when killed. The student had not been carrying a briefcase, but he had been carrying a wallet in which were certain papers of a highly confidential nature.

The Los Angeles Field Office of the F.B.I. was tipped off by an employee of the undertaking parlor about the intense interest of important Japanese in the death of the obscure language student. The F.B.I. agent in charge in Los Angeles instructed the personnel of the undertaking parlor not to show the contents of the student's wallet to anyone until a G-Man got there. When the wallet was examined it was learned that young Torii was a Lieutenant Commander in the Imperial Japanese Navy "on active duty." This was the first concrete evidence that any Federal investigative agency had come upon to corroborate a long-standing suspicion that Japanese language students in American universities were actually engaged in espionage activities for the Japanese government.

Thus it was that the F.B.I. agent at the undertaking parlor had made it a point to trace one particular telephone call—another inquiry about the dead language student—that came in shortly after his arrival. The call had come from a telephone at 117½ Weller Street—the new address that Count von Kietel was to give to the New York stationer more than a year later. Naturally the F.B.I. was more than routinely interested when it was learned that the Weller Street address was that of a private hospital run by a Japanese.

And so, in October, 1933, when the distinguished-looking Count von Kietel called at the private hospital on Weller Street, he forthwith became a figure of importance to the F.B.I., although they did not yet know who he was. Anyone who called at the medical building was by this time a figure of importance because of what the F.B.I. had found out, since the Gardena traffic accident the year before, about Dr. Takashi Furusawa, the proprietor of the private hospital.

Dr. Furusawa was tall for his race, standing almost five feet nine inches. He was in his early fifties, of military bearing and extremely genial manner, and he had the habit of carrying a gold-headed cane with a distinctive air. In the Japanese colony of Los Angeles he was regarded as an authority on Japanese art. His office and consulting room were on the first floor of the Weller Street house; the second floor was taken up by a private hospital; and the Doctor and his wife Sachiko lived on the top floor.

During the entire time that Dr. Furusawa's medical building had been under surveillance, none but Japanese patients had been seen to go into the place. Many of the patients drove up in taxis and, it was clear to watching G-Men, approached the building in a manner that indicated they had never been there before. Such visitors had often remained in the building for several days, despite the fact that their appearance when entering and when leaving indicated that they were in robust health.

After a time, the G-Men began following such patients. Several of them, after a few days or a week or two at Dr. Furusawa's, during which time they never set foot outside of the building, left just in time to catch steamers bound for the Orient from Los Angeles, San

Francisco or Seattle. When it became obvious that a "patient" of Dr. Furusawa was going to sail, G-Men would manage to get one or more photographs of him with a special camera concealed in the palm of the hand or, if circumstances permitted, with a camera equipped with a telescopic lens. If there was time to have the film developed prior to the departure of the vessel, the picture was sent along by a courier planted on the ship; if there was not time, the undeveloped film was given to the courier to be developed at sea.

Meanwhile, while the ship was at sea, the intelligence was relayed to our consular officials in Japan, and when the "patient" arrived in Nippon an American agent was at the ship to get the picture of him from the courier. It was thus possible to trail the "patient" in the Orient and establish his true identity, since such people usually traveled under assumed names while making a trans-Pacific crossing or while staying in the United States. In instance after instance, Dr. Furusawa's "patients" were found to be officers of the Imperial Japanese Navy or men suspected in Tokyo of being Japanese intelligence operatives.

Of no less interest to the investigators than Dr. Furusawa was the physician's attractive wife Sachiko. She was active in the affairs of the Southern California Federation of Women's Societies, the offices of which were located at 117 North San Pedro Street; she was an officer and an "adviser" of the Koyasan Buddhist Temple Women's Society, which met regularly in a Buddhist temple at 342 East First Street; and she was one of the prime movers of the Los Angeles branch of the Women's Patriotic Society of Japan, the headquarters of which was located at 7425 Franklin Avenue, which in turn was the official residence of the Japanese Consul.

The F.B.I., in fact, had quite a dossier on Sachiko Furusawa, which had slowly but certainly been fattening since the medical building on Weller Street and its occupants and visitors had been objects of surveillance. From authentic sources in both California and the Orient, it had been established that Sachiko had precisely the sort of background, personality, mental equipment and connections that would make her an ideal Japanese Mata Hari. She was the daughter of low-caste parents, having been born near Tokyo about 1887, which made her at least forty-five years of age in 1933. She was remarkably young-looking for the middle forties, however, a fact no doubt due principally to the extreme care she had always taken of herself and her long-time participation in fencing, wrestling and dancing. She was tiny and doll-like, and possessed of an electric grace. Had it not been for her yellow skin, she could have been taken for a Spaniard or a member of one of the other Latin races; in fact, in photographs, she looked very much like a Spaniard. Her clothes were always the last word in chic, and her coiffure the very latest thought up by the fashionable hairdressers of Los Angeles and Beverly Hills.

When Sachiko Furusawa was about fifteen, her remarkable beauty had attracted the attention of a much older man—a Commander in the Japanese Navy. But, according to information in the F.B.I. dossier, and believed to be authentic, Sachiko, although she had never been out of Japan at the time of her marriage to the officer, had somehow picked up and embraced occidental ideas. Among other things, she had not been content with the obscure role played by the average Japanese wife; she had insisted upon remaining a personality in her own right. And so, after less than five years of marriage, Sachiko left her husband and came to the United States. For a while she worked as a chambermaid in Los Angeles hotels, then as a waitress in various restaurants in Little Tokyo. It had been while working as a waitress that she met Takashi Furusawa, a very industrious Japanese who was then a medical student in his late twenties. Young Furusawa had hardly one nickel to rub against another and was having a difficult time earning enough money at odd jobs to complete his medical course. The pretty young waitress, however, had saved quite a bit of money from large tips she had received from restaurant customers whom she had favored in one way or another. If Furusawa was attracted to her beauty, she was attracted to his brains. She saw great possibilities if the two of them merged their destinies. The young medical student, too, had occidental ideas; he wanted a wife who was a personality in her own right.

Thus it was that when Furusawa was through medical school, he and Sachiko, who had in the meantime obtained a divorce from the Naval Commander, were married. At first he had the same struggle that most young doctors have in getting started. But he developed into an outstanding physician and surgeon and presently his fame spread throughout Little Tokyo. After some years passed, Dr. Furusawa became president of the Southern California Japanese Physicians' Association. He went in for sports, including golf and fishing, and eventually became president of the Southern California Fishing Club.

It can be seen, then, that the German, Count von

Kietel, was in direct contact with a Japanese man and a Japanese woman who would unquestionably assume, from the investigative point of view, greater and more sinister stature as time went along. By observing the entrance of the medical building on Weller Street from their secret vantage points, the F.B.I. was able to make the deduction that important Japanese in the Los Angeles area had been looking forward with keen interest to the arrival of Count von Kietel on the Pacific Coast. Two nights after the German's arrival a large party was given for him by Dr. and Mrs. Furusawa at the Kawafuku Tei, a well-known Japanese restaurant in Los Angeles. Attachés of the Imperial Japanese Consulate and other important men of their country were present.

During the remainder of von Kietel's stay at the Weller Street medical building, attachés of the Japanese consulates in Los Angeles, San Francisco, Portland and Seattle visited the private hospital. Among those in attendance at a departure dinner that Dr. and Mrs. Furusawa gave in von Kietel's honor, also at the Kawafuku Tei, was an alien Japanese named Momota Okura, who was a Japanese war veteran and the commandant of the Southern California Imperial Veterans' Association, most of whose members were, as Japanese citizens and war veterans, under the jurisdiction of the Imperial Japanese Government. What eventually made Okura of more than passing interest to the F.B.I. was the fact that his son, Kiyoshi P. Okura, a Nisei (or American-born Japanese) was an examiner for the Los Angeles Civil Service Commission—a routine recorded fact that was one day to become of vital importance.

When von Kietel departed for New York in November, 1933—almost a year since he had first put in an appearance at the stationery shop near Manhattan's Hudson Terminal—it was obvious that the purpose of his visit to the United States was to act as a go-between to link up and pool German and Japanese intelligence, probably confining himself to naval intelligence. The F.B.I. had looked into the Count's background through attachés of the American Embassy in Berlin and had established beyond doubt that he was one of the ranking figures of German naval intelligence. Von Kietel was an assumed name, the F.B.I. learned. But the man using the name was a real and typical Baltic Count whose wealthy, powerful and autocratic family had always thrown a good deal of weight around, no matter what kind of government was in power. The Count, however, had been one of the early climbers aboard the Hitler bandwagon. In the last war he had been an officer in the lines and then an intelligence operative. Between wars he had for the most part devoted himself to vast commercial holdings, but at the same time, with an eye to the future, he had remained in close touch with the realm of treachery throughout the Reich. Thus he was, all things considered, an ideal advance agent for the coming day of doom.

CHAPTER 2

The Plotters of
East Sixty-sixth Street

WHEN THE COUNT arrived in New York on the Twentieth Century Limited, after his stay in Los Angeles, he was trailed by F.B.I. agents to his Park Avenue apartment, which was only a five-minute taxi ride from the terminal. Now, for the first time, the F.B.I. knew the Count's New York address. They soon learned about Manfred, the bald-headed butler, about the Japanese visitors that the Count and Countess frequently entertained until almost daylight, and about the secret study.

Von Kietel had been back only a short time when Manfred, the butler, came out of the building and entered a taxi. He was trailed to the offices of the South Manchuria Railway on East Forty-second Street. These offices were staffed entirely by Japanese, and the F.B.I. agents had no way of learning just who it was that Manfred was meeting there.

Late that same night, agents covering the Park Avenue apartment building observed a sly-looking Japanese visiting the Count's quarters. By this time, although it was only a few hours after the Count's arrival, two agents were not only covering the building; they were living in it. Their apartment was directly across the court from the rear part of the von Keitel apartment.

Posing as out-of-town businessmen, they were not known as G-Men even to the superintendent of the building.

By trailing the Count's visitor when he left about two o'clock in the morning, the G-Men ascertained that his name was Roy Akagi, manager of the New York offices of the South Manchuria Railway. This added up. Akagi undoubtedly was the man whom Manfred, the butler, had met immediately after the nobleman's arrival from California. It was only reasonable to suppose, therefore, that Akagi was engaged in some sort of espionage work.

Akagi forthwith became a person to reckon with. He lived in a palatial home in suburban Mount Vernon, in Westchester County. There was more than an acre of landscaped grounds around the house, and even the most casual observation would have indicated that the occupant of the place was not merely wealthy, but extremely wealthy. The F.B.I. had no way of finding out, immediately at least, what Akagi's salary was as manager of the New York offices of the Japanese railway line. Not that it was necessary to get such information, for obviously a man in such a post, even at a top salary, could never have maintained on his salary alone the kind of establishment that Akagi was keeping up. The answer was simple, at least to the G-Men. Roy Akagi's job with the railway was merely a front to cover up espionage activities; the difference between his salary and the amount necessary to maintain his scale of living was unquestionably being made up by the Japanese government.

Two days after Akagi first came into the picture for the F.B.I., he was followed to the Whitehall Building at 17 Battery Place, in downtown Manhattan. This was the address of the German Consulate. Akagi didn't go into the Consulate, but proceeded to the Whitehall Club, a swank eating place in the building. There he met a man whom the G-Man recognized as George Gyssling, German Vice Consul in New York. On the surface, Gyssling's job seemed comparatively unimportant, and his salary was only about twenty-five hundred dollars a year in American money. Yet the fact that there was a meeting between him and Akagi promptly made him, like Akagi, a man whom there was more to than met the eye.

Gyssling was only twenty-eight years old. He was a compact fellow with a hard, square face and a Heidelberg haircut. He was married, and had two children, but his wife and family had remained in Germany. Although he had been occupying the post of Vice Consul since March, 1933—more than eight months prior to his contact with Akagi—the F.B.I. had known about him since February, 1932, at which time he had come from Germany as a member of the German bobsled team competing in the Olympic Games at Lake Placid, New York. There Gyssling had won the personal unpopularity sweepstakes hands down by his obnoxious behavior in the Lake Placid Club. Among other things, he had made sarcastic remarks about the American depression and the unemployment situation, usually topping things off with the unsolicited advice that what we needed was a great man like Adolf Hitler.

Concurrently with the appearance of Akagi and Gyssling in the investigative focus in New York, there emerged on the Pacific Coast a new and fascinating figure—a visitor to Dr. Furusawa's medical building on

Weller Street. He was Torzichi Kono, one-time valet, chauffeur and general handyman for an alien motion-picture star. Kono, a squat little man of middle age whose black eyes, peering from behind silver-rimmed glasses, missed nothing, looked like first-class investigative material, not only because he visited Dr. Furusawa's establishment but because a cursory check-up on the man disclosed that he lived in a sumptuous flat on Bronson Street in Hollywood and drove two custom-built cars, yet had not worked in years. At the request of the F.B.I., the State Department sent a coded cable-gram to the American Embassy in Tokyo asking that intelligence operatives working out of the Embassy find out what, if anything, was known about Kono in the Japanese capital. An answer within a few days brought the not surprising news that the one-time butler visited Tokyo annually to spend his vacation at a luxurious estate that he maintained on the outskirts of the city. Moreover, an Americanized Japanese, who, if he wasn't Kono was certainly Kono's double, had been seen visiting the Japanese Foreign Office at times concurrent with Kono's visits to the Orient.

On the New York scene, F.B.I. agents were marking time, awaiting the developments that they felt sure would come. Von Kietel was no longer working his code from the window of the stationery shop near Hudson Terminal for the simple reason that the shop had meanwhile gone out of business for lack of trade. The watchers had not yet come into possession of the facts relating to von Kietel's visits to the stationer's, and they were therefore quite curious about a visit made by von Kietel to an empty store near the Hudson Terminal.

One night late in December, 1933, Akagi, who had

been working overtime in his office, was trailed to the entrance of the Foreign Press Association at 110 West Fifty-seventh Street. There he waited until he was joined by a second Japanese, who came out of the quarters of the press association, which numbered in its membership the ranking correspondents in the United States of most of the important foreign newspapers and press services.

The person whom Akagi picked up was quickly spotted as Chuzo Hagiwara, the New York chief of Domei, the leading news service of Japan. Hagiwara, upon his arrival in this country not long before, had naturally been the subject of a casual inspection by the F.B.I., since he had been chosen for a key post by an important organization whose headquarters were in a potential enemy country. Hagiwara was that rarity among Japanese—a man who couldn't hold his liquor. He was of middle age and rather fat, and his eyes, which always seemed to be partly closed, gave him the appearance of being always sleepy. In fact, staff members of the Associated Press, where Hagiwara had his office, and colleagues at the Foreign Press Association had conferred upon him the appellation of "Sleepy Joe." Naturally, Sleepy Joe was placed high on the suspect list as soon as he was seen meeting Akagi.

Akagi and Hagiwara proceeded by taxicab to 5 East Sixty-sixth Street, just off Fifth Avenue. This was a large private home that had in 1933 opened as The German Club. G-Men had never succeeded in getting inside this club, but they knew that it was one of the most exclusive organizations in New York. They had learned that it was sumptuously furnished, that it boasted a bar and a dining room second to none in

Manhattan, and that in private rooms on the upper floors Germans coming to New York from Europe—persons of obvious importance but ones whose identities were not always easily established since ship passenger lists might list them under fictitious names—were ensconced during their stay, apparently to have privacy for some very sound reason of their own.

G-Men who had long suspected a Japanese-German tie-up for espionage purposes had, up until this December night in 1933, been keeping an eye in vain on The German Club for the appearance there of Japanese. But either Akagi or Sleepy Joe Hagiwara, or both, had an open sesame to the place, for they were immediately ushered in by a doorman. Shortly after the arrival of the two Japanese, Gyssling, the arrogant little German Vice Consul, entered the club. And a little while later Count von Kietel went in.

It was along toward two in the morning when von Kietel and Akagi came out together and then proceeded to their homes. Not until an hour later did Gyssling and Sleepy Joe Hagiwara emerge from the club. Both men were in a high state of intoxication. They walked unsteadily, arm in arm, the few steps west to Fifth Avenue, which here parallels the east side of Central Park. They crossed the Avenue and walked along on the park side until they came to a monument which was erected after the last World War in memory of American heroes.

For a couple of minutes the German and the Japanese stood in front of the monument, regarding it drunkenly and talking to each other in German. It so happened that two G-Men who were watching them could not understand German, but what the Vice

Consul and Sleepy Joe of Domei were discussing presently became apparent when they desecrated the monument by an act that is technically known in police circles
as disorderly conduct. The act, while it was committed
by two men who were drunk, was nevertheless very significant to the G-Men, since it seemed to be an expression of the deep-seated feelings of two persons high in
espionage circles—one for Japan, the other for Germany.

The situation, then, in December, 1933—eight years
before Pearl Harbor—was in official focus to the extent
that Count von Kietel was a key figure so far as German-
Japanese espionage work was concerned. Although von
Kietel's precise role in the drama that was being en-
acted was far from clear, it was a foregone conclusion
that eventually the Baltic nobleman would pay rich
dividends to those who stuck on his trail. In fact, he
had already turned up figures of undeniable importance—men like Vice Consul Gyssling, Roy Akagi and
Sleepy Joe Hagiwara. And, while the F.B.I. had had
Doctor Furusawa, the Los Angeles physician, and the
Doctor's wife under surveillance prior to the time that
the Count had walked under the official magnifying
glass, the fact that von Kietel had dealings with the
Furusawas was in itself of paramount importance.

On the Pacific Coast, Dr. Furusawa's pretty wife was
very busy. Whenever a Japanese passenger liner put
into the harbor of Los Angeles, its officers were usually
entertained by Mrs. Furusawa at the Kawafuku Tei,
that same restaurant where the Furusawas had given
dinners for the visiting Count von Kietel. Sometimes
Mrs. Furusawa would be driven down to the pier of an
incoming ship and would personally welcome the officers. On other occasions she would board a ship just

before its departure for the Orient, and at such times she usually carried either a briefcase or a large package on board and came off without it.

In May, 1934, Kono, the former butler of the screen star, was observed one night passing through several red lights as he drove one of his custom-built cars from Hollywood to the medical building on Weller Street. Obviously, Mr. Kono had received an urgent message of some kind from Dr. Furusawa. He entrained for San Francisco on a midnight limited, with G-Men following him. In that city the next morning he hired a taxicab and was driven to the campus of Stanford University. He succeeded in shaking G-Men when he popped into one of the dormitories on the campus, and the investigators could not pick up his trail until he came out again. It seemed certain that Kono had been visiting one of the Japanese students, but there were quite a few at the university and the F.B.I. simply could not spare the agents to investigate all of them at that time.

When Kono returned to Los Angeles, and to Dr. Furusawa's, he remained only overnight, then took a transcontinental limited for Chicago. G-Men trailing him across the country in relays followed him from Chicago to New York on the Twentieth Century. In New York, the investigators were hardly surprised to see Kono proceeding to the apartment house on Park Avenue where Count von Kietel lived. That night, Kono and the Count caught a midnight train for Washington. When they arrived in the capital, they went to the Alban Towers on Massachusetts Avenue—the residence of Commander Josiyuki Itimiya of the Japanese Navy, the Naval Attaché of the Japanese Embassy.

G-Men had some time previously succeeded in obtaining several good pictures of the Count by means of cameras equipped with telescopic lenses and the small, specially made cameras that F.B.I. agents conceal in the palms of their hands. Thus it was that while Kono and the Count were visiting Commander Itimiya's quarters on the fourth floor of the Alban Towers, G-Men learned, by getting identification of von Kietel's photographs, that he had visited the Japanese Attaché.

Whatever it was that Kono and von Kietel had to take up with Commander Itimiya was discussed within a few hours. The remainder of the day was taken up by sightseeing in Washington; and Mr. Kono, who carried a little camera with him, took several pictures of public buildings. Kono and the Count left on the overnight train for New York. The next afternoon Kono took a train for the Pacific Coast, and the Count, after seeing him off, went by taxi to Akagi's office. Apparently he acquainted Akagi with the purpose of Kono's visit to the east, for as soon as the Count left Akagi's office, the Japanese hurried over to the Associated Press, where he met Sleepy Joe Hagiwara, apparently by an appointment made by telephone. Thereupon Hagiwara went down to the German Consulate at Battery Place, remaining there until about seven o'clock in the evening, when he and Vice Consul Gyssling went to The German Club on East Sixty-sixth Street.

During the course of the evening, Akagi and von Kietel also went into The German Club, as did two attachés of the Japanese Consulate in New York. This marked the first time that as many as four Japanese had ever been observed in The German Club simultaneously, and G-Men realized that something big was in the wind, although they didn't know what.

The impression that various governmental investigative agencies pool their information is erroneous. This does not mean, necessarily, that there is friction between one agency and another; oftentimes one agency is not aware that another agency is working simultaneously on the same case, or on some other angle of the same case. Since the war a high degree of coordination has, of course, been necessary, but that situation did not prevail in 1934. For one thing, both the F.B.I. and the Office of Naval Intelligence were badly understaffed at that time, and it was all many of the agents could do to keep up with their work, let alone confer with other agencies until such time as it was absolutely necessary. Nor were certain operatives within one organization necessarily acquainted with work being carried on by other operatives in the very same organization. All of which is by way of explaining the series of letters that follow, and the series of events that follow the letters.

CONSULATE OF JAPAN

Chamber of Commerce Bldg.

1151 South Broadway

LOS ANGELES, CALIFORNIA

June 28, 1934.

Mr. H. A. Van Norman,
Chief Engineer and General Manager,
Bureau of Water Works & Supply,
209 South Broadway,
Los Angeles, California

Dear Sir:

If you have any books or pamphlets covering the entire water system of this city we shall appreciate it very much if you will kindly forward us copies of same.

We should like to have information that will explain

every point of the system, including reservoirs, quantity of water, supply, number of consumers, filtering, purifying, pipe pressure, kind of pipes used, office organization, number of employees, etc.

We shall be glad to defray any expenses in this connection.

Thanking you for your kind attention to our request, we are

> Very truly yours,
> CONSULATE OF JAPAN
> By: (Signed) K. Kageyama,
>   Chancellor

*   *   *

June 29, 1934

United States Department of Justice
Division of Investigation
PO Box 536
Los Angeles
California

Gentlemen:

Attached is a copy of a letter received from the office of the Consulate of Japan. It seems to me that they are asking for a great deal of detailed information. Maybe it is only for use in the development of water systems in their country, but before I comply with their request, if I do at all, I would like to have an expression from your office as to the advisability of supplying the data asked for.

> Yours very truly,
> (Signed) H. A. Van Norman
>   Chief Engineer & General Manager

HAV
CRM
Enclosure

*   *   *

U. S. Department of Justice
Bureau of Investigation
P.O. Box 536
LOS ANGELES, CALIFORNIA

July 6, 1934

Mr. H. A. Van Norman
Chief Engineer & General Manager
Bureau of Water Works & Supply
Department of Water and Power
Los Angeles, California

Dear Sir:

I am in receipt of your recent letter dated June 29, 1934, enclosing a copy of a letter you received from the Consulate of Japan, dated June 28, 1934, requesting to be advised the details of the water system in the City of Los Angeles.

It is not within the jurisdiction of this office to pass on the question as regarding whether it would be advisable to supply the data to the Consulate of Japan and, therefore, I regret that I can be of no help to you in connection with this matter.

I would suggest that you communicate with the Commanding Officer, Fort MacArthur, San Pedro, Calif., as that officer may be interested in knowing about this situation.

Very truly yours,
(Signed) J. E. P. Dunn
Special Agent in Charge

BES-T

* * *

July 10, 1934.

Commanding Officer
United States Army
Fort MacArthur
San Pedro
California

Sir:

Attached is copy of a letter received from the office of the Consulate of Japan. It seems to me that they are asking for a great deal of detailed information. Maybe it is only for use in the development of water systems in their country, but before I comply with their request, if I do at all, I would like to have an expression from your office as to the advisability of supplying the data asked for.

Yours very truly,
(Signed) H. A. Van Norman
Chief Engineer & General Manager

HAV
CRM
Enclosure

*   *   *

In reply
refer to:
671 G

HEADQUARTERS

HARBOR DEFENSES OF LOS ANGELES

OFFICE OF THE COMMANDING OFFICER

Fort MacArthur, San Pedro, Calif.
July 11, 1934.

Mr. H. A. Van Norman,
Chief Engineer & General Manager,
Bureau of Water Works & Supply,
Department of Water & Power,
207 South Broadway,
Los Angeles, California

My dear Mr. Van Norman:

In reply to your letter of July 10th, enclosing a copy of a request from the Chancellor, Consulate of Japan, for information concerning the water system of the City of Los Angeles, it is requested that you defer action on the above request until the matter can be referred to higher Government officials.

On this date I am forwarding your letter, together with enclosure, to the Commanding General, Ninth Corps Area,

Presidio of San Francisco, requesting instructions. Pending receipt of such instructions I would consider it extremely inadvisable to supply the data asked for.

Your thoughtfulness in referring this request to me is appreciated.

Very sincerely yours,

(Signed) H. R. Oldfield

Lt. Colonel, 63rd Coast Artillery
Commanding

*   *   *

In reply
refer to:

HEADQUARTERS

HARBOR DEFENSES OF LOS ANGELES

OFFICE OF THE COMMANDING OFFICER

Fort MacArthur, San Pedro, Calif.
July 17, 1934.

Mr. H. A. Van Norman
Chief Engineer & General Manager
Bureau of Water Works & Supply
Department of Water Works & Power
207 South Broadway
Los Angeles, California

My dear Mr. Van Norman:

Referring further to your letter of July 10 enclosing copy of the request from the Chancellor, Consulate of Japan, for information concerning the water supply system of the City of Los Angeles, you are advised that instructions have been received from the Commanding General, Ninth Corps Area, Presidio of San Francisco, California, this date, to the effect that the request of the Japanese Consulate does not pertain to the peace time functions of the regular army and that, therefore, military personnel are not in a position to advise the Bureau of Water Works and Supply, Los Angeles, in this matter.

It is suggested that you contact the Bureau of Investigation of the Department of Justice, located in the Federal Building, Los Angeles. It is believed that office can either advise you on the matter or refer you to the proper government official.

Thanking you for your interest in this matter, I am

> Very truly yours,
> (Signed) H. R. Oldfield
>> Lt. Colonel, 63rd Coast Artillery
>> Commanding

RHK/rk

It is not a matter of record what expressions Mr. Van Norman gave voice to upon completion of this cycle of remarkable correspondence, nor is it recorded how much his blood pressure went up. It is a matter of record, though, that Mr. Kageyama, the Chancellor of the Japanese Consulate, made repeated calls to Mr. Van Norman's office to ask how soon, please, would the information about the Los Angeles water system be forthcoming. Mr. Van Norman stalled Mr. Kageyama off as long as possible, on a polite basis; but when Mr. Kageyama showed a singular lack of talent at taking a hint Mr. Van Norman was obliged to become firm and let the Japanese know that the information was not going to be forthcoming so long as he, Mr. Van Norman, was the chief engineer and general manager of the Bureau of Water Works and Supply. "Oh," said Mr. Kageyama, "so disappointed." Development of later events, however, was to prove that Mr. Kageyama succeeded in overcoming his disappointment by means of one of the boldest moves to come to light in the entire investigation into Japanese espionage and sabotage activities in the U.S.A.

The agents trailing Count von Kietel and his bald-headed butler, Manfred, noticed the Count visiting a printing and stationery shop on Third Avenue. When he had gone, the proprietor was questioned. The Count had ordered some stationery. When he called for it several days later, he began the same routine which he had gone through with in dealing with the stationer near the Hudson Terminal. Operatives took rooms in the neighborhood of the Third Avenue stationer and noticed Japanese stopping to look in the shop window where the Count had instructed the stationer to place samples of the von Kietel letterheads and calling cards.

This time the agents were in a position to follow the Japanese and find out what was going on. Over a period of weeks, during which the Count ordered more letterheads and more calling cards, in various styles of type, the watchers were able to establish the fact that the arrangement of the von Kietel work in the shop window, as supervised by the Count himself, was a code, the basis of which had obviously been carefully pre-arranged. The sum and substance of the whole thing was that when a Japanese espionage worker looked in the window and made note of the latest arrangement of the von Kietel letterheads and calling cards, he was able to ascertain, from the style of type and from the juxtaposition of the calling card and the letterhead, just where he was to go to meet a German who would turn information over to him. Apparently the days of the week on which information was to be exchanged had been established in advance, as had areas of the city where the exchanges were to take place. The style of type that the Count chose indicated which one of several predesignated areas—such an area usually covered several city blocks—was to be used. The position of the calling card in relation to the letterhead would indicate to the Japanese the street intersection in a given area where he could expect to be met by a German who would turn information over to him.

The Count's idea of enlisting the unwitting assistance of a stationer was a clever one. Over a period of time, numerous contacts between Japanese and Germans were made. The meetings always took place in spots that wouldn't normally have been covered, and had the F.B.I. not gotten on to the Count's trail when he had first appeared at Dr. Furusawa's medical building in Los Angeles a considerable time previously nothing would have been known about the street-corner meetings between the Germans and the Japanese.

The men who were meeting on street corners were the small fry in the espionage set-up, but vitally important nevertheless. These small fry had vital information passed on to them by the big men—men who by the very fact that they were big men could not afford to move around as easily as more nondescript individuals. For example, Roy Akagi, the manager of the South Manchuria Railway's New York offices, might have had very legitimate contact with such a man as Sleepy Joe Hagiwara, New York chief of Domei, and vice versa. But Akagi and Hagiwara would naturally have been too clever to meet a German at, for instance, a street intersection on the lower East Side.

The F.B.I. was curious to find out if the Count had used the window code anywhere else before he had come under their observation. It was recalled that he had gone one time to the vicinity of Hudson Terminal, his destination having apparently been a store that was vacant when he got there. So the F.B.I. looked up former occupants of the place and eventually they located the stationer with whom the Count had done business in December, 1932, and for almost a year afterward. It was too late, of course, to get onto the trail of the several Japanese who had stopped to look at the window displays in the shop. But it was not too late to attempt to get an identification of the Japanese who had accompanied the Count on the occasion of his first visit there.

The F.B.I. had by this time collected quite a gallery of photographs of Japanese—such men as Sleepy Joe Hagiwara, Roy Akagi, various consular attachés and other Japanese newspapermen working in New York. A stack of such photographs was handed to the stationer without regard to the order in which the pictures had been placed. The F.B.I., as a matter of fact, didn't have the slightest idea as to who the Count's Japanese companion might have been.

The stationer shuffled through the photographs thoughtfully. When he had gone more than halfway through the stack, he picked one out. "This is the man who came with the Count that day in 1932," he said simply.

An agent took a look at the picture and smiled. "You're absolutely certain that this was the man?" he asked the stationer.

"Absolutely certain."

"Thanks very much," said the agent. He didn't mention to the stationer the identity of the subject in the photograph. The man was Roy Akagi of the South Manchuria Railway.

CHAPTER 3

Intrigue in Chevy Chase

ON THE AFTERNOON of August 1, 1934—more than seven years before the Japanese attack on Pearl Harbor—a copy of *The Service of Information and Security,* a highly confidential book printed expressly for a very limited number of high ranking Navy officers, disappeared from Room 2649 of the Navy Building on Constitution Avenue in Washington.

Lieutenant Commander Leslie G. Gehres of the Naval Examining Board, from whose desk the volume had vanished, knew that the book had been within arm's length less than an hour before. To make matters more mysterious, Lieutenant Commander Gehres had not left his desk between the time that he had last noticed the book and the startling moment when he saw that it was gone.

There had been only one other person in the room during that time—forty-one-year-old John S. Farnsworth, a former Lieutenant Commander in the Navy. Farnsworth, a dapper, high-flying, hard-drinking man of considerable personal charm, had been cashiered out of the service seven years previously after a scandal arising from his borrowing money from an enlisted man.

Though Farnsworth was in official disgrace, the attractiveness of his personality enabled him to continue close friendships with a large number of officers he had known back in his Annapolis days. He had often dropped in to chat with Lieutenant Commander Gehres. "I can't get the Navy out of my blood," was a remark that he frequently made to the Examining Board officer. He had, in fact, spoken those very words when he smilingly departed from Room 2649 about five minutes before Lieutenant Commander Gehres noticed that the book was missing.

Deciding that Farnsworth had taken the book, no doubt by mistake, Lieutenant Commander Gehres felt relieved. The officer's first fear had been that the volume had somehow been removed by an agent of a foreign power—Japan, for instance. Even as far back as 1934 the United States Navy Department wasn't deluding itself into believing that Commander Josiyuki Itimiya of the Japanese Navy—the same Commander Itimiya that Count von Kietel and Kono had called on at his personal quarters in the Alban Towers—wouldn't have given anything in his possession, including even his life, for a copy of *The Service of Information and Security.*

The Office of Naval Intelligence, which did not know that an F.B.I. trail had also led to the Alban Towers, had learned from maids employed in the apartment building that Commander Itimiya had never permitted them to set foot in two rooms of the apartment when they went to clean. The O.N.I. had further learned from the maids that acrid odors had seeped out under the closed and locked doors of the rooms in question—odors that the maids associated with a photographic dark room. Lieutenant Commander Gehres could well imagine Commander Itimiya's happiness if the Japanese could somehow get a copy of *The Service of Information and Security,* photostat its pages, have the book returned, and send the photostats to Tokyo in a diplomatic pouch.

The volume on naval information and security was one of the most secret publications extant. Even the printers who set the type for it had been thoroughly investigated beforehand, and the portions of the manuscript assigned to any one printer were deliberately so unrelated that they made little sense by themselves. The binding of the volume, as well as the printing, had been carried on under the strictest official surveillance. *The Service of Information and Security* distilled between its covers all existing confidential data relating to equipment, tactics, smoke screens, formations and the findings arrived at in the latest secret maneuvers, all of which, to a foreign power, would have added up to one of the prize plums in the whole history of espionage.

Later in the day, Lieutenant Ccmmander Gehres succeeded in reaching the cashiered officer by telephone at the Farnsworth home on Meadow Lane in fashionable suburban Chevy Chase.

"This is Les, Jack," said Gehres. "Say, did you walk off with my *Service of Information and Security* by mistake?"

Farnsworth laughed at his friend's discomfiture. "Gee, Les," he said, "I'm terribly sorry. I thought I mentioned to you that I was borrowing it."

"It's quite all right, Jack," Gehres replied, so relieved at having located the book that he momentarily forgot that it should never have been in Farnsworth's possession, even though the Navy was, in Farnsworth's words, in his blood. "But get it back to me first thing in the morning, will you?"

"Sure," said Farnsworth. "I just want to go through it tonight for some tactics. I've never given up hope of getting reinstated, you know."

When Farnsworth returned the book to Gehres the next morning his eyes were bloodshot and his face was drawn, as if he had slept very little if at all. Apparently he divined that Gehres was noting his appearance.

"I haven't had a wink of sleep," Farnsworth said. "I couldn't put this book down. The newest tactical stuff is fascinating."

Several days later, Captain William D. Puleston, Chief of the Office of Naval Intelligence, frowned when he glanced at a routine report which detailed the circumstances by which the copy of the book had been out of Lieutenant Commander Gehres' office overnight. Captain Puleston held John S. Farnsworth in something less than esteem. He buzzed for an aide, sent for the dossier on Farnsworth and began to take a quick refresher course on the cashiered officer.

John S. Farnsworth was born in Cincinnati of mid-Western parents. After graduating from high school at the head of his class, he developed an ambition to become a naval officer. He succeeded in getting an appointment with his Congressman, the late Nicholas Longworth, and so impressed Longworth with his personality that the Congressman got him an appointment to Annapolis. That was in 1911, when Jack Farnsworth was eighteen. Although he concentrated on such extra-curricular activities as grog and girls while at the Naval Academy, Farnsworth nevertheless attained brilliant

scholastic marks and was graduated in 1915. The Naval
Academy year book of 1915 had some prophetic things
to say about young Lieutenant Farnsworth. One statement about him was:

Had he lived long ago he would have been famous for
his desperate deeds and hairbreadth escapes.

Another sentence read:

His daring and reckless conduct has been the utter despair
of the executive department during his four-year sojourn.

The poet Milton was quoted by way of a frank
prophecy that Farnsworth would never utilize to the
utmost his native ability:

"He can, I know, but doubt to think he will."

In the first World War Lieutenant Farnsworth saw
service on several destroyers. In 1922, having become
interested in aviation, he returned to Annapolis to
study aeronautical engineering, and in 1923 pursued
the subject further at the Massachusetts Institute of
Technology. Upon leaving M.I.T. he was promoted to
the rank of Lieutenant Commander and taught at the
Navy's air school at Pensacola, Florida. Subsequently he
was placed in command of a squadron base at Norfolk,
Virginia.

Somewhere along the line Farnsworth had become a
hard drinker. He had married a society girl, but wasn't
proving much of a success as a husband. Some of his
friends thought that his charm was fatal to him. He was
tall, trim and dashing. His head was well shaped and
his hair closely cropped and prematurely gray at the
temples. Facially, he bore more than a passing resem-

blance to the late John Gilbert, the movie star. People instinctively liked him and he was the life of the party at cocktail gatherings in fashionable homes and in speak-easies. His charm resulted in his invitation to so many parties that he was soon spending virtually all of his Lieutenant Commander's pay entertaining those who had entertained him.

Farnsworth began borrowing money from other officers and eventually, when he had exhausted his credit in his own official circles, he borrowed fifty dollars from an enlisted man. It is against Navy regulations for an officer even to fraternize with an enlisted man, let alone borrow money from him. It is worse yet when an officer refuses to repay the loan and finds himself in the embarrassing position of being dunned by a gob. The sailor made a formal complaint to Farnsworth's superiors and the Lieutenant Commander was court-martialed out of the service in 1927, at the age of thirty-four.

What the source of Farnsworth's income had been between the time of his court-martial and the day he had taken the book from the Examining Board was a disturbing question to Captain Puleston. The dossier on Farnsworth disclosed the arresting fact that the cashiered officer seemed to have more money now than he had ever had, despite the fact that his means of support was invisible to the naked eye. The O.N.I., which had not had Farnsworth under surveillance but which had nevertheless routinely noted anything about him that came to its attention, had observed that Farnsworth had lately been in the habit of passing crisp one-hundred-dollar bills over the bars of the swanky bistros that he patronized.

The O.N.I. was short-handed, and it wasn't practicable to assign agents to cover Farnsworth twenty-four hours a day, particularly in view of the fact that whatever suspicions Captain Puleston had in his mind were not based on anything really tangible. So the Captain's instructions were that Farnsworth's activities in general be noted against the possible day when it would be necessary to assign full-time shadows to him.

For several months after the incident of the borrowed book, Farnsworth, still having unexplained access to a seemingly inexhaustible supply of one-hundred-dollar bills, turned up at various naval points between Newport News and Boston. He sought out old acquaintances and was quick to suggest that they join him in a drink. Invariably, Farnsworth switched the conversation to naval matters, still insisting that the Navy was in his blood and that he hoped for eventual reinstatement. How was a new gun performing in tests? How many knots was that new destroyer making? What salient truth had been arrived at in the most recent secret maneuvers?

Such questions rolled endlessly from the tongue of Jack Farnsworth. When an O.N.I. agent happened to be looking on, he would see Farnsworth's dark eyebrows lowering attentively as he listened to the answers he was getting. Then Farnsworth would finger the waxed ends of the trim sandy mustache he had recently grown and think up other questions to ask.

It was entirely possible, of course, that Farnsworth was sincere in his expressed desire to be reinstated and that he was meeting friends to keep abreast of naval developments with reinstatement in mind. Nonetheless, Captain Puleston came to the conclusion that Farnsworth was coming into possession of entirely too much information, even for a man who had one time been an officer in the Navy and who, theoretically, could be trusted with information relating to national security. And so specific instructions were issued by the O.N.I. to all naval officers forbidding them to discuss naval matters with John S. Farnsworth.

In the meantime, out in Long Beach, California two young men—one in his twenties, the other not yet eighteen—sat talking in a small Murphy-bed apartment on Linden Street. The two—Harry Thomas Thompson, formerly a yeoman in the United States Navy, and Willard James Turntine, a boy from St. Louis—had recently struck up an acquaintance, and Thompson, the stronger-willed of the two, had invited young Turntine to come and live with him.

At first the boy from St. Louis, who had gone west on the break beams of a freight train, only to find it difficult to obtain employment there, had regarded Harry Thompson as a Samaritan extending a helping hand. But lately young Turntine had come to have certain misgivings about the one-time yeoman in the Navy. For one thing, he wondered about the source of Thompson's income. Thompson was always flush with cash, but where he got it was a matter of deepening mystery to his friend.

"Harry," asked young Turntine this night the two sat talking, "what do you work at, anyway?"

"I'll tell you one of these days," said Thompson, "because I think you can be of help to me." The former yeoman was an even-featured, run-of-the-mill young man whose outstanding characteristic was his eyes. They were gray, cold and crafty.

Young Turntine now began to attach significance for the first time to certain activities of Thompson during the several months of their acquaintanceship. Turntine had, for no particular reason, accompanied Thompson when the erstwhile yeoman visited friends aboard the dreadnaughts *Colorado, Mississippi* and *Texas,* the radio-controlled target ship *Utah* and the destroyer *Brooks,* anchored at various times off San Diego and San Pedro. On these visits he had heard Thompson ask of acquaintances in the Navy what now seemed to have been very pointed questions—questions relating to gunnery and tactical information and to maneuvers of the Pacific fleet.

Once when Thompson and Turntine were in San Diego, the former took a small pair of scissors from his pocket and snipped off part of a sheet of paper from a Naval Training Office bulletin board. Turntine had read the contents before Thompson brought out the scissors and he knew that the information Thompson had taken detailed the maneuvers of a battle force.

At the time, Turntine had asked his friend why he had taken the information. "I just like to keep in touch with what's going on," Thompson had replied. But now that suspicion had entered Turntine's mind as he sat in the little Long Beach apartment with the former yeoman, he saw sinister implications in Thompson's previous behavior.

Thompson, Turntine had come to realize, was a very shrewd man; fortunately, as shall presently be seen, the boy from St. Louis was shrewd too. "How do you want me to help you, Harry?" he asked.

Thompson, relaxed, had nothing more on his mind than emptying a fifth of rye whiskey. Turntine poured him another drink and Thompson downed it before answering. "Kid," he asked, "can I trust you a hundred per cent?"

Turntine nodded. "You're my friend, Harry," he said. "I'd do anything for you."

There was a tense silence for the next few minutes, during which Thompson had another stiff drink. He had finished more than half of the bottle now and his eyes were watery and his face flushed. It was about eleven o'clock at night.

"There's a war coming one of these days, kid," said Thompson. "And there's a lot of money to be made out of it for a couple of smart fellows like you and me."

"I don't get you, Harry," said Turntine.

"Look," said Thompson. "What's this country ever done for you? You couldn't get a job in St. Louis and you couldn't get one out here. Right?"

Turntine nodded.

"So the world owes you a living, don't it? Okay, if your own country don't give it to you, another country will."

"*Another* country, Harry?"

"Japan."

"How? I don't get it, Harry."

Thompson was silent again and didn't speak until he had downed another drink. "Where do you suppose I'm getting my money?" he asked at length.

"From Japan, from what you just said."

"That's right, and I can cut you in on it. I need help for the work I've got to do. A smart kid like you will fit right into the picture I got in mind."

Turntine debated with himself as to how far he could safely pursue questioning. Thompson was pretty drunk now; he might divulge a good deal, but on the other hand, he might suddenly get suspicious. Turntine decided to be cautious; there would be other opportunities to ask questions. Thompson's talk rapidly deteriorated into meaningless alcoholic mutterings, and by half-past eleven he had dropped off to sleep.

In the morning, when he opened his bloodshot eyes, he asked Turntine, "Say kid, what did I tell you last night—about what I do, I mean?"

Turntine forced a laugh. "You said you were a secret agent for Japan," he said.

Thompson stiffened and looked steadily at Turntine.

"You don't believe that, do you?" he asked.

"No, Harry, I figured you were only kidding."

"Yes," said Thompson, "I was only kidding."

Several weeks passed, during which Thompson was frequently absent from the Long Beach apartment for two or three days at a time. During such absences Turntine made careful searches of the former yeoman's effects, but found nothing by way of evidence to confirm his suspicions. Nor did Thompson, after that one drunken night and brief reference to it the next morning, bring up the subject of Japan or Turntine's help again.

On the morning of November 1, while Thompson was away on an undisclosed mission, a letter came for him postmarked San Francisco. The envelope bore the name of the St. Francis Hotel in that city, but the sender had not placed his name on the envelope, only his room number. Turntine held the letter up to the light but couldn't manage to make out any of its contents because it had been folded lengthwise and then crosswise, so that there was only the jumble of writing resulting from four thicknesses of paper.

When Thompson came in, early that evening, it was obvious that he had been drinking heavily. Turntine mentioned to him that a letter had come for him. Thompson, who had never received any mail since Turntine had been living with him, didn't appear very interested until the youth mentioned that the letter was from San Francisco. Thompson read the letter eagerly, then stuck it in his inside jacket pocket, opened a bottle of whiskey he had brought home with him and drank until he dropped into a stupor. Turntine reached into Thompson's pocket and glanced at the letter. It was from a person who signed himself Tanni and it said, in effect, that Tanni wished to meet Thompson at nine o'clock the following evening—November 2— at a certain designated point on San Pedro Street in Los Angeles.

Late the following afternoon, Thompson invited Turntine to accompany him into Los Angeles. "I am going to meet a very important man, kid," he said, "and I want you to meet him, too. I've told him about you and one of these days he might have a good job for you."

On the way into Los Angeles, Thompson explained that Turntine was not to speak unless he was spoken to during the meeting. Turntine asked the name of the man they were to meet. "His name is Tanni," replied Thompson.

Thompson and Turntine reached the rendezvous at exactly nine o'clock, due to Thompson's stalling in the vicinity so that he would not, as he explained it, arrive early. Immediately upon their arrival a car drew in to

the curb. The driver—the sole occupant of the vehicle
—was a Japanese, about thirty years old and nattily attired. He smiled to Thompson and motioned the former yeoman and Turntine to get in. Thompson sat in
the front seat and the Japanese indicated that he wished
Turntine to sit in the rear. The car started, and for
several minutes wove through traffic without any of the
occupants saying a word.

Then the Japanese spoke. "Mr. Thompson," he began, "is this the young man you spoke to me about?"

Thompson answered affirmatively, then turned to
Turntine. "Mr. Turntine," he said, with unusual for-
mality, "this is Mr. Tanni."

"How do you do," said Turntine.

"How do you do," said Mr. Tanni, without turning.

The car went through several more blocks of traffic
without anything being said. Then Turntine heard Mr.
Tanni saying, "Mr. Thompson, you are doing very fine
work. Your job will be permanent."

"What about Mr. Turntine?" asked Thompson.

"I shall decide about that later," said Mr. Tanni.
"Mr. Turntine seems to be a very alert young man.
Eventually we will have a place for someone like him."

"I've been wondering about money," said Thompson.

"Money?" asked Mr. Tanni.

"Yes, you see two hundred dollars a month isn't very
much, especially when I have to buy a lot of drinks for
sailors down around San Diego, Long Beach and San
Pedro."

"We will be glad to take care of any expenses, naturally," Mr. Tanni answered. "In fact, we have no intention of continuing to pay you such a small sum as
two hundred dollars a month for salary. Eventually you

will be getting many times that much." The car drew
to a stop on a dark street. "Mr. Turntine," said Mr.
Tanni, "I wonder if you would be kind enough to take
a walk around the block while I discuss something confidential with Mr. Thompson."

Turntine took ten minutes to round the block and
when he returned to the parked car Thompson asked
him to go around the block again. Upon his return the
second time, Turntine was invited to get back into the
car. Then Mr. Tanni drove without speaking to the point
where he had picked up Thompson and Turntine, and
there bade them a pleasant good night.

For some time after this Turntine heard nothing
more about what was going on, and he deemed it pru-
dent not to question Thompson. The ex-yeoman was
frequently away on overnight trips. Then another letter came for Thompson, this one postmarked Palo Alto
but bearing no return identification. Turntine got a
chance to look at it when Thompson was out a few days
later. He copied it down word for word:

My dear Mr. Thompson—

I received your letter just now after my pretty long trip.
I am very glad to know that you are doing very good. Don't
be in a hurry. Since now your monthly salary will be sent
not later than the first of each month and tomorrow $300.00
will be sent including your December salary, clothes and
Christmas present.

I shall have a long trip from the middle of next month
and may return in January, but not sure. I will send your
January's salary before I start here. Will you send me the
schedule (details) of Force Tactics which will commence
from the fifth of December if you can have that before the
time and send me before the third of December. Please remember that you need not send me the reports for my

questions all at one time. One report should be sent at the time that you get it.

Sincerely,
Tanni

Not long afterward another letter came from Mr. Tanni, which Turntine found the opportunity to read. This one brought up a somewhat monotonous spy problem—money for expenditures. Judging from what Mr. Tanni said in the letter, Thompson had complained again about his large expenditures in entertaining sailors at various Pacific Coast ports.

By January, 1935—about six months after Turntine had first met Thompson—it became apparent to the St. Louis youth that either Thompson or Mr. Tanni, or both, had decided that he was not to be assigned to work for Japan. Turntine was disappointed at this turn of events for he was a patriotic young man and was interested in getting as far into Japanese confidence as possible for the purpose of gleaning information that would be of value to the United States.

On the last day of January, when he suspected that Thompson was out of town, Turntine made his way to the flagship *Pennsylvania*, at the time anchored off San Pedro, for the express purpose of acquainting the Navy with what Harry Thomas Thompson was obviously up to. It is a singular fact that in the years preceding Pearl Harbor spies of both Germany and Japan were able to move in restricted areas almost at will, while patriotic Americans were tangled up in red tape. Certainly that situation prevailed on the January afternoon when Willard James Turntine attempted to get aboard the *Pennsylvania* and disclose his information. It was only after struggling through regulations for several hours that he finally found himself in the presence of an officer on the staff of Admiral Joseph M. Reeves of the United States fleet. The officer made careful note of everything that Turntine had to say, thanked him, swore him to secrecy and instructed him to resume his relationship with Thompson as if nothing had happened.

When Admiral Reeves had heard the St. Louis boy's story he communicated with the Office of Naval Intelligence. Officials of the O.N.I. and special agents of the Los Angeles Field Office of the F.B.I. were soon on the job. The investigators slipped down to Long Beach and picked Turntine off the street to hear him tell his story again. The boy impressed them with his intelligence and his sincerity, but neither the O.N.I. nor the F.B.I. was taking any chances. There always remained the possibility of such information being in the nature of a red herring designed to divert attention from something more serious. So young Turntine's background was put under the official miscroscope by agents of the F.B.I.'s St. Louis Field Office. In twenty-four hours, the youth had a clean bill of health and the F.B.I. and the O.N.I. really went to work.

The first problem to be tackled was to ascertain the identity of Mr. Tanni. It was felt that the name was an assumed one. An agent from the F.B.I.'s San Francisco Field Office looked over the register of the St. Francis Hotel of October 31—the date of the postmark on the letter that Thompson had received in connection with the Los Angeles meeting with Tanni on November 2. The register disclosed that a man giving his name as T. M. Tanni and his address as Los Angeles had checked into the St. Francis on October 30 and remained until the morning of November 2, when he had taken a daylight express for Los Angeles.

Inasmuch as some three months had elapsed since the visit of Mr. Tanni it wasn't possible for the F.B.I. to pick up any clues about him from employees of the hotel. It occurred to G-Men, however, that if Tanni had used a false name at the hotel he had probably also used a false city when marking his home town on the register.

Developing this line of thought, the investigators concluded that Mr. Tanni's real address was probably Palo Alto, inasmuch as the second Tanni letter that Turntine had seen had been postmarked from that point. With Palo Alto in the picture, it was a simple matter to deduce that Mr. Tanni was probably a student at Stanford University there, since several Japanese students were studying at the college. The F.B.I. was not unmindful of the earlier visit of Count von Kietel's friend, Kono, the one-time butler, to the campus.

The investigators did not have the benefit of a possible actual identification of Tanni by Turntine, because Turntine had not had too good a look at the Japanese the night he had seen him. Moreover, the boy from St. Louis had told F.B.I. agents, "I don't even know a Jap from a Chinaman."

The Japanese studying at Stanford were for the most part language students and "observers." An observer was theoretically a young Japanese who had been sent to observe customs and business methods in the United States but, as it was to turn out, most of them were observing far more than that. Handwriting seemed to be the best and quickest way to pick out Mr. Tanni from the Japanese students at Stanford, if indeed he was a student there. It was a simple matter for the F.B.I. to arrange with the university authorities to get samples of the penmanship of the various Japanese. When this was done the penmanship of each student was compared with Mr. Tanni's handwriting in the San Francisco hotel register. It thus developed, unmistakably, that Mr. Tanni was a student at Stanford and that his real name was Toshio Miyazaki.

Immigration records disclosed that Miyazaki had entered this country by way of San Francisco on August 24, 1933—almost a year and a half before the F.B.I. and the O.N.I. got on his trail. He was thirty years of age but, like many Japanese, looked much younger because of his short stature. As soon as he was identified, coded cables began to pass back and forth between Secretary of State Cordell Hull's office and the American Embassy in Tokyo. The result of the exchange of intelligence was development of the fact that the language student at Stanford was no less a personage than a Lieutenant Commander in the Imperial Japanese Navy.

CHAPTER 4

The Photostat Clue

WHEN NAVAL OFFICIALS in Washington pondered the intelligence from the Pacific Coast, there was no doubt in their minds that the Miyazaki-Thompson business there and the case of former Lieutenant Commander John S. Farnsworth in Washington constituted two ends of a secret pincers, controlled in Tokyo, which were one day designed to close in on every naval and military secret possibly obtainable in the U.S.A. Not that the O.N.I. had entertained any previous doubt that the Japanese had important espionage plans relating to this country. But the initial evidence relating to Harry Thompson was something definite and concrete; here was an officer of the Japanese Navy, masquerading as a language student in an American university, who was obviously paying Thompson, a former yeoman in the United States Navy, for information to which Thompson had access.

The fact that Lieutenant Commander Miyazaki had hired a white man to do the actual collecting of information confirmed a theory that the O.N.I. had held for some time—that Japanese would prefer to hire white men for certain types of espionage work. The Japanese, unlike the Germans, had a color obstacle to overcome. The very appearance of an Oriental made him a marked individual among white men and therefore an object of scrutiny wherever he went, which constituted a situation hardly compatible with smooth spying operations.

If the Pacific Coast technique was for the Japanese to use the white race to circumvent the color obstacle, it was only reasonable to assume that John S. Farnsworth, if he were a spy, was working for the Washington counterpart of Lieutenant Commander Toshio Miyazaki. And the counterpart of Miyazaki in the capital would be Commander Josiyuki Itimiya of the Japanese Navy —the Naval Attaché at the Japanese Embassy, who was suspected of doing considerable photographic work in secret rooms in his apartment in the Alban Towers.

Thus, during February, 1935, almost seven years before Pearl Harbor, the O.N.I. knew about both ends of the Japanese espionage pincers. So did the F.B.I., though concentrating on different individuals.

On the second day after the Stanford student's identity was established, Miyazaki was trailed into San Francisco late on a Friday afternoon, after his classes were over for the week. He spent some time drinking in a hotel bar, after which he went down to Fisherman's Wharf and had a seven-course sea-food dinner. Following that, he did some more drinking, sticking to the Japanese favorite—whiskey and soda. That very first night Miyazaki established himself as a difficult man to tail. In his rounds of the city, he sometimes changed taxicabs for no other reason, obviously, than that he wanted to shake off anyone who might be following him. But the F.B.I. has ways of overcoming difficulties that they encounter in such circumstances. Toward nine o'clock Miyazaki went to an address which the investigators quickly established as a house of ill fame, inhabited only by white girls.

The Lieutenant Commander remained in the house until an hour when he permitted himself just enough time to catch the overnight train for Los Angeles. He was not carrying any baggage; only a briefcase. Two G-Men also boarded the train for the south, taking no chances on the possibility that the Jap naval officer might get off somewhere along the line. But Miyazaki went all the way to Los Angeles, and took a cab from the Union Pacific station to the three-story house at 117½ Weller Street where Dr. Furusawa had his private hospital.

Lieutenant Commander Miyazaki remained in the medical building on Weller Street from the time of his arrival Saturday morning until early Sunday evening. Then he got into a taxi and was trailed to Long Beach. The shadows were hardly surprised to see the cab proceed to Linden Street and draw up in front of the apartment house where Harry Thomas Thompson, the traitorous ex-yeoman lived.

As it turned out later when young Turntine reported to the F.B.I., Thompson was apparently expecting a visit from the Japanese Lieutenant Commander who was at that moment being trailed by G-Men. For, an hour previous to Miyazaki's arrival in Long Beach, Thompson had said to Turntine, "Kid, go take yourself some fresh air, and don't come back before eleven. I've got a doll coming."

G-Men and O.N.I. agents had made careful preparations beforehand for the appearance of the Japanese in Thompson's apartment. Masquerading as salesmen who had come to Long Beach to do door-to-door canvassing, three investigators had taken a small apartment in a building that afforded a view into the quarters occupied by Thompson and Turntine. With the aid of strong field glasses, the watchers were able to cover approximately half of the floor space occupied by Thompson.

Thus the watchers saw the entrance of the Jap who posed as a language student, and observed Thompson shaking his hand vigorously. The two took chairs at a bridge table that was normally used for eating purposes. The F.B.I. had reasoned that if Thompson and his visitors had cause to go over any papers or documents they would use this bridge table for the purpose. The table had not originally been in full view of the watchers, so the F.B.I. had instructed young Turntine to move it, inch by inch, over a period of days, until it was in full view. Turntine had been cautioned not to shift the table in one move, lest Thompson's suspicions be aroused.

Seated at the table, Lieutenant Commander Miyazaki reached into his inside jacket pocket and brought out a wallet. He carefully counted out some bills and handed them to Thompson. There seemed to be a discussion going on after the Japanese replaced his wallet, and after a couple of minutes Miyazaki brought out his wallet again and handed Thompson more bills.

Next the visitor took from his brief case a large piece of paper and began pointing to what was on it. Thompson rose from his chair, which was at right angles to that of the Japanese, and took up a position behind Miyazaki's back and looked over his shoulder. The Japanese was doing all of the talking, and Thompson looked on at what was being pointed out to him for fully ten minutes.

Next Thompson vanished from the view of the watchers and when he returned to his seat at the table he was carrying a handful of papers. He handed these to Miyazaki one at a time, and there was considerable pointing and discussion about each paper as it changed hands. When Thompson had turned over everything, Miyazaki put the papers in his brief case.

When the Japanese left Thompson's, it was after ten o'clock. He went to Los Angeles by taxi, spent three-quarters of an hour in a house of ill fame and then caught an overnight limited for San Francisco. On Monday morning he was attending classes at Stanford University.

The investigator next wanted to know where Lieutenant Commander Miyazaki did his banking, and they shadowed him until he visited a bank—the Yokohama Specie Bank of San Francisco. A quiet perusal of the microfilmed records of checks relating to Miyazaki's account, turned over by a white employee, disclosed that for more than a year he had been paying Harry Thomas Thompson two hundred dollars monthly. The source of his deposits was found to be the Japanese Embassy in Washington, which had long been suspected by the O.N.I. as the fountainhead of whatever espionage the Japanese had in mind for the U.S.A. And all the while the Japanese Embassy had been maintaining oh-so-cordial relations with the State Department and the White House.

The day after Miyazaki's visit to Long Beach, Thompson bought himself a petty officer's uniform. When he returned to the apartment wearing it, he announced to young Turntine, "Kid, I'm back in the Navy. The Navy's in my blood."

That remark had a familiar ring to O.N.I. agents

when it was passed on to them. They had heard about the Farnsworth case three thousand miles away.

Turntine, carefully coached by the investigators as to just what to say and what not to say to Thompson under given circumstances, was instructed to question the former yeoman mildly about his apparent change of heart and plans. Turntine opened the subject this way, "Harry, I thought we were going to make some money together, you and I."

"How do you mean?" asked the man who was illegally wearing the petty officer's uniform.

"Don't you remember one night you said maybe I could help you?"

"Oh, *that.*"

"Whatever happened? I've got to get something to do, you know."

"Kid," said Thompson, "that's all off. Forget all about it."

"Whatever happened to that Mr. Tanni that I met that night in Los Angeles? Did you have a fight with him or something?"

Thompson turned and faced Turntine. His whole body seemed stiff and his eyes were wide with rage. He grabbed Turntine by the shoulders and shook him violently. "I told you to forget all about that! If you ever mention that again—or if I ever hear that you've breathed a word of it to a living soul—you'll be no good for work of any kind."

Next Thompson was followed to San Pedro. He hung around waterfront haunts of sailors, and when he saw a group of bluejackets clustered together he made it a point to join them and buy them a round of drinks. Then, after the drinking started, F.B.I. and O.N.I.

watchers, who managed to infiltrate themselves into the places patronized by the sailors by dressing as waterfront habitués, would hear Harry Thompson asking the same type of question that agents on the other side of the continent had heard former Lieutenant Commander Farnsworth asking of Navy men. Most of Thompson's questions centered around gunnery and tactical problems, and on more than one occasion the investigators heard the bluejackets and other petty officers coming across with information that was correct in every detail —data that would be of inestimable value to an enemy in time of war.

Although immediate steps had to be taken to shut off the source of Thompson's supply of information, the investigators on the Pacific Coast, like those keeping an eye on Farnsworth on the Atlantic seaboard, had to be extremely careful. The State Department, although kept fully informed of what was happening on each coast, and despite the fact that the Farnsworth and Thompson investigations were regarded as mere straws in the wind heralding graver things to come, was bending backward so as not to offend the Imperial Japanese Government, technically a friendly power. It had long been axiomatic that Japan was a touchy nation, and although the investigators already had enough evidence on Lieutenant Commander Miyazaki to send him to prison for espionage, the State Department made it plain to the Justice Department and the Navy Department that it did not want Lieutenant Commander Miyazaki arrested, or embarrassed *under any circumstances.* Had there been more two-fistedness in the State Department—the same State Department that in later years pursued a policy of appeasement with the Franco government in Spain—and had Lieutenant Commander Miyazaki been picked off, brought to trial and imprisoned, the course of history might very well have been changed—and for the better.

If the American public had been informed, in 1935, about what the State Department knew was going on, instead of being kept in the dark—not only in relation to the behavior of Lieutenant Commander Miyazaki, but about many other things—public opinion would have had a chance to make itself felt. And public opinion, based on knowledge in possession of a fully-informed populace, could have brought about action in the form of preparation for war. This preparation, beginning in 1935 instead of years later, could have canceled the head start that Japan and Germany got on us, and could have conceivably shortened the war to a considerable degree.

The same technique as was applied in shutting off Farnsworth's information was employed in stopping the data that was flowing in to Thompson. Confidential word was passed to all men of the Pacific fleet not to answer questions of anybody under any circumstances. The effect of this was to cause great distress to Thompson. Turntine was still living with him and still reporting to the investigators. He disclosed that Thompson had suddenly become moody and was drinking harder than ever.

One night, when Thompson was drunk and somewhat talkative, he said to Turntine, "Kid, I think I'm in trouble."

"What kind of trouble?"

"Never mind, but it's trouble, all right."

Later in the evening Thompson began to mumble to himself, and Turntine thought he heard him saying something like, "I'll resign and wash my hands of the whole damned thing."

But for several months the former yeoman continued to wear his petty officer's uniform. There were several more meetings with Lieutenant Commander Miyazaki at Thompson's apartment in Long Beach, and at the St. Francis Hotel, in San Francisco, where Miyazaki continued to register as Mr. Tanni. During one of the San Francisco hotel meetings, the investigators succeeded in getting a room next to that of the Japanese, and listened in on a conversation that took place between Miyazaki and the traitor.

"Commander," said Thompson, "I'm afraid I'll have to resign."

"Why, Mr. Thompson?"

"I think something has leaked out. I don't seem to be able to lay my hands on any information any more."

"You are afraid of going to prison, perhaps, Mr. Thompson?"

"You can say that again."

"Do you suppose, Mr. Thompson, that that young man you live with—young Mr. Turntine—has talked to anybody?"

"I'm wondering."

"Ah, then you *have* told him that you are working for Japan."

Thompson coughed. "No, not exactly. But remember, you asked me to bring him with me that night we met in Los Angeles. Naturally, I had to give him some sort of an explanation."

"That is correct, Mr. Thompson, but he could have met me without knowing that our work was espionage for my government."

"But don't you remember, Commander, when I recommended to you that he assist me you said the idea sounded good, especially if he looked young enough not to cause suspicion when he went places or asked questions?"

"But the fact remains," said Lieutenant Commander Miyazaki, "that you informed young Mr. Turntine that you were working for my government."

"Well," said Thompson, raising his voice for the first time, "if you want me to admit that, okay. I *did* tell him."

The listening device amplified a chuckle from Miyazaki. "There is no need, Mr. Thompson," said the Japanese, "to get, as you Americans say, hot and bothered. The solution to our problem is very simple."

"What are you driving at, Commander?"

"We will just arrange to have young Mr. Turntine go out on a fishing boat. He will think he's getting information that he will some day turn over to J. Edgar Hoover, for instance. But he won't come back. What could be simpler than that, Mr. Thompson?"

"Look here, Commander! I'll get all the information I can for you, but I don't want to get mixed up in a murder rap!"

Young Turntine was tipped off by the investigators to be very careful at all times to see that he was not maneuvered into a position where any one could kill him. He was further told that a job was going to be found for him, out of Long Beach, so that he would have a plausible excuse for no longer living with Thompson. The job was not to be found right away, for if Turntine were to move too quickly after the San Francisco hotel conference, Thompson might get suspicious. There would remain, then, a period of perhaps two weeks during which the young man who was doing counter-espionage would find himself wading in highly danger-ous waters.

Meantime, in Washington, John S. Farnsworth had been divorced by his wife. He had married again, but his second marriage was no more successful than the first, and he was soon separated from his second wife. He continued to circulate at social gatherings in Wash-ington, Philadelphia and elsewhere, particularly gather-ings where Navy men were present. He continued to seek information, and the fact that his naval acquaintances were now and had been for some time very close-mouthed only seemed to make Farnsworth more persistent. His supply of one-hundred-dollar bills, whatever the source, showed no signs of diminishing.

Farnsworth's Washington bank account was looked into confidentially. Microfilm records of checks that had passed through the bank disclosed none that would account for the Farnsworth affluence. It was obvious that the former officer was obtaining his money direct from wherever it was coming from. Certainly the source was not an employer—that is, an employer in the usual sense of the word. For Farnsworth had no such em-ployer.

Since his second marital break-up, the former officer had lived at the New Willard Hotel and other first-rate hotels where it had been comparatively simple for the O.N.I. agents to keep track of his comings and goings. Sometimes for days on end he had gone no further than to the bar, where he spent several hours in solitary drinking. During these protracted stays in a hotel he had no visitors nor did he make a single outside telephone call. The source of those hundred-dollar bills became a matter of such curiosity that the Secret Service actually made it a point to get a couple of them from bars around Washington and examine them to see whether they were counterfeits. But they weren't.

At the Washington bank where Lieutenant Commander Josiyuki Itimiya, Naval Attaché at the Washington Embassy, did business, microfilm check records disclosed that in addition to his salary, the Japanese official was receiving from the Embassy frequent large checks, some of them for as much as ten thousand dollars, for undisclosed purposes. O.N.I. operatives further learned at the bank that when the Naval Attaché cashed the checks he always requested new one-hundred-dollar bills. In view of the known relationship between the Japanese naval official and the traitor on the Pacific Coast, it now seemed probable that there was a link between former Lieutenant Commander Farnsworth and the Naval Attaché at the Washington Embassy, particularly when Farnsworth's supply of hundred-dollar bills was considered.

There was, though, one feature of the suspected tie-up between Farnsworth and Itimiya that was totally different from the relationship between the Pacific coast Japanese and the traitor there. Farnsworth had never been seen to confer with Itimiya. Certain government agents who had tapped Farnsworth's phone, since wire tapping was legal at that time, had not come upon a single clue for all their trouble. Any calls that Farnsworth received or made were either purely social or had nothing whatever to do with naval matters. But, everything considered, it was decided to have Farnsworth shadowed twenty-four hours a day. The F.B.I. was called in. Never once from now on would Farnsworth be very far from a watcher. The agents were, in police-detective parlance, going to get Jack Farnsworth up in the morning and put him to bed at night.

In Long Beach, Turntine announced to Thompson that he was leaving for San Francisco, where he had obtained a job in a department store as a salesman. Thompson was immediately suspicious. He wanted to know exactly where Turntine was going to work, what he was going to do, how much he was going to make and how he had gotten the job. The F.B.I. had prepared Turntine carefully for such an eventuality. The youth from St. Louis pulled a want ad from a San Francisco paper out of his pocket—an ad that the F.B.I. had inserted. Then he showed Thompson a copy of the letter of application he had written for the job, and another letter, written on the stationery of the store itself, telling him that he had been accepted. Thompson appeared satisfied.

After Turntine left, Thompson seemed to go to pieces. The operatives looking into his apartment from their secret vantage point saw him doing considerable solitary drinking, sometimes for days on end. Not long after Turntine's departure, Lieutenant Commander Miyazaki paid him a visit. Apparently the Japanese was angered at finding Thompson in the midst of a protracted spree, for the watchers saw him gesticulating in a manner that indicated he was giving his white employee a verbal dressing-down.

When Miyazaki had gone, the operatives watched Thompson spending a long time at the bridge table, writing what was apparently a letter. After several minutes of effort he would destroy what he had written and start again. They realized that he must be trying to compose a letter of some importance, and was having difficulty in expressing himself properly.

The investigators had come to know Thompson as something of a show-off—an ignorant though fundamentally shrewd man who tried to impress people by his flowery language. The F.B.I. search into his background had disclosed that in his native Maryland he had a reputation for trying to appear important. In an effort to compensate for his lack of more advanced schooling, he had done sporadic reading and had picked up a smattering of information on a wide variety of unrelated subjects. The result was that he appeared to some people to be a fairly well-educated, well-informed young man.

Now, as the investigators watched him, they saw the floor alongside the table become littered with discarded paper. Finally, after an hour's time, he seemed to succeed in getting down on paper what he wanted to say. Then he copied what he had composed. Having placed his last effort in an envelope and sealed it, he picked the discarded paper from the floor, tore it up and threw it into the wastebasket. This done, he went out and posted the letter.

The F.B.I. could not legally enter Thompson's room to examine the contents of the wastebasket, although such a move would have been comparatively easy. So the agents arranged to get the refuse from the apartment building the next day. They finally came upon what Thompson had written and, when one particular sheet of paper was pasted together, the F.B.I. found itself in possession of the following communication—apparently the one that Thompson had copied and mailed:

My dear Mr. Tanni:

I respectfully request that this letter be treated as my resignation from the service of your country and the country of which I have been serving. It is with great reluctance and regret that I tender this resignation to the Japanese Government as I can only state that I have enjoyed every moment I have spent in the service of your country and hope all information that has come to you through me has amply repay for the salary paid me.

This resignation is to take effect as of the date of our last meeting. This is my own doing and free will and for the safeguard of my own person and has nothing whatever to do with anything you or your country has done or should do.

In saying good-bye I extend to you my heartiest congratulations and hope that anything you may undertake will prove of a successful nature.

Harry Thomas Thompson

Shortly after receiving this letter from Thompson, Lieutenant Commander Miyazaki returned to the Orient. There were rueful expressions on the faces of O.N.I. and F.B.I. investigators as they watched the ship bearing him out through the Golden Gate to safety. But for the State Department's policy of not offending a touchy foreign power, Miyazaki would have been en route, not to the Orient, but to the place where he should have been—behind prison bars.

Strategy called for letting Thompson have his freedom, for a little more time, at least. The investigators were curious to see what he would do next. They had thought he might lead them to other traitors, and there was still that possibility.

More time passed, and then it was decided to pull Thompson in. Only after his arrest did the F.B.I. learn that Thompson had approached the Japanese with the proposal to do espionage work for them, not the other way about, as had been supposed all along. Thompson had gone to the Japanese Consulate in Los Angeles, offering his services for a fee, and the Japanese had shadowed him for weeks to make certain he was not an O.N.I. operative doing counterespionage work. When they had satisfied themselves that he was what he represented himself to be—an American who was willing to turn a quick dollar in any way he could, even as a traitor—he was put to work.

The F.B.I., after arresting Thompson, found out more about the man's character on further checking. They learned that he had not been popular with fellow bluejackets in the Navy, and that they had applied to him the term, "wise guy." Somewhere along the line he had acquired the attitude that the world owed him a living. He had become cynical and bitter, and while in the Navy he had been openly envious when other men were advanced. His total lack of ethics, plus his desire to be somebody, had no doubt added up to his being considered by the Japanese as ideal for betrayal work.

Reconstructing his acquaintance with Turntine, the investigators could see why Thompson had offered to share his apartment with the younger man. A check back on the time disclosed that when Thompson took Turntine in, the former yeoman was already negotiating with the Japanese; and what better cover could he have for his activities than an association with an innocent youth from the Middle West? There was no doubt, either, that Thompson thought he saw in young Turntine a possible valuable aide in espionage work.

The story of Thompson's arrest broke in the newspapers on March 5, 1936. It was played up big in Washington. There, investigators shadowing Farnsworth were curious to see what effect, if any, the story would have on him. It seemed to have none whatever. That meant one of two things; either Farnsworth was absolutely innocent of what he was suspected of, or he was a far bolder and craftier man than the investigators believed.

A few days afterward, Farnsworth was shadowed from Washington to Annapolis, and there was seen going to the home of Lieutenant Commander James E. Maher of the Navy.

Farnsworth was in the Maher home for more than an hour. When he left, G-Men called on Lieutenant Commander Maher, while others followed Farnsworth. The cashiered officer checked into Carvell Hall, a fashionable Annapolis hotel.

At the Maher home, G-Men learned that Farnsworth had called there on more than one occasion in the past, speaking of Navy matters on each visit to both the Lieutenant Commander and his wife. The Mahers, like others in Farnsworth's one-time circle, had felt sorry for Jack, as they called him, and they had believed his story that the Navy was in his blood and that his chief object in life was eventual reinstatement.

However, when G-Men hinted to the Mahers that Farnsworth might be something other than he appeared to be, both the Lieutenant Commander and Mrs. Maher were able to place a sinister interpretation on Farnsworth's visits. On numerous occasions, when the Lieutenant Commander had been out of the room, Farnsworth had asked very pointed questions on naval matters of Mrs. Maher—questions that he had asked of her husband before the latter had left the room and which Maher had not answered.

On this most recent visit, for example, Farnsworth had been particularly solicitous about information relating to a new destroyer—the *Baddlitt*. Lieutenant Commander Maher, noticing for the first time that Jack Farnsworth was rapidly going downhill from drink, had politely refused to answer any questions about the destroyer, fearing that Farnsworth, while drunk, might divulge the information to persons who shouldn't hear it. Lieutenant Commander Maher had then been called to the telephone, and while he was gone Farnsworth leaned over confidentially to Mrs. Maher and said, *"Please* tell me about the *Baddlitt;* I've *got* to know."

When Farnsworth checked into Carvell Hall, the agents shadowing him tried to get a room adjoining his. It so happened, however, that the rooms on either side of the one assigned to Farnsworth were occupied. Farnsworth checked out the next morning and returned to Washington. The hotel records disclosed that he had made a telephone call—just one—to Washington during his stay at the hotel. The call had been a toll call, and a record had therefore been made of the number. The F.B.I. checked the number in Washington and found that it was an unlisted one, not in the directory. So an agent called it, just to see what would happen. When he was greeted with a "Hello" on the other end of the wire, he asked for a fictitious party. Thereupon the person he was talking to—a man—answered, "You must have the wrong number." At this the agent asked if he weren't talking to such-and-such a number. "I said you have the wrong number!" replied the man on the other end, angrily. "Sorry," replied the F.B.I. agent, "my mistake."

The man who had answered the number had spoken

with an unmistakable Japanese accent. Moreover, when the unlisted phone was checked with the telephone company it was found that the number that the former Lieutenant Commander in the United States Navy had called was that of a phone located in an apartment on the fourth floor of the Alban Towers—the private residence of Lieutenant Commander Josiyuki Itimiya, Naval Attaché of the Japanese Embassy.

The fact that Farnsworth had been in touch with the private phone on the fourth floor of Alban Towers was all the more sinister when it developed that Lieutenant Commander Itimiya no longer lived there, but had gone back to Japan. The new Naval Attaché of the Japanese Embassy—Lieutenant Commander Akira Yamaki—had moved into his predecessor's private quarters, apparently to take up where Itimiya had left off.

Itimiya's departure from Washington had been carried on with typical Japanese secrecy, and he was back in Tokyo and his successor was in Washington before officialdom in the capital knew anything about the change. This secret transfer of Lieutenant Commanders between the Japanese and American capitals constituted to the investigators *prima facie* evidence that the Japanese were neck deep in intrigue with the former United States Navy officer. The deduction by the O.N.I. and the F.B.I. as to Itimiya's secret departure and subsequent replacement was that the Japanese had obtained naval information of such a vital nature that he couldn't trust it even to a diplomatic pouch but thought it essential to carry it to Tokyo either in his own luggage or in his head.

If, reasoned the investigators, Farnsworth had been bold or stupid enough to make one long distance call to the private quarters of the Japanese, he had probably made several. With this in mind, then, the F.B.I. began to check up on the registration records of Carvell Hall. It was learned that Farnsworth had stopped at the Annapolis hotel on at least seven occasions within a period of two years. The hotel's telephone records for the dates in question were then looked into, and it was learned that Farnsworth had called the unlisted Washington number at least once during every visit he had made to Carvell Hall. On one occasion, he had called the Washington number no less than three times within four hours.

Now the investigators began a similar probe into the records of other hotels at which Farnsworth had stayed —in Boston, Philadelphia, New York, Baltimore and Norfolk. In every instance, it was found that he had telephoned to the Washington number. The trail went back as far as January, 1933—some three and a half years prior to that point in the investigation that concerns us at the moment.

In a Boston hotel, where Farnsworth had been registered in January, 1933, the telephone records disclosed that he had called another number in Washington besides that of the unlisted phone in the Alban Towers. A check-up of this second number revealed that it was that of a man who called himself a correspondent for Domei News Agency—a Japanese named Sato who lived on Morrison Street in Washington and who had for some time moved in only the highest official circles in Washington because he had come to be regarded as a sort of a semi-official representative of the Japanese government. Apparently there was more to Mr. Sato, too, than met the eye.

The investigators began to look into Sato's actions and they found that he frequently dined with the new Naval Attaché, Lieutenant Commander Yamaki, in such fashionable spots as the Presidential dining room in the Mayflower Hotel and at Harvey's sea-food restaurant. After such a dinner had come to an end, the correspondent would return to his home and Yamaki to the Alban Towers.

Surveillance of both places seemed to indicate that the correspondent and the Naval Attaché did not get together again the same evening after dinner. Yet maids in the Alban Towers, who were by this time keeping an eye on things for the investigators, reported that the newspaper correspondent frequently appeared on the fourth floor along about one o'clock in the morning, was let into the Naval Attaché's quarters, and remained until almost dawn. This was puzzling to the investigators, until they began to cover the back entrances of both the Alban Towers and the newspaper correspondent's home. Then they found that the correspondent, after a dinner with Yamaki, returned to his home, slipped out the back way, took a circuitous route to the Alban Towers, and entered the apartment building from the rear. The very fact that the correspondent was using a surreptitious means in going to and from the Alban Towers was a pretty clear indication to the investigators that he, too, was deeply involved in espionage work.

Farnsworth was at this time living in the New Willard Hotel, and the watchers got the idea that he, too, was perhaps going to the Alban Towers by leaving the hotel by a service entrance and entering the apartment building from the rear. Several weeks wore on, however, and Farnsworth was not observed using anything except the normal entrances to, and exits from, the New Willard, nor was he seen in the vicinity of the Alban Towers or the home of the Japanese newspaper correspondent. Farnsworth, in fact, seemed to be comparatively inactive. The deduction was that the arrest of Harry Thompson on the Pacific Coast had caused everyone, particularly Lieutenant Commander Yamaki, to become very cautious. It was, indeed, quite possible that the turn of events in California had caused the Japanese to regard Farnsworth as a man who could be of no further use to them.

In the meantime, the investigators were digging deeply into the activities of the former naval officer during the period when the facts had not warranted full-time surveillance of him. It was learned that Farnsworth had visited establishments of concerns making commercial photostats in both Washington and Baltimore. There were no copies available of the photostats that Farnsworth had, from time to time, ordered. Nor did employees of the establishments recall with any detail the subject matter that Farnsworth had brought in to be copied. They did remember, however, that Farnsworth never left anything that he brought in, but always remained while the work was done, so that when he left he took with him the original and the copies.

While the people who had done this work could recall no details about the subject matter, they did remember distinctly that the Farnsworth jobs had always related to naval matters. This had not caused suspicion at any time inasmuch as Farnsworth had always appeared very open and aboveboard. He had, in fact, informed an employee of one photostat concern that he was a Lieutenant Commander in the Navy and that the subject matter that was being copied was in the nature of official business. Farnsworth's claim that he was still in the Navy put a different light on things. There could not be the slightest question now that the man had from time to time laid his hands on official Navy data and had it photostated expressly for the Japanese government.

The probe into commercial photostat houses fanned out to other cities that Farnsworth had visited for a period of more than three years. A photograph of the man was shown to employees of photostat establishments from Boston to Norfolk. His features were recalled in three different places as those of the man who called himself a Naval officer and who had come in with official data to be copied.

The O.N.I. had long since suspected that two rooms in the apartment of the Japanese Naval Commander in the Alban Towers had been utilized for photographic and photostat work, since maids in the building who were never allowed in those rooms had identified odors seeping through the doors as those common to photographic dark rooms. The maids still smelled the same odors. The move that the investigators most wanted to make was, of course, to get a search warrant for the Japanese quarters. But once again the appeasement policy of the State Department stood in the way. An official of the Japanese government could not be offended!

Just to make certain, however, that their suspicions were well founded and that there were photostat machines in the apartment, the investigators began a canvass of all manufacturers of such equipment in the United States. They soon came across the records of one such concern which disclosed that two photostat machines had been shipped to the fourth floor of the Alban Towers within a month after the arrival in Washington of Lieutenant Commander Itimiya.

Now that the cat was out of the bag, so to speak, and the Japanese were apparently being very cautious and having little if anything to do with Farnsworth, the investigators felt safe in being a little more open about the questions they asked while covering certain phases of the probe. The identities of various officers and enlisted men with whom Farnsworth had talked and drunk in various cities along the Atlantic seaboard had been carefully recorded. Now these men were sought out and questioned in great detail. The investigators no longer had to fear that they would tip off Farnsworth, for the official feeling was that the circumstantial evidence against the former officer was now sufficient to warrant his arrest at any time if quick action became necessary.

What the bluejackets and the officers told the investigators cannot be detailed here. It can be said, however, that they had unwittingly turned over to the charming cashiered officer information that would probably have resulted in a quick and decisive defeat for American sea forces had war with Japan come just then! Among other things, Farnsworth had obtained data relating to the effectiveness of every gun on every warship and information relating to the vital performance records of the aircraft carriers *Saratoga* and *Ranger*.

The next development of importance was the sudden return to Japan of Lieutenant Commander Yamaki. Sato, the so-called correspondent, moved to New York. Once more the investigators found themselves watching a departing liner from a Pacific Coast port going out with a man who should have been on his way to prison instead of to his native land.

In July, Harry Thomas Thompson was brought to trial in Los Angeles. Young Turntine was one of the principal witnesses against him. The traitor was found guilty and sentenced to fifteen years on McNeil Island.

Farnsworth had showed no visible signs of being affected when Thompson had been arrested more than three months previously. But now, when he was seen to purchase a newspaper in the New Willard Hotel lobby, a G-Man standing alongside him noticed him stiffening as his gaze lit on the headline telling of Thompson's sentence. Farnsworth read the entire story avidly, then went in to the bar and got very drunk. The next morning he was trailed to the National Press Building. He had been trailed to this same building in the past, but investigators had never been able to find out just where he had gone there. They had been reluctant to shadow him too closely for fear of uncovering themselves. Farnsworth was again dropped at the entrance of the National Press Building, but the reason for his visit there, and all the details about it, were soon to be in the possession of the investigators.

Farnsworth went to the offices of Universal News Service, a Hearst news-gathering organization. He announced to a receptionist that he had a very sensational story that he wished to sell, and he soon found himself in the office of John Lambert, head of the Washington Bureau. "My name's Farnsworth—John S. Farnsworth. You probably recall the name. I—"

"Yes," interrupted Lambert. "You're the Farnsworth who was cashiered out of the Navy about ten years ago."

Farnsworth nodded.

"So what can I do for you?" asked Lambert, who was very busy at the time.

"I'd like to sell you a story on the activities of Japanese spies here in Washington."

Lambert looked at Farnsworth. The ex-officer's eyes were bloodshot and there was liquor on his breath. Lambert didn't know whether to take the man seriously or not, nor did he have time to find out personally. But no newspaperman passes up the possibility of a good story, so Lambert excused himself and went over to the desk of one of his star reporters—Fulton Lewis, Jr., who has since become renowned as a radio newscaster. "Talk to this bum, Fulton," said Lambert.

Lewis was affable to the visitor and quickly put Farnsworth at his ease. "We're always interested in a good story, Mr. Farnsworth," he said, "so go ahead and spill what you have. I understand it's about the Japanese."

Farnsworth nodded.

"That's very interesting, Mr. Farnsworth. May I ask how you come to know about Japanese espionage?"

"I've been working for them," said Farnsworth.

Lewis raised his eyebrows. "So?"

"That is," Farnsworth went on, "*pretending* to work for them. I've been stringing them along by supplying them with false information, so that I could find out what their plans were."

"And you found out?" asked Lewis.

"Plenty."

"Before we go any further, Mr. Farnsworth," said Lewis, "suppose you straighten me out on just how you first got in touch with the Japs."

Farnsworth said that he had originally met a newspaper correspondent—a man who had lately returned to Japan—who had in turn introduced him to Lieutenant Commander Itimiya.

"I understand," said Lewis, who was then, as he is now, one of the best-informed men in Washington, "that Itimiya had three photostat machines in his apartment in the Alban Towers."

"No," said Farnsworth, "he had only two." Lewis had learned through sources of his own that there had been two photostat machines in the Alban Towers apartment, but he had used the old newspaper trick of making a mis-statement so that he would get confirmation of a fact by means of a correction. Farnsworth's correction of the Lewis statement proved beyond any doubt in Lewis' mind that Farnsworth had indeed been in close contact with the Japanese.

"What kind of stuff did you supply the Japs with?" asked Lewis.

"Oh, old worthless Navy stuff."

"Did you have any of it photostated yourself?"

Farnsworth nodded.

"Where?"

"In different places. One place was right here in the National Press Building—the Abel Photostat Agency."

"Do they know you down there?" asked Lewis.

"Sure, come on along and I'll prove that I've taken stuff in there for some time to be photostated."

Lewis went with Farnsworth to a different floor of the National Press Building to the Abel agency. The former officer sought out a lady named Mrs. Grace Jamieson, an employee of the photostat establishment. "Remember me?" asked Farnsworth of Mrs. Jamieson.

"Certainly, Mr. Farnsworth; glad to see you again."

Farnsworth turned to Lewis. "See," he said. Lewis asked Mrs. Jamieson, "What sort of stuff has Mr. Farnsworth here been bringing in to be photostated?"

"Documents for the Navy Department, where he is employed," was the answer.

Now Lewis looked at Farnsworth. "I'll explain that later," said Farnsworth. The two men left and returned to Lewis' desk. "If you were only stringing along the Japs," said Lewis, "why did you claim to be employed in the Navy Department?"

Farnsworth's answer was all ready. "I didn't want the Navy to know what I was doing, because I was doing it on my own."

"Does the Navy know about this business yet?" asked Lewis.

Farnsworth shook his head. "I want you people to know about it first, because I want some money—a lot of money—for my story."

Farnsworth's story, as he outlined it, was along these lines: One Japanese newspaper correspondent, and the two Lieutenant Commanders—Itimiya and Yamaki—had importuned Farnsworth to use his Navy connections to get information for them. At first Farnsworth said he considered turning the matter over to the naval authorities. But then he said he felt that if he did a good counterespionage job on his own and turned his information over to the Navy when the job was done his fine work might result in his reinstatement.

Lewis began to question Farnsworth as to the nature of the false information he said he had turned over to the Japanese. Farnsworth's answers to these questions were far less definite than his answers to other queries, and Lewis felt sure that Farnsworth was lying to him. But he did not let on.

"Now about price," said Lewis. "What figure did you have in mind?"

"This should make a long, important series," said Farnsworth. "It should be good for several weeks, with a story every day. I figure about twenty thousand dollars."

"I'll have to take that up with the front office," said Lewis. "Can you come back tomorrow, or can I call you somewhere?"

"I'm staying at the New Willard," said Farnsworth. "And I forgot to mention, there's a condition attached to the series. The stories are not to start running until I have reached Germany."

Lewis raised his eyebrows. "How come?" he asked.

"That's a personal matter that has nothing to do with the series," said Farnsworth. "I would want to get out on the *Hindenburg*." The ill-fated zeppelin which blew up over Lakehurst, New Jersey, a year later, was making frequent trips between Germany and the United States in 1936.

When Farnsworth left, apparently unaware of Lewis' suspicions, the reporter went over to the Navy Department and had a talk with Captain William D. Puleston, Chief of the O.N.I.—the same man who had originally become suspicious of Farnsworth a long time before when he saw the routine report to the effect that the cashiered officer had "borrowed" *The Service of Information and Security* from Room 2649 of the Navy Building. Lewis' information lent itself very readily to sinister interpretation by Captain Puleston. Farnsworth, dropped like a hot potato by the Japanese, was desperate for money. He was also badly frightened because of the turn of events on the Pacific Coast. He saw only one way out—to pretend that he had been a counterespionage agent, rather than a spy, collect a large sum for his information and flee the country.

But it didn't work that way for Jack Farnsworth. He was arrested only a few hours after he had talked to Fulton Lewis, Jr. The two Japanese Naval Commanders who had returned to Japan were indicted for espionage but were of course beyond jurisdiction. Farnsworth wasn't brought to trial until February, 1937. G-Men and O.N.I. operatives gathered an imposing array of evidence against him. He stood to be sentenced to as high as forty years on two different espionage counts, which carried maximum penalties of twenty years each.

As the trial was about to begin, Farnsworth, who had previously maintained a stout show of innocence, suddenly changed his plea to *nolo contendere* which, in legal parlance, meant that he did not contend the charges against him but, calling himself neither guilty nor innocent, threw himself on the mercy of the court. Actually, there had been some behind-the-scenes activities between the naval authorities and Farnsworth. The decent side of the man—that side of him that had once made him a respected officer in the United States Navy—was appealed to. He was told that he had already betrayed his country, and that to continue to plead innocent and cause the Navy publicly to disclose much of the evidence against him would constitute a further betrayal, inasmuch as a considerable part of the evidence was of a nature that the Navy did not want publicized. And that's why Farnsworth changed his plea to *nolo contendere*. He was sentenced February 23, 1937, by Federal Justice James M. Proctor to serve not less than four years or more than twenty years in a Federal penitentiary.

CHAPTER 5

Pigeon Photographers

THERE WAS PLENTY going on, early in 1935, in addition to the Farnsworth and Thompson investigations—and the probes into the activities of such men in New York as Count von Kietel, German Vice Consul Gyssling, Roy Akagi, manager of the South Manchuria Railway offices, and Sleepy Joe Hagiwara, New York manager for Domei News Agency; and such people on the Pacific Coast as Dr. and Mrs. Furusawa, and Kono, the affluent ex-butler. The F.B.I., the O.N.I., G-2 (Army Intelligence) and other investigative agencies were having difficulty, naturally, in ascertaining where fiction left off and truth began when they looked into tips that had by now assumed flood-tide proportions. While there was plenty of fiction in what was reported, there was also plenty of fact—fact so incredible that hard-boiled investigators chose their words when reporting to their superior officers so that they would not be accused of romancing.

All sorts of messages and instructions were passing between Tokyo and both American-born and alien Japanese in Pacific Coast cities. The methods that the Japanese were using to keep such messages from prying eyes were for the most part none too subtle. Notes intercepted by Customs inspectors at various California ports had been placed inside of toothpaste tubes, bars of soap and chocolate bars. There were instances of messages concealed in the linings of neckties worn by Japanese departing for or arriving from the Orient, and some women travelers were found in possession of strangely embroidered handkerchiefs which, when folded a certain way, reproduced a map of military importance.

Of course the Japanese fishermen operating out of California had long been suspected of being more than they appeared to be, although in 1935 it had not been definitely established that many of these seemingly nondescript fisherfolk were actually high officers in the Imperial Japanese Navy.

Various so-called Japanese-American societies, operating under apparently innocent guises, were, like the fishermen, on the suspect list. The various Buddhist temples and Shinto shrines, particularly around Los Angeles, were believed to be either already integrated or in the process of being integrated into the Japanese espionage machinery in Southern California. Naval Intelligence operatives, for example, had for some time observed carrier pigeons arriving in the rear of a Shinto mission in the Little Tokyo section of Los Angeles. The pigeons always arrived at about the same time—three o'clock in the afternoon on Mondays, Wednesdays and Fridays. By continued surveillance, investigators ascertained that the pigeons always came in from the same direction, which might mean that the birds had flown over certain areas vital to the security of the United States. The pigeons usually flew very high until they neared the Shinto mission which was their destination, so the operatives got the idea of bringing down one of the birds with a shot before it reached the mission.

Nailing a pigeon on the wing is no easy matter, even

for a good marksman. Eight pigeons were fired at from a vantage point within a block of the mission, over a period of seventeen days, before one was brought down. When the bird was retrieved, Naval Intelligence was astonished to find that it had attached to it a small, specially constructed camera, of German origin, which was something of a cross between a regular camera and a movie camera. That is, the device could be set so that it would automatically snap a picture at any given time through a special lens which, because of the manner in which the camera was fastened to the pigeon's belly, pointed straight down at the ground.

The film took a total of twelve pictures. When these were developed, three of the twelve photographs were found to be clear enough for identification purposes. Two of these three pictures showed portions of large military objectives, while the third would have been of no value at all to espionage operatives. It was easy enough to deduce what the Japanese had done. They had merely worked out a route for the pigeons to traverse time and time again—a route that took the birds over military objectives. Distances and flying speed had been taken into careful consideration, and the timing devices on the tiny cameras adjusted so that pictures would be taken when the birds were over points of interest to the Imperial Japanese Government. There were, of course, uncontrollable factors involved. For example, if a pigeon took it upon itself to circle around more than usual at the time of departure, the whole schedule would be thrown out of kilter, and when the camera clicked the bird would not be over the points that interested the Japanese. But the Japanese were apparently operating on the law of averages; they knew they would get what they wanted if they had enough birds and enough film—and they had plenty of both— and if they tried long enough.

Countermeasures adopted by the intelligence services to thwart the feathered spies cannot be detailed here. But it can be said that appropriate measures were taken, and turned out successfully.

By the beginning of 1935 separate investigations were proceeding on various fronts, both on the Pacific Coast and the Atlantic seaboard. While many of these probes were separate and complete in themselves, such as those relating to former Lieutenant Commander Farnsworth and to ex-yeoman Thompson, each investigation was nevertheless part and parcel of the over-all picture. For example, Count von Kietel was continuing to use his ingenious code in the Third Avenue stationery store. The Japanese whose activities were governed by this code had no direct connection, for instance, with Doctor Furusawa's medical building in Los Angeles; yet it was perfectly clear, in the minds of the investigators, at least, that the activities of the Japanese in New York bore a relationship, however indirect, to the activities of Doctor Furusawa. By the same token, the intelligence that was being surreptiously relayed by carrier pigeons all fitted in with the work that Roy Akagi was doing in New York, despite the fact that in all probability Akagi knew little, if anything, about the pigeon photographers. The investigators were picking up pieces of a gigantic jig-saw puzzle wherever they found them; it was not always apparent where a specific piece of the puzzle would fit, but they knew that eventually each piece would contribute to the whole picture.

On a certain night early in 1935, Little Tokyo in Los

Angeles teemed with a medley of activity, and two Japanese attracted no attention as they loitered just beyond
the glare of an orchid neon sign advertising the Little
Tokyo Club. The establishment was, so far as met the
eye, a social organization where both alien and American-
born Japanese foregathered just to sit around and talk,
gamble and drink saké. It was suspected by certain
members of the Los Angeles Police Department and
Federal narcotic inspectors, however, that crafty little
Yoshiaki Yasuda, president of the club, was trafficking
in dope and in white slaves, but surveillance had thus
far failed to result in evidence.

It was almost midnight when the two Japanese took
up their vigil outside the club. They had to wait for
three hours before they saw what they had come for—
Yasuda, the club's president. As usual, Yasuda was accompanied by two bodyguards whose tight-fitting jackets
clearly outlined the shapes of the guns they carried in
their hip pockets.

Yasuda and his bodyguards got into a car standing at
the curb and spurted away. The two loiterers, who had
also come by automobile, hurriedly got into their car
and followed Yasuda's. They must have heard Yasuda's
name being called out in a warning tone by a friend
of the club president's who had happened along and
seen the two diminutive figures rushing suspiciously
into the pursuit car. But if the two who were following
Yasuda heard the warning cry, Yasuda did not.

Yasuda lived within a five-minute drive of his club.
The area in front of his home was pitch black when his
bodyguards deposited him and drove off. In the meantime the two men who were following him had parked
their car down the street, and walked to a point near

the house. Yasuda had forgotten the key to his front door, so he aroused his wife, a slant-eyed beauty. When she switched on a hall light and opened the front door, her husband presented a grimly attractive silhouette to the two stealthy watchers. The silence of the neighborhood was broken by the sound of shots, and Yoshiaki Yasuda spun around and dropped to the porch floor, a corpse.

The police questioned Yasuda's bodyguards. They wouldn't talk. Then, from Yasuda's acquaintance who had seen the two men trailing him from the club, detectives learned that one of the pair had borne more than a passing resemblance to an infamous character named Sigo Nojiri. This man Nojiri had once been associated with Yasuda in the operation of the Tokyo Club, but the police learned that the two had quarreled violently over money matters during the past year.

Three and a half weeks after Yasuda's murder detectives caught up with Nojiri, but the man was dead. He had met precisely the same fate as the man he had been suspected of killing. Although the Japanese have a singular talent for masking their inner feelings, detectives nevertheless noticed a certain satisfaction on the faces of Yasuda's friends and business acquaintances following the finding of Nojiri's bullet-riddled body.

Murders in the Japanese underworlds of Los Angeles and other Pacific Coast cities had long been a dime a dozen, and the police never became too exercised about them. The Los Angeles Police Department, understandably enough, saw nothing more in the murders of Yasuda and Nojiri than an expression of bad blood among bad people. Certainly it never occurred to the detectives working on the two cases that there was a direct link between these rather nondescript crimes and the incalculably evil program of espionage being carried on by the Japanese government on the Pacific Coast more than six years before Pearl Harbor.

The man who murdered the murderer of Yasuda was himself taken care of in the due course of events—bullets in the dark again—and then the perpetrator of the third homicide was laid to rest in a Japanese cemetery with thirty-odd slugs in his body. The murders continued; only a few months after the first one, killers in the Japanese underworld of Los Angeles had applied a sort of a chain-letter principle to their hideous handiwork and, before the smell of gunpowder had dissipated, more than a score of Japanese had died of what the underworld calls lead poisoning.

Although it was a patent impossibility for white detectives to get on the inside of goings-on within the Little Tokyo Club, it became obvious, from outside surveillance, that there was something about the place that did not meet the naked eye. The Los Angeles Field Office of the Federal Bureau of Investigation had by this time become interested in the Little Tokyo Club, not because any of the murders were Federal offenses, but because it was quite obvious that the fountainhead of so much lethal strife—Yasuda—must have been quite an important man. When the F.B.I. dug a little deeper into the situation, it was learned that Yasuda had apparently had connections with similar social clubs in San Francisco, Portland and Seattle.

Then the F.B.I. learned that burial arrangements for some of the murder victims had been made by a gentleman they were already acquainted with—Doctor Furusawa, operator of the suspicious medical building on Weller Street.

If a man who was up to what the Weller Street physician was suspected of being up to had exhibited such interest in murder victims who had been closely linked to the Little Tokyo Club, it was only reasonable to suppose that the club itself somehow fitted into the espionage jig-saw puzzle.

The F.B.I. and the O.N.I. made the simultaneous discovery that Yasuda, the first of the murder victims, had been a frequent visitor not only to Doctor Furusawa but to the Japanese Consulate in Los Angeles. The Consulate, as well as the private hospital, had for some time been under surveillance, and visitors there were followed. Not long after the last of the shootings, Dr. Furusawa one day had a visitor who had for almost a year been a person of interest to Federal investigators. The man was a particularly evil-looking little Japanese called Kanekichi Yamamoto. His eyes were large, intensely dark, and crafty. His mouth was misshapen and cruel, and his nose, battered in many a fight, was so broad at its base that it was about one-third as wide as his whole face. He was known to the F.B.I., the O.N.I. and the police of Portland, Seattle, San Francisco and Los Angeles as the Yellow Al Capone, undisputed leader of the Japanese underworld from the Mexican border to the Canadian line. You can imagine, then, that the Federal investigators were interested when they saw Yamamoto calling at the private hospital on Weller Street, and when they learned that the first of the score of murder victims had been his Los Angeles representative.

Doctor Furusawa and the Yellow Al Capone were trailed from the medical building to the Japanese Consulate, and they were in there for more than two hours. When they came out they parted, the physician going back to his hospital and Yamamoto proceeding to, of all places, the Little Tokyo Club.

Immediately after the gangster's arrival at the club, Japanese hoodlums began filtering in. It was late in the afternoon and the hoodlums and Yamamoto didn't depart until early the next morning. The hoodlums went to their respective places of abode, and Yamamoto, whose home at the time was in a Seattle hotel operated by Japanese, spent the night in the personal quarters of the Japanese Consul in Los Angeles.

It all began to add up. Since it was suspected, although far from proven, that the two principal clearing houses for espionage information in Los Angeles were Doctor Furusawa's hospital and the Japanese Consulate, the deduction was that Yamamoto, the gangster, was something more than a suspected trafficker in dope and white slaves. It was a known fact that Japanese consular representatives wanted no truck with common hoodlums of their race. When a man slept in the personal quarters of the Consul himself, that man was an important figure to the Japanese government, and no two ways about it.

Various Pacific Coast police departments had known about Yamamoto for more than a decade. He was now a man of about forty. When he had arrived in the United States in the early twenties, he had jumped the freighter that he had come over on as a seaman, and lost himself in the Japanese colony in Seattle. He was so illiterate that he could hardly speak his native language, but he had been there when the brains were passed out.

Unscrupulous in the extreme, Yamamoto had come up, in the space of a decade, from a laborer in the Washington lumber camps to a racketeer of major stature. Like the Chicago gangster that he came to be named after, Yamamoto turned his hand to practically anything that would bring in quick, big and easy money. As it was to develop later, he had succeeded in fooling customs agents for years by smuggling in dope in such an ingenious manner that to dwell on the method here would only put ideas in the heads of other criminals. He had trafficked in women, both white and yellow, and he was, early in 1935, the proprietor of a string of gambling houses and houses of prostitution that stretched from Seattle to San Diego.

The secret of Yamamoto's apparent immunity from interference by the police departments of the cities where he operated lay in the fact that he was paying graft—and not peanuts, either—to certain crooks in certain police departments. The F.B.I. and the O.N.I. were later to learn this.

Convinced that somewhere along the line they could unearth additional clues from Yamamoto's past if they probed far enough, the F.B.I. conferred with officials of the United States Customs Service.

Thus it was that the F.B.I. was able to attach considerable significance to certain data relating to Yamamoto which had for three years been in the possession of Inspector Melvin Hanks, one of the aces of the Customs Service. In 1932, Hanks had come upon evidence in Seattle that convinced him that Yamamoto was the big shot behind Pacific Coast dope smuggling. Unfortunately, however, Hanks didn't have enough to go into court against Yamamoto. He decided to enlist the aid of Japanese officials in getting the goods on Yamamoto.

One particular dope shipment that was seized bore the imprint of a drug manufacturer in Osaka, Japan. Since there was a law in Japan requiring all manufacturers of opium and other dope (manufacture of such narcotics being legal there) to supply the Japanese government with the names of individuals to whom the stuff was shipped, the American customs official decided to have inquiries made in Japan as to the identity of the consignee for whom the seized Seattle dope had been intended.

Hanks forwarded his request to Martin Scott, Treasury Attaché of the American Consulate in Osaka. Scott took the matter up, by letter, with the Chief of Police of Osaka. His letter went unanswered, so he wrote again. When there was no answer forthcoming to the second communication, Scott called personally on the Chief of Police. The Chief was very polite but said that he was sorry, there was nothing he could do.

As soon as he left the Osaka police headquarters, Scott had the feeling that he was being followed. He had means of ascertaining whether there was anything to his suspicion—and his suspicion was confirmed. For several weeks afterward, Scott and other attachés of the American Consulate in Osaka had their footsteps dogged wherever they went, by sly little Japanese who were strangers to them. At length they resorted to counteraction, just to find out who the shadows were, and they soon learned that the men were detectives of the Osaka Police Department.

Customs officials in Seattle had noticed a flurry of activity around the Japanese Consulate there at a time, it later developed, that coincided with the receipt by the Osaka Police Chief of the first letter written by the Treasury Attaché of the American Consulate in that city. Customs agents in Seattle found that they, too, were being shadowed by Japanese. They resorted to counteraction also and learned, not exactly to their surprise, that one of the shadows was a minor employee of the Japanese Consulate in San Francisco who had apparently been brought up to Washington for the job, and that another one was none other than a trusted underling of the Yellow Capone.

For three years, then, the customs authorities had regarded the shadow work in Osaka and Seattle as an outcome of caution being exercised over Yamamoto's close shave with one particular dope shipment. But now the F.B.I. was able to put an entirely different and far more sinister interpretation on the behavior of the Japanese, both in Osaka and Seattle, three years before. As early as 1932, the F.B.I. decided, Yamamoto had been a figure of paramount importance to Tokyo.

Not long after the F.B.I. had seen him visiting Doctor Furusawa's, Yamamoto took over control of the Little Tokyo Club. Strife in the Los Angeles underworld stopped as if by magic. Whereas in the past the Little Tokyo Club had been frequented by relatively unimportant run-of-the-mill Japanese, with Yamamoto's presence it became the rendezvous of important men of that race. Doctor Furusawa, for example, visited it three nights running, and various attachés of the Japanese Consulate, including the Consul himself, began to make the place a hang-out.

Soon the small run-of-the-mill people were in the minority; the big shots had virtually taken over. Among the visitors were several "patients" in Doctor Furusawa's private hospital—men who, when they were trailed back to the Orient, were found to be officers of the Imperial Japanese Navy and persons who were received with open arms at the Japanese Foreign Office.

Among others who visited the Little Tokyo Club while on a flying visit to Los Angeles was Commander Josiyuki Itimiya, the Washington Embassy Naval Attaché, who was under surveillance at the moment by both the O.N.I. and the F.B.I. in connection with the Farnsworth case. Apparently Commander Itimiya had come west for a conference with Dr. Furusawa and Lieutenant Commander Miyazaki, the latter under observation in the investigation into Harry Thomas Thompson, the ex-yeoman. Miyazaki and Itimiya spent several days in the private hospital on Weller Street and then, after a dinner given in their honor by Dr. and Mrs. Furusawa at the Oriental Cafe, a Japanese restaurant, Miyazaki returned to his masquerade as a language student at Stanford, and Itimiya went back to Washington.

The investigators by this time had Yamamoto's relationship to the over-all Japanese espionage machinery pretty well figured out. Bit by bit, they had pieced together evidence showing that the Little Tokyo Club which he had taken over in Los Angeles was only one of many similar clubs in other Pacific Coast cities, all of them apparently the mediums through which the Yellow Capone carried on his various racket enterprises. He had hundreds of henchmen who operated out of these places between the Mexican and Canadian borders. It was obvious to the Federal probers that Yamamoto had made individual arrangements with crooks in various police departments for local protection so that he could go on with his racketeering unmolested. But what concerned the Federal detectives was that the Imperial Japanese Government was apparently in the process of integrating Yamamoto's gangster set-up into the espionage machinery, if indeed that had not already been accomplished.

CHAPTER 6

Scale Models for Disaster

Toward the end of 1936, while the investigators were sticking close to Yamamoto, Count Hermann von Kietel shifted his activities to Los Angeles, taking an apartment at a fashionable hotel there. His wife, the beautiful Countess, had, during all those years, shuttled back and forth across the Atlantic between New York and Hamburg, no doubt acting as a courier of information. The same held true of Manfred, von Kietel's bald-headed butler. Customs inspectors in New York had always been particularly thorough in examining the baggage of both Countess von Kietel and Manfred, but had found nothing. Whatever it was that these two were carrying, they were carrying it in their heads. At no time had any Federal law-enforcement agency obtained evidence upon which to base an arrest.

Not that the F.B.I., to name one agency, had been anxious to arrest either the Countess or the man who posed as a butler. It is axiomatic that, up to a certain point, a spy on the loose is more valuable than one who is locked up—for two reasons. First, a spy traveling at will often leads to other spies. Second, a spy at liberty can often be used to advantage by counterespionage agents who contrive to feed him with false information that is of more harm than good to an enemy.

The Countess had not led the investigators anywhere during her presence in New York, but Manfred
had. He had been observed from time to time meeting
Japanese on street corners and in out-of-the-way restaurants, and had thus turned up many suspects that
the F.B.I. might not otherwise have learned about.
Both the Countess and the butler were now in Germany, and American agents keeping tabs on them there
reported that they were showing no disposition to return to the United States.

In Los Angeles, the Count, who was now calling
himself plain Hermann Kietel, was seen meeting certain Japanese who were known to be close to Yamamoto. The very fact that the Count had an indirect
connection with Yamamoto forthwith increased the
sinister aspects of Yamamoto's character. Apparently
the Count was on the Pacific Coast because the Japanese espionage and sabotage program was really getting
started there in a big way. Gyssling, the German Vice
Consul in New York, and Akagi, the Japanese with the
railway-office front, were obviously taking over in the
east the Count's work of co-ordinating German and
Japanese intelligence.

Japanese consulates in eastern and western cities were
increasing their staffs, although the bulk of legitimate
business at the consulates had not increased. The fishing boats manned by Japanese and operating out of
California ports were getting bigger and better and
greater in number. Shinto and Buddhist priests in the
shrines and temples of Southern California were seen
associating more and more on the outside of their religious domains with men to whom religion patently
didn't mean a thing. The various Japanese social or-

ganizations in Pacific Coast cities seemed to be drawing within themselves and getting more secret with the
passage of each month.

It was not long after the conviction of Farnsworth
that the F.B.I. confirmed its suspicions of the stature, in
the eyes of the Japanese government, of the man named
Yamamoto, the Yellow Al Capone. A Korean in his
early thirties, Kilsoo K. Haan, one of the organizers of
a secret anti-Japanese organization called the Sino-
Korean Peoples' League, had succeeded in deceiving
attachés of the Japanese Consulate in Honolulu into
believing that his sympathies lay with Japan. Haan was
a young man who knew his way about the Orient. In
addition to his native language, he spoke Chinese and
Japanese fluently.

Some time in 1935 Haan had sold attachés of the
Japanese Consulate in Honolulu on the idea that he
could convert the Hawaiian Koreans into seeing things
Japan's way, and the Japanese had arranged for him to
take a job as a bellboy in a Honolulu hotel to act as a
cover for his real activities on their behalf. The plan,
as the Japanese had it figured out, was for Haan to
present the picture of a poor bellboy rather than a
person of affluence, and he was to circulate at Korean
gathering places in Honolulu and begin a propaganda
campaign of selling Japan to his own people.

It was this young man who sent information about
Yamamoto to the headquarters of the Sino-Korean Peoples' League in Washington. Haan, during his "plant"
in the Honolulu hotel, made it a point to listen in on
every Japanese conversation within earshot. When, for
example, he was summoned to a room occupied by
Japanese to serve whiskey-and-soda, he would stall

around on various subterfuges, or suddenly pop back into the room for something he had forgotten. It was in this way that Haan, on more than one occasion, heard the name of Yamamoto mentioned by important Japanese who stopped at the hotel while passing through Honolulu. The men who mentioned Yamamoto's name had all been, in Haan's considered opinion, espionage operatives, either on their way to the United States or on their way from it. While the young Korean had never heard Yamamoto's name mentioned in any particular connection, it was clear to him that this Mr. Yamamoto, whoever he was, was considered important by the Jap agents who carried information from the United States to Nippon.

J. Edgar Hoover was no sooner in possession of this latest intelligence from Hawaii, than the Sino-Korean Peoples' League received a coded wireless message from Haan reading, in translation, as follows:

I HAVE DEFINITELY LEARNED THROUGH A CONVERSATION 1 HAVE JUST OVERHEARD IN THE JAPANESE CONSULATE HERE THAT YAMAMOTO AND HIS ORGANIZATION ARE ABOUT TO BEGIN AN INTENSIVE COURSE OF STUDY FOR THE PURPOSE OF COMMITTING SABOTAGE IN CALIFORNIA, OREGON AND WASHINGTON WHEN WAR COMES. THE NIGHT CLUBS THAT YAMAMOTO OPERATES ARE TO BE THE HEADQUARTERS FOR THIS TRAINING AND THE TRAINING WILL INCLUDE THE CONSTRUCTION AND STUDY OF SPECIALLY BUILT SCALE MODELS OF BRIDGES, ELECTRIC POWER PLANTS, WATER SUPPLY SYSTEMS, RAILROAD YARDS AND OTHER SUCH STRATEGIC POINTS. AN N.Y.K. LINER DUE IN SAN FRANCISCO NEXT THURSDAY IS CARRYING TWO MEN WHOSE NAMES I HAVE BEEN UNABLE TO FIND OUT AND WHO ARE BRINGING INSTRUCTIONS FOR YAMAMOTO.

Forty Japanese got off the liner when it docked, but both the F.B.I. and the O.N.I. were well prepared.

Every last one of them was shadowed. Of the forty, thirty-eight either remained in San Francisco, went to Los Angeles, or entrained for the East. Two, traveling together, called briefly at the Japanese Consulate in San Francisco and then took a train for Seattle. They occupied a drawing room, and it was obvious to agents who boarded the same train that the Consulate had purchased their passage in advance, since the new arrivals had not gone near the ticket windows at the railroad station. When, halfway to Seattle, a Western Union boy came aboard with a coded message for one of the agents, they felt that they were on the trail of the two men who had come with the sabotage instructions. For the wire stated that Yamamoto had left Los Angeles by plane for Seattle and that the plane would arrive considerably ahead of the train on which the agents were traveling.

When the train reached Seattle, who was at the station to meet the two men who came out of the drawing room but Yamamoto himself.

There could be no doubt now that the right men were being trailed.

The new arrivals and the Yellow Capone went to the latter's suite in a Seattle hotel. The three were together for two solid days, never once setting foot outside the hotel. The pair from the Orient left Seattle just in time to catch a train that connected at San Francisco with a steamer of the Dollar Line sailing for the Orient.

There was a heavy concentration of O.N.I. and F.B.I. agents around Yamamoto's hotel after his visitors left. Almost immediately after their departure, Yamamoto went to his club in Seattle. He had apparently telephoned ahead that he was coming, for just before he got there more than fifty Japanese underworld characters drifted into the place.

The meeting in the Seattle club lasted all night. In the morning Yamamoto went directly from the club to an airport and boarded a plane for Portland. There he went to his club in that city. Again his arrival had obviously been expected, for half a hundred underworld characters—all Japanese—awaited him there. This meeting lasted most of the day.

Yamamoto then went to the Japanese Consulate in Portland until it was time to catch an overnight limited for San Francisco.

In San Francisco, virtually the same situation that the agents had observed in Seattle and Portland was duplicated. When he took a late afternoon plane for Los Angeles, the agents knew pretty much what to look for at the Yamamoto club in that city. And they were not wrong.

All told, Yamamoto had held conferences in four cities since the departure of his friends from Japan, and he had talked with approximately two hundred underworld characters in long conferences—apparently giving all of them instructions of some sort.

It was not possible for the Federal agents to trail every one of the Japanese who had attended the meetings called by Yamamoto. But the agents managed to fasten themselves on the trails of enough of these men to arrive almost immediately at the conclusion that they were bent on assembling information for future sabotage.

While the details of what Yamamoto's underlings did cannot at this time be disclosed in detail, it can be stated that immediately following the meetings with their chief they dropped whatever they had been doing and infiltrated themselves in and around strategic military and naval locations the entire length of the Pacific Coast. Through powerful field glasses, the Federal sleuths, stationed at secret vantage points, were able to observe many of Yamamoto's men taking photographs of strategic points. Not that this matter of Japanese taking photographs was anything new. They had been doing that for years. But these pictures seemed to be taken with definite angles in mind—angles that would enable engineers, for example, to duplicate what had been photographed. For instance, one particular underling of Yamamoto's spent three solid days in the vicinity of a certain bridge. When he was through with his photographic work he had unquestionably duplicated on his negatives every part of the bridge that could possibly be photographed.

By March, 1937—some two years after the first of the killings at the Little Tokyo Club in Los Angeles—the photographic work was pretty well completed. Yamamoto had been running up and down the Pacific Coast like a harried executive, holding meetings at his clubs. It was an interesting fact to the investigators that for many months now, dope shipments from the Far East had dropped considerably. This was taken as an indication that Yamamoto was too occupied with his more important current work to bother with mere smuggling and racketeering.

Both the F.B.I. and the O.N.I. could, of course, have closed in on the two hundred Japanese who were running around gathering photographic and other information for Yamamoto. But that wouldn't have been good strategy. There was one major question in the minds of

the investigators, and that was just who would be employed to reduce the information gathered by the gangsters into actual scale models for the use of potential
saboteurs. The investigators decided that by continued
shadowing of Yamamoto, and of the various Japanese
Consulates and Doctor Furusawa's private hospital in
Los Angeles, the answer would come to light sooner or
later.

One afternoon in April, 1937, two smart-looking Japanese showed up at the private hospital on Weller
Street. If ever two men looked to be in good health,
these two did. Yet evening came and the night passed,
and they didn't come out of the place. The next day at
noon, while they were still in there, Yamamoto, who
had come in from San Francisco on a morning plane,
was driven to Weller Street by a chauffeur who had met
him at the airport. He stayed in the private hospital until early evening, and when he came out he was accompanied by the two men who had gone in the previous
day. They were new figures in the investigation, these
two, and the Federal detectives were most anxious to
find out who they were.

Yamamoto and the two men went from Furusawa's to
the Japanese Consulate. The three spent the night in
the Consul's personal quarters. In the morning, when
they appeared on the street, they split up. Yamamoto
took a plane for Seattle; the two others went to a downtown Los Angeles office building. There it was found
out that they were two of the most prominent Japanese
engineers on the Pacific Coast! There was no doubt now
as to who was going to construct the scale models from
which saboteurs would work.

The engineers were trailed for more than a week.

They visited hardware stores, lumber companies and other establishments where one would go to buy material for the construction of scale models of bridges, harbors and the like. The technique of the agents was simple. They just waited outside a store until the Japanese had made their purchases, then went in and found out what had been bought.

Now the engineers began to burn the midnight oil in their offices in downtown Los Angeles. They had for a long time been engaged in legitimate work, but now clients who called found the doors of the offices closed, even during regular business hours. The watchers in the meantime had succeeded in renting an office on the same floor, as representatives of a southern fabric company.

After the two engineers had been at work for more than a week, they began to have visitors. Doctor Furusawa called and so did the Japanese Consul and several of the attachés of the Consulate. Yamamoto came down from Seattle and spent all of one morning with the engineers.

Even had the agents not known what the two men were up to, their suspicious behavior would eventually have come to notice. The two Japanese had notified the superintendent of the building, in no uncertain terms, that under no circumstances were cleaning women to let themselves into their offices at night. The superintendent, curious, asked why. He didn't like Japanese. "Because," replied one of the engineers, "we are working on something in there that we don't want anyone to see."

"Working on what?" asked the superintendent.

"Something secret; it's for the government."

In a way, the Japanese was telling the truth, but he didn't say *what* government.

By May, 1937, the two Japanese began leaving their office building at odd hours of the night—anywhere from eleven o'clock to three in the morning—carrying large suitcases. Sometimes they proceeded by taxicab to the Japanese Consulate and deposited there whatever was in the suitcases. The watchers knew that when the men left their office, the suitcases they carried were filled with something heavy; that was obvious from the way the bags weighed them down. When they left the Consulate, it was just as obvious that the bags were empty. Sometime the engineers went directly from their offices to Furusawa's; at other times they went to the Little Tokyo Club, but they never appeared there unless Yamamoto himself was there.

The deliveries of what were obviously the scale models went on for some time. But no delivery was ever made except to one of three places—the Consulate, the private hospital or the Little Tokyo Club. The investigators wondered if the engineers were making models of only strategic points in and around Los Angeles. If that were so, then other engineers must be making models of locations in Washington and Oregon—engineers not discovered yet. Finally, however, watchers at the three focal delivery points noticed men going in with empty bags and coming out with filled bags, and departing for San Francisco, Seattle, Portland and other points. This seemed clear indication that the two Los Angeles engineers were making all of the scale models.

In the meantime, half a dozen American-born Japanese who were known to be acquaintances of some of Yamamoto's underlings who had done the photographic work were carefully investigated by Federal operatives and found to be trustworthy. These men were approached, very carefully, and asked to learn all they could about the men they knew in Yamamoto's employ. They were warned, however, to be extremely cautious and instructed by all means to pass up even the most promising information if following through would cause the slightest suspicion to fasten itself on them.

The Federal agents made elaborate arrangements whereby the six Japanese counterspies would report to them without being found out by any of Yamamoto's men. For several weeks the arrangement worked to great advantage. Two of the six Japanese counteroperatives, in fact, disclosed to the Federal men the broad general plan of the Imperial Japanese Government for sabotage on the West Coast when war came. The details of that are still a government secret but it can be said that the information was of the most vital sort and among the most revealing unearthed since Japanese spies had begun to operate on a large scale.

The investigators had high hopes of worming their way right into the heart of Yamamoto's organization through the medium of the Japanese counterspies. All six of these men had by this time succeeded in being accepted in the Little Tokyo Club, where the membership requirements were growing increasingly rigid. While none of the counteroperatives had as yet succeeded in attending any of the meetings at which Yamamoto presided over his hoodlums, they had nevertheless learned that the men were getting intensive courses of instruction in just how to take care of important strategic points when war came, with the scale models being used by the instructors.

According to information picked up by the counter-operatives, Yamamoto himself sometimes acted as instructor. At other times, one or both of the engineers who had built the scale models talked to the men who were being trained for sabotage. This latter information checked with what the agents had already suspected, for they had lately observed the engineers traveling to the Yamamoto club in Los Angeles, either together or singly, and up to the San Francisco, Portland and Seattle clubs, always when there were large meetings.

One day, after a Los Angeles meeting, Yamamoto took a plane for San Francisco. A Federal operative was on the same plane, and another Federal man was waiting at the airport in San Francisco. When Yamamoto arrived there he was handed a note by his chauffeur. While he was usually as adept as other Japanese at masking his feelings, Yamamoto this day gave way to plain rage when he read the contents of the note. There was a plane leaving for Los Angeles within a few minutes, and he was on it.

Federal operatives, waiting at the Los Angeles airport for Yamamoto's return, wondered what had upset him so. When he reached Los Angeles, he waved aside his chauffeur there, and got into a taxi instead. During the next hour he led his shadows around in circles, changing taxis, going into buildings through one door and coming out another, and resorting to other dodges employed only by a man who realizes he is being tailed. The agents immediately feared the worst; they feared that perhaps someone in Los Angeles had found out about the counterespionage operatives who were worming their way deeper into the Little Tokyo Club. It could only have been a matter of the gravest importance that would have caused Yamamoto to display such anger and to return immediately to Los Angeles.

The agents succeeded in getting in touch with four of the six counterespionage men. They warned them to go into hiding. The other two weren't at home, and could not be reached.

Mr. Yamamoto had only begun. The next morning, the two counterespionage operatives were found in Little Tokyo, murdered.

CHAPTER 7

Mystery of the Bubbling Acid

SHORTLY AFTER THE MURDER of these two men, a hard-hitting San Bernardino attorney named Benjamin Harrison was appointed United States Attorney for Southern California, with offices in Los Angeles. Then the United States Government really began to coordinate data relating to Japanese espionage activities on the Pacific Coast. Harrison, a capable public servant—as are most United States Attorneys, in contrast to the many political hacks who get to be County Prosecutors—had hardly taken the oath of office when he began an investigation into a situation that had long alarmed thinking Californians—the suspected activities of fishing boats operating out of California ports and manned by Japanese. The new United States Attorney had, like everybody else in California whose hearing was unimpaired, heard fabulous stories about espionage activities of the Japanese fishermen. What he had in mind was an investigation designed to separate fiction from truth, and then proceed accordingly.

Among other things, United States Attorney Harrison was a scholar. He went into the history of Japanese fishermen and learned of an incident that had taken place more than thirty years before—in 1905—that was of such lingering significance to the Japanese people that it had a direct bearing on what was taking place in 1937. In the year 1905, two Japanese fishing boats had observed the approach of the Russian battle fleet in the Straits of Tsushima and thereupon rushed to the Japanese naval base at Sasebo, where the fleet of Japan was at anchor. Admiral Togo was in command of the Japanese fleet, and because of the intelligence relayed to him by the two fishing boats he was able to align his forces in a favorable formation before engaging the Russian fleet. To this day, naval strategists are of the opinion that Togo's final victory over the Russians was made possible through the intelligence carried to him by the two fishing boats. The United States Attorney learned that even in 1937, in the little town of Sasebo, in Japan, the Japanese living in the area each year celebrated the anniversary of the arrival of the fishing boats at Sasebo at a Shinto shrine erected to the memory of the fishermen of 1905.

If, reasoned United States Attorney Harrison, the Japanese still thought so much about this incident of more than three decades ago, it was only reasonable to suppose that they were, as rumor had it, depending to a large extent on Japanese fishermen in California to supply them with intelligence against the United States.

In 1937 there were about nine thousand fishermen operating off the California coast. Four thousand were Americans, two thousand were Italians and three thousand were Japanese. Of these three thousand, five hundred operated out of Terminal Island at San Pedro—the harbor port of Los Angeles, where all of the important freighters and passenger liners calling at Southern California anchored. Terminal Island itself was preponderantly Japanese. All told, five thousand people lived there, and three thousand of them were Japs. There were seven big fish canneries on the island, a bank, a postoffice, and thirty-six business establishments, mostly Japanese. It was the only community of its kind in the United States.

The American Legion and other patriotic organizations were, in 1935 and in 1937, behind bills introduced in the Legislature at Sacramento to confine commercial fishing licenses to American citizens, such as had already been done in Oregon and Washington. This would have been a big blow to the Japanese fishermen, for the bulk of them had been born in Japan and therefore could not hope ever to become citizens. But at both legislative sessions—and at the 1939 session as well—the bills died in committee.

Some canneries, principally ones operated by white men on Terminal Island, organized a powerful lobby that brought pressure to bear on certain so-called statesmen who made laws at Sacramento. The canneries, you see, stood to have their operating costs increased if they could no longer employ Japanese fishermen, who were a good deal cheaper than white fishermen. There is nothing in the records to show that any of the operators of the canneries suffered from defective hearing; therefore they must have heard the stories that were being circulated about the Japanese fishermen doubling in brass as spies. There is no evidence, either, to show that the cannery operators had severe cases of astigmatism or any other kind of eye trouble that would have prevented them from seeing what the Japanese were pulling under their very noses—open espionage operations. Yet these men, supposedly patriotic Americans, thought more of a dollar than they did of the security of the country that made their success possible. There can be no question that their successful fight against the proposed statute that would have seriously hampered Japanese espionage operations in California six full years before Pearl Harbor was in the nature of a major contribution to the Japanese government. Time after time, watchmen employed by the canneries on Terminal Island told their employers that the Japanese fishermen were unquestionably engaged in espionage, particularly after the fall of darkness; and the watchmen were told, in effect, to mind their own business if they wanted to keep their jobs.

All of this was found out by the new United States Attorney. He found out something else, too. The cannery lobby was not the only form of pressure that was brought to bear on the legislators in Sacramento. Investigators for Mr. Harrison learned that important members of the Communist Party in California had also exerted considerable influence in having legislation blocked, both in 1935 and in 1937. All of which indicates that certain American citizens—big businessmen and Communists alike—were willing to do the United States a bad turn for reasons of their own.

The boats that the Japanese used were valued at anywhere from twenty thousand dollars to two hundred thousand dollars each. Many of them were held under dummy owners. The bulk of them were powered by Diesel engines, and some of them had cruising ranges up to six thousand miles. Special officers of the Los Angeles Police Department, stationed at Terminal Island, found out for a fact—and so did investigators for United States Attorney Harrison—that the larger boats, especially the tuna clippers, were equipped with short-wave radios and radio telephones that could communicate direct with Tokyo. One Terminal Island policeman, a particularly alert cop, sneaked onto a boat one night and saw that it was secretly armed from stem to stern.

It wasn't long before the United States Attorney found to his chagrin that he was up against a stone wall, so far as anti-Japanese legislation was concerned. That didn't stop Harrison, however, from continuing to find out everything he could about the Japanese fishermen. He conferred frequently with F.B.I. officials and with a certain Captain of the Office of Naval Intelligence. The Captain, who understood the Japanese language thoroughly, intercepted, in August, 1937, a radio message that had apparently emanated from a Japanese ship somewhere in the Pacific. The message stated that a boat known as the *Flying Cloud* was to meet a freighter named the *Edna* at a certain point seventy miles off the coast of Lower California.

The O.N.I. Captain had long since compiled a list of the names of the fishing boats that the Japanese operated, and he knew that the *Flying Cloud* went out for tuna for the Van Camp Fish Packing Company, which had a cannery on Terminal Island. He assigned O.N.I. operatives, masquerading as wharf rats, to infiltrate themselves into Terminal Island and find out if the *Flying Cloud* was riding at anchor.

The *Flying Cloud* was. Moreover, Yamamoto, the Yellow Capone, was aboard her. The only question now was when the tuna clipper would depart for her rendezvous with the *Edna*. In intercepting the message, the Captain had not been able to catch the time of the

rendezvous, but that made little difference. He knew
where the rendezvous was, and his men on Terminal
Island had, by observing the *Flying Cloud,* been able
to approximate her speed. When the boat left, it would
be but reasonable to suppose that she was headed for
her rendezvous; and calculations could easily be made,
based on the hour of departure, the boat's speed and the
location of the rendezvous point, which would determine in advance when she would meet the *Edna.*

The *Flying Cloud,* carrying an all-Japanese crew, departed at two o'clock one morning. Word was flashed
to the O.N.I. Captain, and he made arrangements to
have a Navy plane in readiness to carry him out over
the Pacific so that he could take a look at what was going on when the two craft met.

The O.N.I. Captain timed things perfectly—in fact,
a little too perfectly. As his plane flew toward the rendezvous and he gazed ahead through powerful glasses,
he saw a freighter heading east and a smaller boat,
which looked like the *Flying Cloud,* going west. The
two craft were about three miles apart. The Captain's
supposition was that he had arrived a little early, and
that the Japanese fishing boat and the freighter had not
yet actually made contact. He ordered the plane to turn
around and go back, keeping out of sight so as not to
arouse the suspicion of either the crew of the freighter
or the smaller boat. The plane circled around, beyond
the view of either of the boats, for about half an hour,
and then headed out to sea again.

The Captain's glasses were such good ones that his
plane did not have to go too close to the boats for him
to see what was going on. By this time the *Flying Cloud*
was standing by, alongside the freighter. The smaller

boat was flying a Japanese flag, although it had been flying the Stars and Stripes when it left Terminal Island. The *Edna* was flying a swastika. Certainly the picture the Captain saw—a Japanese fishing boat secretly meeting a German freighter—did not add up with Hitler's protestations that he wanted only peace, and with the smiling assurances of Japan's ambassador in Washington that Japan had no designs on the United States.

Through his glasses, the Captain saw that some large drums which looked like gasoline containers were being unloaded from the German freighter to the Japanese fishing boat. On one end the drums were painted a brilliant yellow, while the rest seemed to be dark brown or dark red.

It was obvious to the Captain that these drums were filled with something of vital importance to the Japanese; just what he could not even surmise. But he intended to find out.

The Captain was a thorough man. He had arranged that a Coast Guard cutter be in the vicinity of the point of rendezvous, but beyond the horizon and therefore out of sight, in order to follow the fishing boat after it parted from the freighter. The *Flying Cloud* was picked up by the Coast Guard cutter, traveling not in a northeasterly direction, which would have taken it back to its base at Terminal Island, but due east. Inasmuch as the rendezvous point was seventy miles due west of Ensenada, in Lower California, the supposition of the men on the Coast Guard cutter was that the *Flying Cloud* was going to put in to Ensenada. There would be two sound enough reasons for a Japanese boat carrying something of a secret nature to put in at Ensenada. It was in Mexico and therefore out of jurisdiction of officers of the United States; and there was a large Japanese population in the Lower California town.

While the *Flying Cloud* was still being trailed on its journey toward land—a ticklish business, inasmuch as the Coast Guard cutter could only show itself over the horizon every so often—word was flashed ahead to the O.N.I. as to the probable landing place of the *Flying Cloud*. The O.N.I. thereupon made arrangements with the Mexican Federal Police to have all wharves at Ensenada carefully watched by detectives, dressed as harbor hangers-on, for some sign of the *Flying Cloud*.

Two Mexican detectives posing as roustabouts who had come down from the hills where, they said, they had been unsuccessfully panning for gold, made it known to the Japanese that they wanted jobs. Thus it was that they were lying on a wharf, apparently the worse for overindulgence in tequila, the potent Mexican drink, when the *Flying Cloud* came over the horizon.

Because the act they were putting on seemed so genuine, the two Mexican sleuths were able to tarry in the vicinity without exciting the slightest suspicion, while the Japanese crew of the *Flying Cloud* transferred the drums with the yellow bottoms from the fishing boat to an abandoned flour mill near the wharf. This work was supervised by none other than Yamamoto, the Yellow Capone.

There were some thirty drums in all, each apparently of one-hundred-gallon capacity. Judging from the difficult job that the Japanese had in rolling the drums from the wharf to the abandoned mill, the detectives concluded that the containers were filled to capacity.

After the cargo was safely stowed away in the flour

mill, the *Flying Cloud* proceeded northward, and the supposition was that she was headed for Terminal Island. When she arrived there two nights later, O.N.I. operatives and a special officer of the Los Angeles Police Department were there to see her putting in to a wharf at the foot of Tuna Street.

Apparently the return of the *Flying Cloud* to Terminal Island was an event of more than passing interest to certain Japanese on the island, for two of them who had for some time been under surveillance by the O.N.I. were waiting at the foot of Tuna Street for her to arrive. These two were a man who ran a restaurant on Tuna Street, and another Japanese from the same street who had a criminal record as a narcotic runner. The restaurant, the O.N.I. had learned, was one of the favorite gathering places of fishermen coming in from long trips, and the restaurant owner's friend, the ex-criminal, was usually present when there was a crowd there. So far, neither of these two Japanese had been observed to meet any important Japanese officials, such as attachés of the Consulate in Los Angeles.

It was about one o'clock in the morning when the *Flying Cloud* actually docked. Her crew and Yamamoto, met by the restaurant owner, got into two sedans that had been parked near the wharf and drove up Tuna Street to the restaurant. The ex-criminal remained at the wharf, apparently as a look-out. Half an hour later, a truck drove up and four Japanese got out. They engaged in conversation with the waiting Jap, and then boarded the *Flying Cloud*.

The Los Angeles policeman and two O.N.I. operatives, secreted at vantage points where they could see what was going on, observed the four men from the truck coming off the boat with a large drum—the same sort of drum as those secretly stored in the abandoned mill in Lower California, even to the bottom painted a bright yellow. Just why the Japanese had chosen bright yellow for the bottom of the drums wasn't apparent, though it seemed that the color was to be a tip-off of some sort. But the Japanese couldn't have chosen a better color so far as the American investigators were concerned, for it had shown up like a beacon when the O.N.I. Captain had watched the drums being trans-ferred to the *Flying Cloud* from the German freighter; and now at Terminal Island, even in the darkness of night, the yellow bottom of the drum being rolled to the waiting truck tipped off the watchers that the *Flying Cloud* had, for some reason, brought back a sample of whatever it was that had been taken off the German freighter and stored in Lower California.

By this time, information forwarded to the O.N.I. from the Mexican Federal Police indicated that what-ever was in the drums was of such a secret nature that the Japanese were taking no chances on anybody finding out about it. The detectives in Ensenada had discovered that the flour mill, which hadn't been used for years, was now under a heavy guard twenty-four hours a day. The mill was owned by an Italian, and the guards—eight in all, working in twelve-hour shifts—included four Italians and four Japanese, evenly divided on each shift. One shift began at midnight and ended at noon, and the next shift worked from noon until midnight. Mexican detectives at secret vantage points near the building where the yellow-bottomed drums were stored, observed through field glasses that every one of the guards was heavily armed.

When the drum was aboard the truck at Terminal Island, the ex-criminal's duties were apparently over for the night, for he walked up to the restaurant on Tuna Street and joined the crew of the *Flying Cloud* in the merrymaking that was going on there. Yamamoto, who had been in the restaurant, walked to the waiting truck and got in.

The truck was trailed into Los Angeles. Its destination was, of all places, a Buddhist temple at 342 East First Street. This temple was known as the Koyasan Beikoko Betsuin. One of the men on the truck got out and went to the entrance of the building, which seemed to be in darkness. But the front doors were flung open as soon as the men from the truck reached them, as if someone inside had been waiting for their arrival. Now the drum was taken inside the temple, and the truck went back to Terminal Island. Yamamoto was apparently remaining inside the temple.

For some time, the O.N.I. had been receiving reports from American operatives in Tokyo to the effect that German chemists, who had been brought to the Japanese capital from Berlin, had been working in a secret laboratory near the Foreign Office on new offensive devices for naval warfare. One American newspaper correspondent in Tokyo had informed an attaché of the American Embassy there that a certain contact of his—a man who had always been reliable in the past —had informed him that among the discoveries which the imported German chemists had made was a liquid substance which was comparatively harmless until mixed with salt water. But the combination of the new secret substance and salt water produced an acid of such intensely destructive properties that it would eat right through steel plate. This substance, according to the information given to the newspaper correspondent, and in turn passed on to the Embassy attaché, was designed to be placed in metal drums, which were, in time of war, to be laid like mines in the waters where our battle fleet would be. Explosive devices attached to the drums would be set off by magnetic devices that would go into operation when a battleship passed over one of the drums, the containers would be shattered and the contents released. Once the contents mixed with salt water, a bubbling acid would be formed, which would quickly rise to the surface and fasten itself in gummy form to the plates of the battleships. The acid would eat completely through the plates within twenty-four hours.

The whole idea of the mystery liquid in the gasoline drums sounded so fantastic to the Embassy attaché that he didn't even make a report of it at the time. He suspected that perhaps the newspaperman had been imbibing too freely of saké and someone had pulled his leg while he was in his cups. But now, in the summer of 1937—with thirty-some drums in that mill in Lower California, and another one of the drums at the Buddhist temple on East First Street—the O.N.I. began to make inquiries of its intelligence sources in Tokyo. Thus it learned the story of the drums and the mystery liquid—and forthwith attached a great deal of significance to it. One O.N.I. official was to say later that he would willingly have given five years of his life to have been able to examine immediately the contents of one of the containers in the Mexican flour mill or the one

container sneaked into the Buddhist mission in the dead
of the night.

Buddhist and Shinto missions, officiated over by Japanese priests, dotted the whole of Southern California. If
these supposedly religious sanctuaries were going to be
integrated into the Japanese spy machine on the Pacific
Coast, the work of the O.N.I., the F.B.I. and other investigative bodies was going to be just that much more
difficult.

There seemed to be no developments at the temple
on East First Street during the rest of the night. But
the first thing in the morning things began to happen.
An attaché of the Japanese Consulate showed up at the
mission shortly after nine o'clock. He was quickly followed by Doctor Furusawa—the physician whose private
hospital on Weller Street had long been suspected as a
focal point for espionage workers. The third person to
call—he arrived only ten minutes after Doctor Furusawa—was a tall, thin Japanese who gave the impression of being a professional man. The three visitors—
the Consular attaché, Doctor Furusawa and the unidentified man—remained in the temple most of the morning. When they came out with Yamamoto about noon,
each carried a small package in his right hand. The
watchers got the impression that each one of the Japanese was being very cautious in order that he would not
drop what he was carrying. When this intelligence was
relayed to the O.N.I. it was concluded that the three
men had perhaps been given samples of the contents of
the drum that had been taken into the temple the night
before. Yamamoto himself returned to Seattle.

The unidentified visitor was followed first to another address on East First Street—Number 1291½. This was the headquarters of a Japanese organization known as the Southern California Imperial Veterans. It was known to the investigators that, while this organization was supposedly merely a social one, the majority of its membership were foreign-born Japanese who were therefore not eligible for American citizenship. Moreover, the bulk of the members had seen service at some time or another in the Japanese Army and, since they were still Japanese citizens, they were therefore subject to orders from Japan's Military High Command.

Shadows on the trail of the unidentified man were not able to establish his identity when he visited the headquarters of the association, nor when he stopped afterward right next door, at the Los Angeles offices of the N.Y.K. Steamship Line. It was only after he was trailed to a handsome home on South Western Avenue in Moneta, a suburb of Los Angeles, that he was identified as Doctor Rikita Honda. A quick though cautious canvass of the neighborhood established the fact that Doctor Honda was a physician of considerable standing and that he had white patients as well as yellow ones. Of more interest to the investigators, however, was the disclosure that Dr. Honda's home was frequently the scene of large nocturnal Japanese gatherings which didn't break up until almost daylight.

That night, just after the quick California dusk had descended, sleuths assigned to trail Dr. Honda, Dr. Furusawa and the Consular attaché who had called at the Buddhist mission, found themselves converging at a point two blocks from Dr. Furusawa's Weller Street hospital. Dr. Honda, who had left his own home in his car, had first picked up the Consular attaché, and now he picked up Dr. Furusawa. The fact that Furusawa was not called for at his private hospital was of some concern to the O.N.I. investigators, and also to the F.B.I. operatives who had in the meantime joined them. For it might indicate that he had caught on to the fact that he was under surveillance. The shadows were interested in a little package that the Doctor was carrying; it looked like the same one he had taken out of the Buddhist temple.

The car bearing the three Japs was trailed in the direction of San Pedro. Once outside the heavy traffic of Los Angeles, Dr. Honda stepped on the gas and sped along at almost seventy miles an hour. As much as they wanted to keep on the trail, the investigators were obliged to drop it. They were following the tried-and-true police rule that it's far better to drop the subject of surveillance than to be uncovered—and certainly they would have been uncovered had they followed Dr. Honda at seventy miles an hour.

One of the O.N.I. operatives telephoned ahead to two O.N.I. sleuths who were staying there at the home of a white resident. Operating on the theory that the Japanese might have tapped the phone, as they had been known to tap other phones for no other reason than to make sure that they knew what was going on, the message to the operatives on Terminal Island was relayed in code. It sounded like an ordinary message between two quite ordinary persons. Actually. it gave the license number of Honda's car and instructed the two operatives to go to a point on Ways Street, through which most traffic from Los Angeles to Terminal Island passed, pick up the car and try and ascertain what its occupants were up to.

The operatives spotted the car when it came along and they saw that it went to a point near the foot of Tuna Street, where the *Flying Cloud* was still anchored. The two Jap doctors and the Consular attaché were met there by the Tuna Street restaurant proprietor and his henchman, the ex-criminal.

The quintet then proceeded to an unoccupied wharf. The Los Angeles police officer, who could move about the island more freely than the O.N.I. operatives, since it was his job to keep an eye on things, had meanwhile been communicated with by the naval sleuths. He followed the five men to a point on an adjacent pier, as close to them as he could get without being observed. He saw one of them kneeling down on the wharf and training a flashlight on a spot about ten feet below, at a point where the water was lapping against the pier. The flashlight was a strong one, and the water where it shone was almost as clearly visible to the policeman as it would have been in daylight.

Then he heard some conversation in Japanese among the five. What they said he did not know, and he had not been told any details of what was suspected about the contents of the yellow-bottomed drums. But he knew what he saw—and what he saw was something being poured onto the area of water revealed by the flashlight, and almost instantly afterward he saw the water bubbling as if it were boiling.

The five Japanese left the pier, got into Dr. Honda's car and went to the restaurant on Tuna Street. There they remained for about three hours. Then they drove to the pier again. The policeman managed to secret himself at the same vantage point as before. There was a ladder near the place in the pier where the Japanese had earlier poured something into the water, and now, with a flashlight in his hand, one of the five men—he appeared to be the restaurateur's friend—descended the ladder to the level of the water. He trained the flashlight close upon the water, then he called up in Japanese to the four others some ten feet above him in a tone of voice that bore good tidings. One by one, Dr. Furusawa, Dr. Honda, the Consular attaché and the restaurateur descended the ladder and examined the spot that the first man had been looking at. There was excited chatter in Japanese while all this was going on. When the last of them had made his examination, the restaurant owner and his ex-criminal friend walked off in the darkness, up Tuna Street, and the two physicians and the Consular attaché drove back into Los Angeles.

Now the officer got in touch with the O.N.I. agents. Since the whole of Terminal Island was literally alive with snooping Japanese, the naval agents, who were almost beside themselves with anxiety to get a look at what had so excited the five men, had to be very careful. It was almost dawn before they decided that the coast was clear enough for one of them to go down the ladder while the other operative and the police officer stood as lookout.

The agent went down to the water level and shielded his flashlight as best he could when he turned it on. His eyes widened when he looked at what the light revealed. A length of cable that ran down the side of the pier and under the water was actually eaten all the way through for about three inches just above and just below the water level.

There was no question now as to what was in the drums that had been transferred to the *Flying Cloud* during the secret rendezvous at sea with the German freighter. There was no doubt now as to the authenticity of that fabulous story the American newspaperman in Tokyo had heard about the discovery of the imported German chemists. There was no question now—and this was more than four years before Pearl Harbor—about the extent of America's betrayal from the east. The two physicians, the Consular attaché and the two Japanese on Terminal Island had conducted a hellish experiment. Japan was preparing well.

The O.N.I. began to lay plans to obtain one of the drums in the Lower California flour mill, but it was realized that such a feat would take time. Yamamoto was still permitted to remain at large, just to see where he would lead.

Doctor Honda's next move, after the experiment at Terminal Island, was to visit the Los Angeles apartment of Count von Kietel. The Count had not been very active on the Coast for some time, at least not in a way apparent to the investigators. But he had no doubt been keeping in close touch with the espionage situation, and had probably been issuing orders now and then. It was quite possible that he had had a finger in the *Flying Cloud* pie. After Honda visited him, the Count went to Seattle to see Yamamoto. They made an incongruous pair, the Count and Yamamoto. One was a man of breeding and polish; the other a hoodlum. The investigators reflected on the fact that espionage, like love and death, recognized no social barriers.

After the meeting with Yamamoto, the Count took a plane for New York, where he met Roy Akagi, the Japanese whose front was the offices of the South Manchuria Railway. Akagi then went to Washington and visited the Japanese Embassy, the Count meantime returning quickly to the Pacific Coast. The whole operation appeared to boil down to this: Yamamoto had reported the result of the experiment to the Count, the Count had reported to Akagi, and Akagi had reported to the Embassy. It would have been much simpler, of course, for the information to have been relayed by mail, but the Count and the Japanese were obviously operating on the theory that their mail was being watched and perhaps being opened.

When the Count returned to the Pacific Coast he tarried in Los Angeles only long enough to visit Dr. Furusawa's medical building for a few hours. Yamamoto was visiting the Doctor at the same time. Yamamoto returned to Seattle and the Count went down to Ensenada, to the abandoned flour mill where the drums were stored.

The Count didn't remain long in Ensenada either. He went from there to Terminal Island, where he was seen holding a conference with the crew of the *Flying Cloud*. When von Kietel left Terminal Island for his Los Angeles hotel apartment, the *Flying Cloud* put out to sea, headed in a southerly direction. The deduction was that the tuna clipper was going to Ensenada to pick up the drums of acid.

In the meantime, intelligence operatives had been quite busy around the flour mill. In a manner that cannot be detailed here, they succeeded, just after the Count had left, in substituting a drum of gasoline for one of the drums in the flour mill. While the *Flying Cloud* was halfway between Terminal Island and Ensenada, Uncle Sam made an analysis of the contents of the drum that had been taken. The analytical findings were so astounding that they seemed almost incredible. Had a quantity of the drums containing the acid been sown like mines beneath waters where our fleet would pass in time of war, and had the contents been released by means of magnetic devices that would have exploded the drums, something would have happened to our fleet that had never happened in all the history of naval warfare. What the German chemists and the Japanese had in mind—and the chemical analysis showed how close they were to their hideous objective—was that the acid from the drums would attach itself in gummy form to the steel plates of our battlecraft and eat right through, so that the ships would be crippled beyond hope of possible aid while far at sea.

Just what countermeasures our government took to avert the danger of Japan's new secret weapon fall into the category of military secrets. It is interesting to note, however, that one of our investigative bodies took the bull by the horns, for, when the *Flying Cloud* was only an hour out of Ensenada, a "mysterious" fire and explosion broke out which destroyed the flour mill and the drums.

CHAPTER 8

The Mata Hari of the Embassy

THERE COULD BE NO QUESTION at the beginning of 1938 as to the extent of Japanese sabotage plans for the United States of America, particularly on the West Coast, when war came. The discovery by the Office of Naval Intelligence of the bubbling acid that German chemists had perfected for their yellow "Aryan" friends was but one of more than a score of similar discoveries, the nature of which will not be disclosed until the war is over, if then. The discovery by the Federal Bureau of Investigation that Japanese engineers were making scale models of Pacific Coast locations that would be key points for saboteurs at the outbreak of the war was only one instance of what the Japanese were doing along similar lines.

Yamamoto, the Yellow Al Capone, was sent to prison, not for espionage but for income tax violations—the only thing that the Federal authorities cared to talk about in court three years before Pearl Harbor. This business of pinning an income tax rap on Yamamoto was a fine piece of behind-the-scenes strategy. It served to cover the fact that the F.B.I. knew what he had been doing by way of prospective sabotage. Thus the F.B.I. was in a position to keep under surveillance all those who had been associated with Yamamoto. The strategy of this was that those already being followed would lead to others that the F.B.I. did not yet know about.

As a matter of fact, things worked out just that way. By December 7, 1941, the F.B.I. had more than thirty Japanese engineers under surveillance, and every one of them was busy making scale models of strategic locations. Potential saboteurs of Japanese ancestry—both aliens and American-born—were being shadowed by the hundreds, from Seattle to the Mexican border, when it became obvious that they were being schooled in sabotage at secret meeting places in more than a dozen West Coast cities.

The work of the investigators was made far more difficult than it should have been because of the prevailing policy of the State Department not to offend the Japanese. The result was that the F.B.I. and other investigative organizations had to lay elaborate advance plans whereby they could keep an eye on every one of the hundreds of alien and American-born Japanese who were making extensive preparations to sabotage the West Coast when war came. The broad general strategy called for striking at these enemies immediately after war was declared and getting them out of circulation before they could carry out their plans. Had the American public known what the F.B.I. and other investigative agencies were aware of as long as three years before Pearl Harbor, this nation would, to put it mildly, have had a case of jitters, and the people of the West Coast would have been in absolute panic. There it was —a keg of dynamite of almost inconceivable enormity —and all the Federal agents could do was sit on it, hoping the lid would not blow off.

As in the case of spies operating exclusively for Germany—the people whose activities were chronicled in *Passport to Treason*—the Japanese had, by 1938, built up an elaborate system for transferring intelligence to Tokyo. Japanese couriers who had previously called at the apartment of Count von Kietel crossed the Mexican border regularly. These people usually carried their intelligence in their heads so that customs inspectors would never find anything on them. Mexican Federal Police, cooperating with the American investigators, trailed many of these couriers to the little settlement of Cuernavaca, some fifty miles from Mexico City. There the couriers were guests in a notorious male homosexual colony of Germans. It was quite obvious that the couriers transferred their intelligence to the homosexuals, because the latter later met prominent Japanese in Mexico City. Subsequently these Japanese were seen to sail from Mexican ports, bound for the Orient. On more than one occasion, Mexican officials saw the Japanese leaving at night in small boats that had been concealed in out-of-the-way coves. These observations, coupled with reports of Mexican fishermen that they had observed surface submarines in Mexican waters concurrently with the departure of the Japanese in the boats, made it reasonable to suppose that certain intelligence was being handed to submarine commanders only a few miles off shore.

By 1938 it was apparent to the one hundred fixed monitor stations of the Federal Communications Commission, located throughout the U.S.A., that Japanese on the Pacific Coast were busy sending short-wave radio messages to Tokyo on outlaw stations. The FCC's traveling monitor stations—automobile trucks with sensitive and highly accurate locating devices—were busy running up and down the Pacific Coast pegging the locations of the outlaw sending stations. All told, they located several hundred such sets. The monitors found out something else, too—that Japanese physicians, notably Dr. Furusawa, proprietor of the medical building on Weller Street in Los Angeles, were using their diathermy equipment for the purpose of sending out short-wave messages.

The Japanese, like the Germans, operated with a code. Ironically enough, when cryptographic experts in Washington broke down the code they discovered that the Japanese were using as the basis for messages emanating from one group of outlaw stations certain pages in a printed version of George Bernard Shaw's play, *The Devil's Disciple*.

Strategy did not call for raiding any but a comparative handful of the outlaw stations. Some of the stations were like some of the spies; they were more valuable to the investigators while operating than they could possibly have been if put out of action. Considerable intelligence in the possession of the Japanese radio operators was learned about for the first time when FCC monitors picked up the messages and sent them to Washington to be de-coded. If it was found that the Japanese had come upon some particularly valuable information, the very basis of the information was altered so that when war came the intelligence that had been sent to Tokyo would do more harm than good. On other occasions, when something particularly hot was going through the ether, the FCC men jammed the air.

Individual spies were by this time looming in their true stature. There were the small fry and there were the big shots, and there were those in between. For example, there was a particularly affable Japanese who worked in a large Los Angeles department store. He was middle-aged, and his aristocratic mien had, during the several years of his employment, made a favorable impression on fellow workers and employers alike. The man went under a very American name which was obviously not his own, but nobody thought anything about that. Over a period of years, he had drawn considerable high-class Japanese business to the department store, so that in the course of a year the profit statements showed that the Japanese salesman had been responsible for actual profits many times in excess of his annual salary. So it seemed good business to keep the man on, despite the fact that in 1938 there was considerable anti-Japanese feeling on the Pacific Coast.

Well, the charming Japanese came under F.B.I. scrutiny as a matter of course. An agent who was planted in the store to keep an eye on him noticed that the salesman's relationship with several customers of his own race, who always spoke to him only in Japanese, apparently extended far beyond a mere commercial realm. Eventually, the F.B.I. agent had a strong conviction that the charming, aristocratic salesman was a "post office" for information. And so he was put under surveillance after business hours. In months of observation he was not seen to meet anyone outside of store hours who was suspected of being involved in espionage activities. Several of his special customers had been trailed, however, and found to be neck-deep in spy guilt.

The conclusion arrived at was that the information turned over to the department store salesman was telephoned by him to his superior in the espionage set-up— whoever that was. Phone-tapping was illegal, but there was a way of legally getting a list of toll calls that the salesman made from his apartment. When this was done, it was discovered that he made long-distance calls to the Japanese Embassy on an average of once a week.

Putting two and two together, the F.B.I. decided that something interesting might turn up if the real identity of the man so close to the Embassy was established. There was a way of doing this too. It involved a look at immigration records and some investigation by an attaché of the American Embassy in Tokyo. And a very interesting piece of information turned up. The charming salesman who used an American name in the Los Angeles department store was actually named Nomura —and that was also the name of the smiling Japanese ambassador in Washington. The similarity of names was more than a coincidence. The Japanese ambassador and the man who was acting as a post office for espionage information in Los Angeles were first cousins!

Which brings us to Ambassador Nomura himself. The Ambassador certainly did his Washington job well. There was something about his very appearance that was quite unlike the sinister aura thrown off by many Japanese. Nomura, a large portion of official Washington and the American public thought, was one man from Tokyo who was really on the level. Yet, as it now develops, Nomura was no better than the rest of the Jap plotters. In fact, he was a blown-in-the-bottle blackguard. Privately and publicly, he professed great friendship for President Roosevelt—the two men had, years before Nomura's appointment as the Ambassador to the United States, found mutual interest in their love of the sea. When he arrived in Washington, Nomura attempted to further this friendship. It was looked upon as a fine and wonderful thing—perhaps the one thing that would eventually smooth the troubled waters. And all the while the smiling old son-of-a-bitch was okaying large expenditures of cash which, it was eventually proved, he knew were being spent for espionage work.

Despite the Nervous Nellie attitude of the State Department, F.B.I. and O.N.I. agents were keeping a close eye not only on the Japanese Embassy in Washington but upon everyone who visited it who looked as if he or she might prove interesting after an investigation. It was through this procedure that the watchers were drawn to an exceedingly attractive girl in her early twenties. They had seen her, over a period of months, drawing up to the Embassy in a taxi, usually on an evening when there was some sort of a social affair going on in Ambassador Nomura's official bailiwick. It wasn't until the summer of 1938, however, that one of the agents —an O.N.I. man—got around to trailing the girl.

The young lady took a train one morning, after having remained in the Embassy overnight following a large social affair, and was shadowed to a city within five hours of the capital. The city in question need not be mentioned here, for such a specific detail would only add embarrassment to certain innocent dupes of the Japanese girl—the dupes in question being her superiors and fellow workers in the public library where she was employed.

Naval intelligence operatives and G-Men made frequent trips to the reading room of the library in question, which afforded a view of the desk of the girl who obviously stood in so well at the Washington Embassy. She was one of the most respected librarians in the place, yet it soon became obvious to the watchers in the reading room that she was, like Ambassador Nomura's cousin in Los Angeles, a "post office." But she was not only a collector of information; apparently she gave out assignments, too, to various important Japanese who visited her apartment at nights.

On certain days no less than a dozen Japanese would stop at her desk in the library. Naturally, they used as an excuse the fact that they were calling with or for books. When a Japanese called with a book, the sleuths planted in the library noticed that before sending the volume on its way to its proper place in the shelves, the yellow Mata Hari would riffle through it and extract either an envelope or a piece of paper. When one stopped to get a book, the watchers noticed that he merely went through the motions of making a selection, and that the selection had actually been made for him in advance by the attractive librarian. Continued observation disclosed that when the girl handed out a book she first slipped either a paper or an envelope into it. When the Japanese were trailed, it was soon established that they were espionage operatives. Some of them, it was later to develop, had white friends who held key jobs in vital production centers.

Japanese were not the only visitors to the librarian's apartment at night. White men—some of them well dressed and apparently prosperous, and some of them rough-looking and seedy—also visited the Mata Hari. Sometimes the white men were in her apartment when the Japanese were there; sometimes they were alone with the girl.

Trailing of the white men served further to corroborate the long-standing belief that Caucasians were employed by the Japanese to pick up information in spots

where Oriental faces would be likely to excite suspicion.
The seedy-looking individuals who called at the girl's
apartment were, as trailing them revealed, merchant seamen, both Germans and Americans, working on ships of
both German and American registry. These men were
undoubtedly couriers who were returning to Germany
with information that had emanated from no less lofty
a source than Ambassador Nomura himself.

Certain invisible links between the Germans and the
Japanese had by this time been detected. One link, it
was fairly well established, began with Ambassador Nomura's cousin—the salesman in the Los Angeles department store—and ended in Berlin. If, for example, a spy
on the Pacific Coast picked up a piece of information
that would be of interest to Germany as well as to Japan,
he would "mail" it at the "post office" in the Los Angeles
department store. Then the intelligence would be telephoned long distance by Nomura's cousin, from his
home, to the Embassy in Washington. From that point
it would be relayed to the librarian while she was in
attendance at a social function at the Embassy. Later, at
her apartment, she would pass the information on to a
German courier who worked on a North German Lloyd
liner plying between New York and Hamburg. A hot
piece of intelligence didn't necessarily have to be put in
writing; it could be passed along by word of mouth, and
cross a continent and an ocean. If, on the other hand,
information was so complicated or detailed that it might
lose some of its value by being transmitted verbally by
way of half a dozen mouths before it reached its destination, it could be put in writing and transferred from one
person to another with comparative security from prying eyes. While the Germans went in for considerable

writing in secret ink—much of which was intercepted by the Imperial British Censorship Laboratory at Hamilton, Bermuda—the Japanese were very cagey when it came to putting anything down in writing. They used either couriers operating on Japanese liners sailing from Pacific ports, submarine crews or the short-wave radio.

Some of the couriers who were trailed to North German Lloyd liners from the apartment of the librarian were picked up in Hamburg by attachés of American Consulates in Germany and trailed. It was found that some of them went to a spy school in Hamburg, near police headquarters in that city, the same spy school where many German operatives were trained for work in the United States and in other countries. It is not generally known, except in official circles, that a considerable number of Japanese were in attendance at this school. Some of these Japanese had been trailed around the world by American intelligence operatives, from Los Angeles, where they had their homes, to Japan, and thence over the trans-Siberian Railway through Russia, after which they entered Germany from the east.

It was in 1938 that Fritz Wiedemann, recognized as one of Hitler's right-hand men since the days of the first World War when Hitler was a corporal under him, was appointed German Consul in San Francisco. At the same time, General Eugen Ott, a close friend of Wiedemann's and long known to American intelligence officials as one of the most resourceful espionage operatives alive, was appointed German Ambassador to Tokyo. Investigators immediately suspected that Ott had been placed in Tokyo for the express purpose of further coordinating German and Japanese espionage operations.

These fears were quickly confirmed. American consular attachés in Tokyo, keeping an eye on Japanese whom General Ott conferred with, tipped off Washington on when the Japanese sailed for the United States. As a result, these travelers were observed when they landed in Seattle, Los Angeles or San Francisco, often being met by Count von Kietel. As was expected, they made a beeline for the German Consulate in San Francisco. The situation also worked in reverse. Japanese travelers who had previously been under observation of the investigators by reason of visits to Dr. Furusawa's private hospital, frequently conferred with Consul Wiedemann, either in the Consulate or in a San Francisco restaurant or hotel, just prior to their departure for the Orient. Arriving in the Far East, the men whom Wiedemann had gone into a huddle with went direct to the German Embassy in Tokyo. Von Kietel now became quite busy commuting between the Pacific Coast and Washington, obviously as contact man between Wiedemann and Ambassador Nomura.

At about the same time that Wiedemann was appointed to his post in San Francisco, George Gyssling, the arrogant little German Vice Consul in New York, was appointed to the important post of German Consul in Los Angeles. This was quite a jump for Gyssling. For one thing, his salary went up, in one bound, from fifty dollars a week to two hundred a week, plus expenses. He brought his family on from Germany, and a governess for the children, and began to cut quite a social swath for himself. He joined a fashionable golf club, where he was in a fine position to overhear information of value when the boys got talking too much at the nineteenth hole.

It so happened that the territory taken in by the Ger-

man Consulate in Los Angeles embraced Lower California and a portion of Mexico proper. Previous German
Consuls in Los Angeles had never shown too much interest in the Mexican portion of their official territory.
But Gyssling was different. He had no sooner settled in
his new job than he made a trip to Mexico. He took his
wife and children with him, and also the children's
governess. That made a party of five in all. Now, because of Gyssling's official rating, not only was his baggage immune to a customs examination at the border,
both going and coming, but the effects of his wife, his
children and the governess were likewise immune to
search. To operatives who were trailing the Gyssling
party, the immunity aspect of the trip assumed grave
proportions. For some time prior to Gyssling's departure
from New York, couriers from North German Lloyd
liners had been traced to his office in the Whitehall
Building. These couriers had been carrying packages
when they went in, but had come out empty-handed. It
was but reasonable to suppose that they had turned over
to Gyssling certain articles of vital importance to espionage operations. The chances were that Gyssling had
still been in possession of these articles when he had
been transferred to Los Angeles, and that he was now
carrying them across the border to Mexico.

Gyssling's family and the children stayed at a hotel
in Mexico City, while the Consul himself took a side
trip to Cuernavaca, where the homosexual espionage
clique resided. It was almost impossible for the investigators to get close enough to Gyssling without running
the risk of betraying themselves, once he landed in
Cuernavaca. Gyssling was carrying two suitcases with
him when he disappeared into the colony of abnormal

German males. When he left, he was carrying only one suitcase.

After Gyssling had returned to Los Angeles, Mexican detectives, keeping an eye on the homosexual colony, saw the son of an internationally notorious German woman leaving the colony. He was a cagey bird, this youth, and he doubled back on his trail and so many times resorted to other dodges of people who suspect they are being shadowed that the Mexican detectives were forced to abandon the trail for fear that they would uncover themselves.

Two days later, the Mexican police received a report from a fisherman to the effect that a youth easily identified as this abnormal young man had stopped at a small hotel on the western Mexican coast, and that he had been there at a time that coincided with the appearance in Mexican waters of a submarine. The whole thing was very simple. The Germans were working, in reverse, the Japanese stunt of passing intelligence from west to east. Whatever it was that had been brought from Germany to New York by the couriers on the North German Lloyd liners was now on its way to Japan via submarine.

Mrs. Furusawa, in Los Angeles, was growing increasingly active as the head of the Japanese Navy Assistance League, an organization ostensibly devoted to the welfare of Japanese merchant seamen, but obviously an espionage outfit. Many of the Japanese fishermen who frequented such spots on Terminal Island as the Yoshioka Café on South Seaside Avenue and the Minatoya Café on Cannery Street were, time and time again, traced either to the Weller Street medical building or to one of two favorite Los Angeles Japanese cafés where Mrs.

Furusawa entertained. It was noted that when the fishermen appeared at either the medical building or as a
guest of Mrs. Furusawa in a café, they were neatly attired in expensive clothes, in striking contrast to their
attire at Terminal Island.

The Japanese in Seattle, particularly certain of the
more intelligent hoodlums who had come under surveillance as a result of the shadowing of Yamamoto, the
Yellow Capone, were resorting to distinctly Occidental
schemes in obtaining information. Of all the hotels in
Seattle, more than half were owned by Japanese, many
of them close to shipyards, power lines and water-supply
systems. This was an old Japanese stunt the entire length
of the Pacific Coast. But one particular hotel in the city
had added value, besides its location in close proximity
to a vulnerable section of the city's gas-supply system.

This hotel, operated by some of Yamamoto's men,
was nothing more or less than a house of ill fame, inhabited by white girls. The girls were a few cuts above
the average run of prostitutes, both in appearance and
intelligence. When the hotel came under surveillance,
late in 1938, it was observed that the clientele was composed almost wholly of Army and Navy men, some of
them officers. This is not meant as a reflection on the
moral make-up of any of the American armed forces,
whose morals are known to be high, and they need no
defense. But there is always a certain percentage of men
in any large group whose behavior is not indicative of
that of the group as a whole, and it was this type of man
who frequented the Seattle hotel.

The O.N.I. soon succeeded in planting an operative
in the hotel. This man went equipped with a listening
device that enabled him to hear what was going on in an

adjoining room occupied by a prostitute. Thus it was discovered that the hotel was the scene of blackmail operations. If, for example, a client of one of the prostitutes happened to be a married man, the prostitute found that out by skillful questioning. She also ascertained the man's home address. When she had that information the stage was all set for the same type of blackmail operation that was quite popular with the Atlantic City underworld before Uncle Sam tagged Knocky Johnston, the crooked political and vice boss, for income tax violations.

The prostitute in the Seattle hotel would maneuver her victim into a position that he naturally wouldn't want publicised. Then, as if suddenly discovering something, she would say, "Look!" and point to a certain spot on the wall. Things had been so arranged that when the man complied, he was looking directly into the lens of a camera that had been placed in the wall.

Later, when the victim was confronted with a photograph of himself and the prostitute, both scantily clad, he was naturally in a tight spot. The O.N.I. man heard one of Yamamoto's gangsters taking up a picture proposition with a victim. "We thought your wife and friends might be interested in getting a copy of this picture," said the Japanese to the victim, who happened to be an officer in one branch of the service. The officer, enraged, seized the picture and tore it up. The Japanese only laughed. "We still have the negative," he said. The officer told his blackmailer that he would report the hotel to the proper authorities. The Japanese only smiled again. "If you do," he said, "we'll mail a copy of the picture to your superior officers."

The Jap had the white man behind the eight ball;

there was no doubt about that. The white officer wanted to know what he had to do to get the negative. The Japanese was quite frank about what he had in mind. He wanted certain details about a certain point of vital strategic value to the U.S.A.

"Why," roared the officer, "you're just a God damned spy!"

The Japanese didn't deny that he was engaged in espionage operations. He felt certain that the incriminating negative in his possession would be enough of a club over the officer's head to prevent him from disclosing what the Jap blackmailer was up to. The officer said he would think things over. "There's no hurry," said the Japanese. "Negatives don't spoil."

The O.N.I. took a hand in this particular case, and in other similar cases. Sometimes the victim was willing to balance personal protection against national protection. Sometimes the victims reported the whole situation to their superiors. When this was done, the intelligence branches of the services were in the enviable position of planting not only false information on the Japanese, but information that would one day do more harm than good. A check back, however, turned up both officers and enlisted men who had been afraid of their own skins and, rather than face personal exposure, had played ball with the blackmailing espionage operatives in the Seattle hotel by turning over all or part of the data that was requested. Fortunately, such men were greatly in the minority. But the situation in Seattle was not an isolated one; similar hotels where the same game was played reached all the way to San Diego.

Thus, a good three years before Pearl Harbor, our investigative agencies had a pretty clear picture of what was going on, the only trouble being that they couldn't move on account of the State Department. Various Japanese organizations, such as the Japanese Navy League, the Imperial Military Veterans and the Japanese Military Virtue Society had in their organizations men who were known to be engaged in espionage work. The Buddhist temples and the Shinto shrines were frequently the locations of secret meetings in the hours before dawn when engineers known to have been engaged in the construction of scale models of bridges, water-supply systems, naval bases and other such strategic locations unquestionably taught sabotage tactics to those in attendance.

By this time the investigators had been able to secret themselves at vantage points that afforded views into such places as the offices of the engineers who were building the scale models and also into certain of the temples and shrines where the sabotage meetings were held. It should be recorded to the everlasting credit of the F.B.I., the O.N.I., G-2 and other Federal investigative bodies that there wasn't a Japanese scheme of major importance that they did not know about before Pearl Harbor. Some day the whole story can be told, but that day is not yet.

CHAPTER 9

Encounter at Treasure Island

AT THE SAN FRANCISCO WORLD'S FAIR one of the exhibits was called the Candid Camera Artists' Models Studio. It was quite a drawing card, for men with candid cameras could purchase admission to the exhibit, where they found several specialists in pulchritude posing in the nude. Just what percentage of men who had no interest whatsoever in photographic work purchased candid cameras to get into the show and look over the subjects is perhaps beside the point. For that nude exhibit happened to serve as the background for the beginning of one of the most fabulous spy plots of modern times.

One of the owners of the exhibit was a former vaudeville performer named Al Blake—an alert-looking, nattily attired man with sharp eyes and a trim mustache. Blake was now in middle age, but he had always taken excellent care of himself and had the physique of a man considerably younger. At one time, Blake had been known as the King of the Robots. He had performed in vaudeville and in department store windows. He possessed the gift of remarkable control over his voluntary and involuntary muscles. Sometimes for hours on end, with a waxlike make-up applied to his face, he would stand in a department store window, alongside a dummy dressed exactly like him. The idea was for those in the crowd in front of the window to decide which was Blake and which was the dummy. It wasn't an easy matter.

Blake's background is important in that his control over his voluntary and involuntary muscles was to be of vital importance to the United States of America in the years 1940 and 1941. On a day in the fall of 1940 a squat little Japanese, with a candid camera on a leather strap around his neck, walked into the Artists' Models Studio. With the eye of the connoisseur, the Japanese looked over the girls, photographed them, and then glanced around at others in the place, just out of a natural curiosity characteristically Japanese. Thus it was that his eyes met those of Al Blake, the so-called King of the Robots. The face of the Japanese creased in a smile and he approached Blake with outstretched hand and said, "How are you? Don't you remember me?"

Blake didn't. Whereupon the Japanese explained that he was Torzichi Kono, one-time valet, chauffeur and general handyman for Charlie Chaplin. Yes, Blake did recall him now. His mind flashed back to 1917, when he had first met Kono in the Chaplin studio in Hollywood. Blake had played a small part in Chaplin's classic war comedy, *Shoulder Arms*. There had been a well-remembered scene in a trench where the water rose higher and higher and gradually submerged Chaplin's bunk, the lower one. Al Blake, who was running the nude show at Treasure Island almost a quarter of a century later, had been the man in the upper bunk.

Blake had seen Kono around Hollywood from time to time for a few years after appearing in *Shoulder Arms*. But he had not laid eyes on him for more than a decade. Kono, now nearly fifty, had put on weight, although his face hadn't changed much. It was a good-looking face, for a Japanese, and quite even-featured. Like many Japanese, Torzichi Kono wore glasses.

Blake asked Kono how things were and what he was doing. "I'm not doing anything," said Kono. "I haven't for some time. You might say I am taking it easy."

There was something vague and mysterious about Kono's behavior that intrigued Blake. The thought crossed Blake's mind that maybe Kono was a Japanese spy, but he told himself that he was too quick to suspect every Japanese of being a spy. Then, after a few moments of general conversation, Blake became suspicious of Kono for a second time when the Japanese said, "Say, Blake, you used to be in the Navy, didn't you?"

Blake nodded. "Yes," he said, "in the last war. I was a yeoman." He wondered how Kono knew that about him.

"Too bad you're not in the Navy now," said Kono.

"How come?" asked Blake.

Kono shrugged and smiled enigmatically. "You could make a lot of money," said Kono.

"In the Navy?"

Kono nodded.

"In the Navy."

Kono walked out of Blake's exhibit, and that was the last the King of the Robots saw of him again until one day in March of the following year—1941. Blake was walking along Santa Monica Boulevard in Hollywood, where he lived, when he met Kono by accident. This time he was anxious to string the conversation along, if possible. Since the previous fall, the thought of Kono's suspicious behavior at the Treasure Island exhibit had intrigued Blake. In fact, Blake had inquired around

Hollywood for several months trying to find out where Kono might be, but nobody seemed to know.

This time Blake was all ready with just what to say. After the opening pleasantries and a little general talk, Blake remarked, "I'm thinking of joining the Navy again if they'll have me."

Kono seemed interested. "It's a great life, the Navy," he said.

"Yeah," said Blake. "I just heard from a friend of mine in the Navy the other day. He's stationed out in Hawaii, the lucky dog."

Kono was fascinated.

"Hawaii?" he repeated.

Blake nodded.

"On what ship?" asked Kono.

"The *Pennsylvania*."

"Oh," said Kono, "the flagship."

"Uh huh."

"Look," said Kono, "if you're going in the Navy again, Blake, or even if you're not but have a friend on the flagship, maybe I can show you how to make a lot of money."

"God knows I could use some money," said Blake, who was actually quite solvent. "The finance company's after me about my car."

Kono's eyes glittered. He was obviously pleased to hear that Blake was in financial distress. He insisted that Blake mark down his Hollywood address and telephone number. "Maybe," said Kono, "you would like to be my guest at dinner. I have some things I would like to talk over with you. I think they would be to mutual advantage."

Kono took Blake's telephone number before the two

parted. Blake was certain that Kono was up to something, but he didn't want to appear too eager for fear of exciting the suspicion of the Japanese.

That evening Kono telephoned Blake and suggested that the two of them get together the following evening for dinner at Kono's apartment on Bronson Street. Blake, not wishing to appear too anxious, made up a story about having a previous engagement that he could not break. Kono thereupon suggested dinner the second evening following, and again Blake pleaded off on the grounds of a prior engagement. "Then what about lunch day after tomorrow, Al?" said Kono, obviously quite eager to see the so-called King of the Robots at the earliest possible moment. So an appointment was made for a Japanese restaurant in Hollywood.

After an elaborate repast for which Kono footed the bill, and during which the talk had been general, the little Japanese got down to brass tacks. "Al," he said, after looking about him to make certain that no one was eavesdropping, "what do you think of the war?"

Blake shrugged. "I don't give much thought to it one way or another, Kono," he said. "Personally, I don't think the war is any of America's damned business."

"How do you feel about Japan and China?" asked Kono. His eyes fairly glittered behind his glasses; it was obvious to Blake that the subject of the war—particularly Japan's participation in it—was of intense moment to the onetime valet.

"I figure," said Blake, who had thought out his answers beforehand, "that if Japan needs more territory, she's entitled to take some. After all, Japan is a pretty smart nation. On the other hand, what the hell has China ever done?"

Kono smiled. "You have a very intelligent view of things, Al," he said, "and that's going to help us a lot."

"Us?"

Kono nodded. "You remember I said," he went on, "that there was a lot of money to be made by somebody like you who was either in the United States Navy or had Navy connections?"

Blake nodded. "Just what's cooking?" he asked. "I'm badly in need of dough, you know. The finance company was around about my car again this morning."

"About this friend you say you have in the Navy, Al—this man who is on the *Pennsylvania*—could you get in touch with him any time?"

"Sure. We're old buddies and correspond frequently."

"What's his name?"

"Campbell," answered Blake. "Jimmie Campbell." The name and the person were, of course, purely fictitious, having been thought up by Blake for the occasion. But, as it was to turn out later, the fictitious man and the fictitious name were to become very real and to play a major role in Uncle Sam's fight against the Japanese Secret Service.

"This Jimmie Campbell," said Kono, "what is he, a sailor or an officer or what?"

"He's a yeoman, like I was."

"Been in the service long?" asked Kono.

"Oh sure, since the last war, when I was in. I got out after the war was over, and Jimmie stayed in."

"Is he a pretty smart fellow, this Jimmie?"

Blake narrowed his eyes dramatically. "They don't come any smarter," he said.

"And he wouldn't be against picking up some extra money, eh, Al?"

"Not unless he's changed overnight."

Kono took his glasses off and wiped them. When he put them on again he peered at Blake intently some time before speaking. Then he said, "Al, are you going to be available almost any time in case I want you to meet somebody?"

"If there's dough in it, Kono," was the answer, "don't hesitate to get in touch with me at any hour—including three in the morning."

Kono laughed at Blake's little joke and the two got up to go. As they parted outside the restaurant Kono said, "You'll be hearing from me, Al."

Late that night Blake's telephone rang. Kono was calling. "Leave tomorrow morning open, Al," the Japanese said. "We've got to get together by noon, but I don't know where yet. I'll call you."

In the morning Kono called to say that Blake was to meet him in the furniture department of a large Los Angeles department store. Blake got there first. When Kono appeared, he looked very excited. Just as he began to talk to Blake, a salesman approached. "Go away," Kono said impatiently. "We're just looking."

Blake noticed for the first time the seething temper that was screened by Kono's bland front. His words to the salesman were uttered in a tone that might have been employed by a military officer issuing instructions to an underling. Then the anger that was on Kono's face swept away as quickly as it had come. Smiling, Kono said to Blake, "I was very foolish yesterday, meeting you in that restaurant where a lot of white people might have seen us. I received instructions last night not to do that any more. In the future we must meet in places like this."

Kono swept the furniture department with a quick glance, then led Blake to a bed upon which the two of them sat. "It's this way, Al," he said. "At noon tomorrow be at the corner of Sunset Boulevard and Wilton Street out in Hollywood. A very important man will be there to talk to you." With that, Kono arose to go. "Don't fail me," he said, in parting. "And wait here for a few minutes after I've gone."

The next day Blake was at the appointed street corner right on the stroke of twelve. He found Kono waiting. The Japanese was smoking a cigarette and his hat brim was pulled low over his brow as if he didn't want anyone to recognize him. When Blake approached, Kono made a surreptitious gesture that clearly indicated that he did not wish Blake to begin talking with him, but rather to remain near so that the two would give the appearance that they were not together but just standing there waiting for a bus.

Presently a sedan drew up to the curb. A Japanese was at the wheel. Without looking at Kono, the man at the wheel reached into the back of the car and opened the rear right door. Kono hurried into the car and then motioned to Blake to get into the back seat with him. Then the machine spurted off. It went into the Hollywood hills, and during a ride of about fifteen minutes not a word was spoken by any of the three occupants. The driver seemed to be a man of about thirty-five, and on the fat side. When at length the car stopped in a desolate spot, he said to Kono, "Introduce me to your friend." There followed a formal introduction that seemed rather ludicrous to Blake.

During the introduction, it developed that the driver called himself Mr. Yamato. He got right down to business. "Mr. Blake," he said, "tell me something about this friend of yours—this Jimmie Campbell, the yeoman on the *Pennsylvania*."

"What do you want to know?" asked Blake.

"Things about his personality. Is he married? Does he like to drink? Does he like girls? Does he like expensive places? Is the Navy in his blood, or is it just a means of a livelihood?"

Blake began to get cagey. He wanted something a little more definite from the Japanese before he went deeper into the deal. He turned to Kono. "Who is Mr. Yamato, anyway, Kono?" he asked. "I'm being asked a lot of questions here, and I don't know what it's all about." Blake paused briefly, then went on. "That is, I've got a pretty good idea what it's about, and I'm willing to string along. But there's got to be definite arrangements—particularly about dough."

Kono looked at Yamato in a subservient sort of way. During all this time the latter had not turned to look at either Kono or Blake, but had used the rear vision mirror to watch the facial expressions of the men in the back seat when he talked to them.

The driver was silent for a few moments. Then he said to Blake, "Would you be prepared to leave for Hawaii, Mr. Blake?"

"I'll leave for Tibet if there's enough money in it," said Blake.

"Mr. Kono will attend to all of the financial details, Mr. Blake," answered Mr. Yamato. "You needn't worry about expenses or remuneration. Be assured you will be treated very well."

"But just what am I to do?" asked Blake. "Have I got it straight that I am to be a spy and to get this friend of mine on the *Pennsylvania* to get information for the Japanese government?"

Yamato looked out over the green Hollywood hills and seemed to be meditating on his answer. At length he replied, "You have the general idea, Mr. Blake. And now, so we won't misunderstand each other, I take it you will be ready to leave for Hawaii any time?"

"Yes," answered Blake, "but I still don't know exactly what I'm supposed to do. I'll take my chances with the next one, but I don't want to wind up in the clink. I've got to have some protection."

This seemed like a great joke to both Kono and Yamato and they began to laugh. Now Kono took the conversation upon himself for the first time. "Al," he said, "you have no idea how much protection you'll get. You simply haven't got a thing to worry about."

"Where can we drop you, Mr. Blake?" asked Yamato.

The situation as a whole was far from clear in Blake's mind, but he decided that it would be futile, perhaps even dangerous, to press the Japanese for more details just then. Obviously these men intended to run the show their own way; Blake told himself that he would learn more in good time. "If you don't mind," he told Yamato, "you can drop me at a bowling alley on Sunset Boulevard. I've got to see a fellow in there about something."

When Blake got out of the car in front of the bowling alley, Kono said, "You'll be hearing from me very shortly, Al," and Mr. Yamato nodded stiffly as he and Kono drove away. As Blake was entering the bowling alley he caught sight of a car, out of the corner of his eye, pulling up across the street. Something told him that this was the same car which, he had vaguely noticed,

had seemed to be trailing the sedan part of the way between the Hollywood hills and the bowling alley.

When he reached the place upstairs, Blake looked
down into the street through a Venetian blind, so that
he could see but not be seen. He noticed that the car
was occupied by two Japanese, one of whom seemed to
be keeping a steady eye fastened on the doorway through
which Blake had entered to go up to the bowling alley.

Blake had a program in mind, and he wanted to carry
out a specific part of it this very afternoon. He wanted
to go to the Office of Naval Intelligence in Los Angeles,
apprise the authorities of what was going on, and be
prepared for anything. But certainly Blake didn't want
to be followed to the building in downtown Los Angeles
where the O.N.I. was located. So he ducked out of a
rear exit and walked by a circuitous route to a corner
where he caught a bus for Los Angeles.

Blake was halfway into Los Angeles when something
prompted him to look at the cars at the rear of the bus.
He was hardly surprised to see, just behind the bus, the
same car with the two Japanese that had been parked
across the street from the bowling alley. If there had
been the slightest question in Al Blake's mind that this
car was following him, it was thoroughly dispelled when
Blake saw the car slowing down every time the bus
slowed down.

Blake decided to change his plans, although he intended still to wind up at the Office of Naval Intelligence. It was obvious that the Japanese did not know
where he was going or they wouldn't have bothered to
follow him, but rather would have gone direct to the
building where the O.N.I. was located, there to await
him.

Blake got off the bus near a large department store in Los Angeles, which was several blocks from the building where the O.N.I. was located. As he went through the revolving doors he resorted to some psychology. The car with the two Japanese had been right behind the bus when Blake got off at the department store. The King of the Robots tried to place himself in the psychological position of the Japanese and decide, if possible, just what they would figure he was going to do. Blake felt that inasmuch as he had tried once to give the slip to the two men in the car, the two Japanese would take that into consideration now. So he decided that they would probably expect him to leave by the opposite entrance of the store, which was one block away. Then Blake, telling himself that he was very smart, made up his mind to cross up the Japanese by backtracking and coming out the very entrance he had gone in.

When he found himself out on the sidewalk again, he also found the car with the two Japanese still there. Obviously, they had anticipated his psychology. Blake, thinking fast, snapped his fingers in a gesture meant to indicate that he had forgotten to get something in the department store. So he went back in again. Now he went in for some more psychology. Certainly, he figured, this time the Japanese would deduce that he would make an exit from the door at the opposite end of the store. So he decided once more to go out the door he had twice entered. Once again the Japanese were still there!

Blake, in something of a quandary, stood near the door looking up and down the street, as if he were waiting for someone. Then he went inside again. This time the Japanese would surely calculate that he would use the exit at the other end of the store. And this time he could succeed in eluding them by using a side entrance that let out on the third street that the store fronted on. Out of this door he went—and there was the car with the Japanese parked at the curb!

There was no use going back into the store again, so he went into a motion picture theater. Even in the darkness of the theater, he couldn't shake off the Japanese. One of them sat only two rows behind him, and the other across the aisle. When the show was over, Blake called it a day and returned to his Hollywood apartment.

Blake knew he had been followed because the Japanese wanted to see whether he was being on the level with them or whether he visited, for example, the F.B.I. Not that he had made any bones about trying to get away from the two who were shadowing him; he intended to tell Kono all about that, just to impress Kono with the fact that he was very alert.

As Blake sat in his apartment thinking things over, his eye suddenly fell on a patch of the rug in his living room that somehow appeared unnatural. There was an indentation in the rug, as if made by a piece of furniture that had long stood in one place but had been moved. The piece of furniture obviously was a heavy chair which had indeed been shifted. There should have been no one in his apartment that day, but apparently someone had been there.

He approached the chair cautiously and examined it. Just as he thought, he came upon a dictograph, planted under one of the arms. The Japanese had removed the cloth covering of the arm and sewed it back on again. The wire attached to the dictograph had then been put through a tiny hole made in the rug beneath the chair, and run under the rug and through a hole in the baseboard of the wall. From that point it had obviously followed the telephone wires outside, and it was not possible for Blake to find out just then whether the listening device on the other end of the apparatus was in the same building or some distance away.

Not long after Blake made the discovery of the dictograph, his telephone rang. Mr. Kono was on the wire. "That was a good meeting we had today, Al," said Kono. "The driver of the car was very impressed by you; he likes you very much."

"I'm glad of that, Kono," said Al. "Where do we go from here?"

"You'll be hearing from me in the morning."

When Blake hung up he was mindful of the dictograph. He saw an opportunity to impress the listening Japanese with his sincerity. "Hooray for me," he muttered to himself, just loud enough, he judged, for his words to clearly carry over the dictograph. "I'm going to be in the money again. Nice guy, Kono. . . ."

Kono phoned again the next morning and another meeting was arranged with Mr. Yamato. At the second conference of the three men in the Hollywood hills, the two Japanese talked in their native tongue for a while, then Yamato said to Blake, "Are you prepared to leave within a week by Clipper for Honolulu?" Blake nodded. "Mr. Kono here," Yamato went on, "will give you full instructions about just what we want when you get there. But to give you a general idea now, you are to see your friend, Jimmie Campbell, as soon as you can after your arrival and make the proper arrangements to get everything that will be of value to the Imperial Japanese Government—such things as codes that the Navy uses, all tactical information, charts of mine fields, and so on."

"What about money?" asked Blake.

"How much do you want?" said Kono.

"Twenty-five hundred down and all expenses," said Blake, "and five thousand more when I deliver."

"That's exactly the figure we had in mind," said Yamato, and Blake had to call upon his ability to control his involuntary muscles in order to keep from laughing at the obvious lie. For Yamato was apparently pleased to hear Blake's figure—a lower one than he had expected him to demand.

That afternoon Blake decided that he would simply have to get in touch with the O.N.I. Once more he headed into Los Angeles by bus, but once more the car with the two trailing Japanese was right behind. This time Blake went right for a motion picture theater. Inasmuch as he had stayed through the entire show the last time he had been followed by the Japanese, he figured on the possibility of the Japanese not following him into the playhouse but waiting outside until the show was over. As luck would have it, they parked in the car across from the theater and did not get out.

Blake had a talk with the manager inside the darkened theater, told him he was being followed, and asked if he could be let out another exit that would give him access to a different street. The manager was willing to oblige him and Blake was soon outside. He walked back to a point that afforded a view of the front of the theater and saw the two Japanese still sitting in the car, apparently quite content to wait until he came out to pick him up.

When Blake reached the O.N.I. and made it clear to an officer there that he had information of a vital nature, he was shown into the office of Lieutenant Leo P. Stanley of the United States Naval Intelligence. Blake told his story in a simple straightforward manner and Stanley never interrupted to say a single word while the narrative was in progress. After Blake had finished, Lieutenant Stanley said, "This sounds very important, Mr. Blake. And it also sounds as if you have to do exactly as the Japanese say."

"How do you mean, Lieutenant?" asked Blake.

"Ordinarily," said Lieutenant Stanley, "a private citizen who turns in information such as this no longer has to be concerned with the outcome because experts in the field of investigation follow through. But in this instance, you will have to carry the ball for us, for it simply wouldn't be possible for us to work things so that anyone could substitute for you."

"You mean that you have no intention of arresting Kono and this Mr. Yamato?"

"None whatever at present," said Lieutenant Stanley.

Blake had meanwhile been wondering if the O.N.I. wasn't just a bit lax—here was an official telling him all this, when he had just walked in off the street and not produced identification of any kind to substantiate anything he said. It was while Blake was speculating along these lines that Lieutenant Stanley began to clear things up for him. "This Kono," the Lieutenant said, "is a thoroughly bad man. We know that he is in the pay of the Japanese government because we have information to the effect that he owns a large estate on the outskirts of Tokyo and that his only means of livelihood is derived from money paid to him through the Japanese Embassy in Washington."

"Oh," said Blake, "so you have known about Kono."

Lieutenant Stanley nodded. "For some time," he said. "Incidentally, before I forget it, I must warn you that an associate of Kono's has planted a dictograph in your apartment in Hollywood."

Blake, startled, inquired how Stanley knew that. "Simply because we have had an eye on Kono and his associates for some time. You see, the fact that you, Mr. Blake, possess the singular ability to control both your voluntary and involuntary muscles is one of the reasons why the Japanese sought you out in the first place. They wish to get a white spy who will have such superb control over himself that he will not betray himself in a tight spot. We intend to use that very quality of yours against the Japanese."

While Blake was growing more astonished over Stanley's knowledge of facts which Blake thought only he himself knew about, the O.N.I. officer consulted some papers on his desk. "We can't be too long with our meeting today," Stanley said as he looked through the papers, "because you will have to get back to the theater before the show ends. Otherwise, the two Japanese in the car outside the theater will get suspicious."

At this Blake was more astonished than ever. He had not mentioned a word to Lieutenant Stanley about where he had been prior to reaching the O.N.I. offices. So he asked, "How did you know about that, Lieutenant?"

Stanley smiled. "We have been following you, as well as those who have followed you, ever since that day last year at Treasure Island when Kono walked into your exhibit. The very fact that you came here voluntarily and informed me of many things we already knew, in addition to many things we did not know—such as the nature of the conversations you had with Kono and Commander Tachibana in the Hollywood hills—proves your good faith."

"Commander Tachibana?" Blake repeated. "That's a new name on me. The man I spoke to with Kono was named Yamato."

"To be sure," said Lieutenant Stanley. "That's the name that has been assumed by Commander Itaru Tachibana of the Japanese Navy. We have known about the Commander for some time. It is important that you should know something about his background." Whereupon Lieutenant Stanley divulged the information they had about the man who called himself Yamato.

Tachibana had been educated at the Japanese Naval Academy and the Naval War College, in Tokyo, and had eventually been commissioned a Lieutenant Commander, rising to the rank of full Commander. He had come to the United States eleven years previously—in 1930—and attended the University of Pennsylvania, where he had specialized in American history and American foreign relations, and later enrolled at the University of Southern California in Los Angeles. For several years Tachibana had been flitting about the Pacific Coast, holding conferences with leading Japanese from Seattle to the Mexican border.

Stanley went on to explain that the O.N.I. would follow through on Blake's bright idea of having thought up a fictitious yeoman on the *Pennsylvania*. When Blake asked how, the Lieutenant explained, "We will put an operative on the *Pennsylvania*. He will be dressed as a yeoman and he will answer to the name of Jimmie Campbell." Stanley laughed. "So you see there actually will be such a person as Jimmie Campbell in the event that the Japanese in Hawaii should go to the trouble of checking up. Moreover, if you are instructed to write to this man and let him know of your coming, the letter will be delivered. It wouldn't be a very good thing, you know, if you sent a letter and had it returned for lack of an addressee, for the Japanese are unquestionably watching your mail." Stanley looked at the clock. "Mr. Blake," he said, "you had better be getting back to the theater. I assume you will have no trouble getting in the same way you came out?"

"No trouble at all," said Blake. "The manager's a very nice guy. When do you want me to get in touch with you again?"

"You are not to come here again. It's too dangerous. You will be contacted at the proper time and told what to do. Meanwhile, do as the Japanese say."

Blake inquired as to what the set-up was to be in Honolulu. Stanley replied that details would have to be perfected, but that he would receive instructions in good time.

That night Kono telephoned to Blake. "Start making your reservation for Honolulu, Al," said the Japanese. "Leave tomorrow by Clipper if you can."

Blake immediately telephoned to Pan-Pacific Air Lines. He was told that all space was sold out for two weeks. Actually, it wasn't, but the Navy needed that much time to make proper preparations in Honolulu. O.N.I. officers knew that in addition to the dictograph, Blake's phone was also tapped, and they figured that if the Japanese heard a false report that Clipper space couldn't be obtained for a fortnight they would have no alternative but to accept the delay.

Blake called Kono and reported the unfavorable news. Kono seemed greatly upset and said he would call back. When he did call back he said to Blake, "Try anything, Al, but get off tomorrow."

Blake put in another call for Pan-Pacific. He begged and pleaded for a reservation, offering to pay a premium, but he couldn't get anywhere. The voice on the other end of the wire—that of a man—was quite authoritative. Actually it was that of an O.N.I. operative planted in Pan-Pacific.

Blake reported to Kono. "This is awful, Al," said the Japanese. "Get ready to leave your apartment; I'll pick you up outside in twenty minutes and you'll have to come with me where I'm going."

Kono drove Blake to a Japanese restaurant in Los Angeles. They didn't go in the front entrance, but through the service door. Blake found himself in the kitchen, where Kono seemed to be well known and treated with deference by the Japanese chefs. One of the chefs, in fact, stopped what he was doing and led Kono and Blake to a room in the basement. There Commander Tachibana, alias Yamato, was sitting in native Japanese costume, drinking whiskey-and-soda. He and Kono spoke in Japanese for a while and then the Commander said to Blake, "Too bad about the Clipper. You'll have to take the *Matsonia* from San Francisco Saturday at noon."

"I'll be on it," said Blake.

On Friday night Kono drove Blake to the Southern Pacific Railroad station where the King of the Robots was to catch the midnight train for San Francisco.

"Good luck in Honolulu," said Kono, pumping Blake's hand vigorously, just before the train pulled out. He reached into his pocket and handed Blake an envelope. "There's a couple of thousand dollars in here," he said. "That will cover your expenses in the meantime."

Blake had not received any instructions relating to a Japanese meeting in Hawaii. It was at the very last minute that Kono brought up certain details, such as the name of the hotel at which Blake was to stop. "It is understood," he said, "that you are to get what you are supposed to get from your friend on the *Pennsylvania*. But just make sure that you are clever enough to avoid being trailed by any operatives of the United States Naval Intelligence. Our people will be keeping an eye on things in Honolulu, and if any further instructions are needed you will receive them." Kono looked searchingly at Al Blake, and Blake for the first time had to make use of his ability not to appear alarmed. Then Kono said, "I would suggest that if you are trailed in Honolulu you go into a moving picture theater and go out the back way while the people who are trailing you wait out front until the show is over."

Blake was really alarmed. Did Kono's remark mean that the Japanese had actually caught on to his dodge of leaving the movie theater when he went to the O.N.I. that day? Or was the remark merely the result of a coincidence—the coincidence of the Japanese thinking of the same subterfuge as Blake had already used?

When he arrived in San Francisco the next morning he went immediately to the Matson Line and applied for passage on the ship sailing at noon. He was informed that all space was sold out and that the next Matson liner wouldn't be sailing for Honolulu for seven days.

When Blake walked out to the street to think things over, a little Japanese slid up alongside of him and whispered, "Follow me, Mr. Blake." Blake followed the man to a Japanese restaurant about two blocks away. He was led into the kitchen, and from there to a side room off the kitchen. The Japanese reached into his pocket and handed Blake an envelope. "This," he said, "is passage for you on the *President Garfield* of the Dollar Line. The *President Garfield* also sails at noon. When we learned this morning that a cancellation that had been expected on the *Matsonia* did not materialize, we decided that it would be just the same if you went out an another line."

Blake, puzzled as to the identity of this Japanese, inquired. The little man grinned. "Who I am is unimportant," he said. "What is important is that you sail today."

The *President Garfield* had hardly passed through the Golden Gate when Al Blake realized that he was going to be under surveillance on the trip to Honolulu. Two gentlemen of distinctively Teutonic appearance shared the cabin to the forward side of Blake's, and two Japanese occupied the cabin that adjoined his to the aft.

The King of the Robots went down to the bar and ordered a highball. The waiter had no sooner brought the drink than the two Germans came in and took a table directly alongside Blake. A little while later the two Japanese sauntered to the bar and sat down near by. The Germans and the Japanese were seated in such relationship to Blake that he couldn't make out whether any signals were passing between the two pairs of men. Summoning up all of his ability to control his facial nerves, Blake sat tight and had two more highballs.

After almost an hour passed, the two Germans got up and left. Five minutes later, when Blake was ordering his fourth drink, the Japanese departed.

Blake remained in the bar for another hour, striking up a conversation with an elderly American and his wife who said they were on their way to Honolulu for a vacation. When he returned to his stateroom, one glance told him that someone had gone through his luggage. This left him comparatively undisturbed, however, for he was carrying nothing in his luggage or on his person that would prove anything against him one way or the other, and he had been under constant surveillance for so many days running that he took shadow men in his stride.

Later on, Blake strolled down to the purser's office and glanced at the passenger list. The names of the two Japanese who were occupying an adjoining cabin meant nothing to him. He noted, however, that both of the Germans were going under the name of Mueller, which is as common a name in Germany as Smith or Jones is in the United States. Blake decided that the Messrs. Mueller were traveling under assumed names and had been rather unimaginative about selecting the names. All of which confirmed Blake's earlier suspicion that the Germans were secret agents operating on behalf of the Japanese government.

As a matter of fact, the O.N.I. could have told Al Blake quite a bit about both the Japanese and the Germans who were occupying rooms adjoining his. For the O.N.I. had been far from idle prior to Blake's departure, despite the fact that none of its operatives had had the opportunity to get in touch with him safely prior to the departure from San Francisco of the *President Garfield*.

Two days before Blake had sailed, O.N.I. agents had trailed Commander Tachibana from Mr. Kono's apartment in Hollywood to the Japanese Consulate in Los Angeles. Commander Tachibana had remained in the Consulate for well over an hour, and when he came out he proceeded to the haberdashery department of a large Los Angeles department store. O.N.I. agents trailing the Commander, and agents shadowing Mr. Kono converged in the haberdashery department when Kono met the Commander there. The two Japanese did not recognize each other outwardly, but when both were trying on hats they placed themselves in front of mirrors in such a way that they were able to catch one another's eye. Then they maneuvered themselves close enough to each other to exchange a few whispered words. Mr. Kono, who had come in after Tachibana, decided he didn't want a hat and left. Tachibana tarried for a little while, going through the motions of making a decision about a hat, finally purchased one and departed.

Tachibana went to the Los Angeles hotel where he was making his home at the time, while Mr. Kono proceeded to 117½ Weller Street—to the medical building operated by Dr. Furusawa. When Kono came out several hours later, after darkness had fallen, he was accompanied by two Japanese. The three men were then trailed to a house of ill fame where they remained until about midnight, when they came out just in time to get to the Southern Pacific station before the departure of an overnight limited for San Francisco. Mr. Kono saw his two friends off, then returned to the house of ill fame.

When the two Japanese arrived in San Francisco in the morning, intelligence agents trailed them to a small restaurant specializing in sukiyaki, located not far from the Dollar Line piers. The agents quickly ascertained that the restaurant was patronized by both Japanese and whites. It was therefore concluded that it would be safe to send an agent in, attired as a waterfront worker. The naval agents were always well prepared for such eventualities, and the result was that one of them, looking for all the world like a dock walloper, walked into the restaurant less than ten minutes after the entrance of the two men who had been trailed from Dr. Furusawa's.

The Japanese were eating at a table in the rear, and they paid no attention to the O.N.I. man. In a little while, two men who looked like Germans came in. They immediately joined the two Japanese, and the four of them were still engaged in earnest conversation when the O.N.I. agent, deciding that he would become an object of suspicion if he tarried too long over his food, left.

The two Japanese and the two Germans came out together. The quartet was trailed to the Japanese Consulate. The remainder of the morning passed, and the afternoon, and when late evening came, with no sign of the reappearance of either of the Japanese or either of the Germans, the watchers concluded that the four were going to remain at the Consulate overnight. In the meantime, a check-up behind the scenes at the Dollar Line offices disclosed that the Japanese had made a reservation for Al Blake on the *President Garfield,* and that they had also reserved the rooms on either side of Blake's cabin. And so, when the *President Garfield* steamed out of San Francisco harbor, the O.N.I. was well aware that the two Japanese and the two Germans going under the name of Mueller were keeping close tabs on Al Blake. And while the American agents had not been able to get in touch with Blake, the O.N.I. had nevertheless managed to do something about the situation, as shall presently be seen.

CHAPTER 10

Masquerade on the President Garfield

FOR THREE DAYS and three nights, Blake knew that he was under the constant surveillance of either the two Japanese or the Messrs. Mueller. He had become so adjusted to the situation by this time, however, that he was able to ignore it. He thoroughly enjoyed himself by playing shuffleboard and bingo and otherwise participating in the diversions offered on an ocean trip. Blake was a good mixer and he struck up friendships all over the ship, but his closest was with the elderly American and his wife—the couple he had met during the first two hours of the journey.

The American's name was Horner, and he said he was a hardware dealer from the Middle West. He spent considerable time in the bar and on more than one occasion his drinking activities apparently seriously interfered with his ability at shuffleboard, much to the amusement of other passengers, including the two Japanese and the Messrs. Mueller.

Among other things, Mr. Horner, as everybody on the ship knew, was constantly expecting a radiogram. His daughter, he had announced, was about to have a baby and the news as to whether the child was a boy or a girl was to be radioed to the Horners immediately.

Mr. Horner seemed very proud of his daughter, and he showed pictures of her to everyone who was within reach when the mood was on him. Sometimes, after a session at the bar, Mr. Horner would approach a passenger to whom he had previously shown pictures of his daughter and insist upon showing the pictures again. Among those to whom he had repeated himself was one of the Mr. Muellers—the elder of the two Mr. Muellers. He was about fifty, while the younger Mr. Mueller was perhaps thirty-eight. The elder Mr. Mueller got very annoyed at Mr. Horner and made it plain that he wished nothing further to do with him or the photographs of his daughter during the remainder of the trip.

It wasn't until the last night out that Mr. Horner received his radiogram. It was quite a long message of its kind, announcing that the baby was a boy and giving the child's weight, the name that had been conferred upon it, who the officiating doctor had been, and other such details. Mr. Horner showed the message to many of the passengers, including the younger Mr. Mueller and both of the Japanese. Then, by way of celebration, he set up drinks for everybody who would accept and was soon quite obviously roaring drunk.

Al Blake was in the Horner party, and finally Mrs. Horner, patently quite embarrassed by her husband's behavior, appealed to Blake to assist her in getting the old boy to his stateroom.

Blake had quite a struggle. Horner resented the interruption to his gaiety and took a swing at Blake, giving the King of the Robots quite a cut under the eye, Blake, angered, wanted nothing further to do with Horner, but the old man's wife pleaded for aid.

Finally Blake got Horner to his stateroom. The old

man bellowed for his radiogram, which he had dropped during the scuffle in the bar, and insisted that Mrs. Horner go and hunt for it. When his wife left, Horner startled Blake by seeming to sober suddenly. "Lock the door," he whispered to Blake. The King of the Robots complied mechanically. By the time he had locked the door and turned around, old Horner had arisen from the bed, where a few moments before he had appeared to be quite the worse for alcohol. Now he was steady, grim and clear-eyed. "Blake," he said, "I have your instructions for you."

"Oh," said Blake. "You're——?"

Horner interrupted by nodding affirmatively, "I'll have to talk fast," he said, "as you'll have to get back to the bar or they'll get suspicious." Blake was reaching into his pocket for pencil and paper. "No," said Horner, "no notes. Just listen: The radiogram I just received contained your instructions." The instructions were that upon his arrival in his Honolulu hotel, Blake was immediately to put through a call for the U.S.S. *Pennsylvania,* which was anchored at Pearl Harbor, and ask to speak to Yeoman Jimmie Campbell—the counter-espionage agent O.N.I. had planted on the ship. "Our people in Honolulu have found out certain things since this ship left San Francisco," Horner explained. "The Japanese there have arranged that you be assigned to a certain room when you register at the hotel. You are going to be watched very closely while you are in that room. For one thing, the two Japanese who are next to you on this ship will be in a room adjoining yours at the hotel. The two Germans on the other side of you on this ship will be on the other side of you at the hotel."

"That's not very smart of them, is it," asked Blake,

"having the same men who flanked me on the ship doing the same thing at the hotel?"

Horner shook his head sideways and smiled. "No, it isn't," he said, "but you'll find as you go along that despite their cleverness the Japanese can be stupid, too. For one thing, I think it was unnecessary for them to have had you under surveillance during this trip, just to see whether you intend to doublecross them or not. Certainly you couldn't have done much doublecrossing here. But to get on. In addition to the eavesdroppers on either side of you in the hotel, there will be a dictograph planted in your room. It has, in fact, already been placed there. It is concealed behind the blind in the upper right-hand corner of the left-hand window in your room—left-hand as you look out. Make certain that most of your conversations with Yeoman Campbell are conducted near that spot."

"When I call Campbell," asked Blake, "what shall I say?"

"Just be natural. Don't have anything made up beforehand. Just act as if Campbell is an old buddy of yours that you haven't seen for some time. Ask him what he's doing and when he can get away for you two to meet."

"And where are we to meet?"

"He'll come to your room."

"How will I know him?"

"There will be a slight tear on the left breast of his uniform." Mr. Horner explained precisely what the tear would look like so that Blake could not mistake it. "After telling each other how glad you are to see one another, you will get down to business. You'll feel him out as to how satisfied he is with life in the Navy, and he'll tell you he's disgruntled—so disgruntled in fact, that that will be your opening to put your proposition to him. He will carry on from there, for the benefit of the spies in the adjoining rooms and for members of the Japanese Secret Service in another part of the hotel who will be listening in over the dictograph. Just remember, all you have to do is to act natural. You are trying to get information from Campbell for the Japanese government and the money that the Japanese are willing to pay for it will benefit both of you."

"Is Campbell going to go for this in a big way?" asked Blake.

"Yes and no," said Horner. "He will act natural, too. The stumbling block, so far as he is concerned, will be the possibility of his getting caught. You are to be a parrot and repeat what the Japanese have told you to say if he should be afraid."

"I get it," said Blake, "but there's just one more question."

"Make it fast," said Horner, starting to get undressed.

"Am I to get all of my instructions through Campbell?"

"Yes," answered Horner. "He will either gesture to you or show you things in writing when you are in your hotel room with him." Horner was undressed by this time and he got back on his bed and into his drunken stupor pose. He came out of the pose long enough to grasp Blake's hand firmly, and say, "Good luck, Blake."

Blake walked out into the corridor. One of the two Japanese was walking toward Horner's room, and Blake couldn't tell whether the man had been standing there for some time. The Japanese smiled and handed Blake the radiogram that Horner had dropped in the bar. "I thought maybe your friend would want this," said the Japanese.

"Thank you," said Blake.

Blake didn't sleep well the last night. He wondered whether the Japanese had seen through the Horner ruse.

Blake followed instructions to the letter, calling Yeoman Campbell on the *Pennsylvania* at Pearl Harbor. He noticed that Campbell had apparently been carefully chosen for his dangerous and important role. Even over the phone, the man sounded like a yeoman.

An appointment was made for Campbell to call at Blake's hotel room that night, and he showed up right on the dot. Blake identified him at once by the small, distinctive tear on the left breast of his uniform. Campbell was a big, hard man of over forty, and he certainly looked the part he was to play, even to the color and texture of his skin, which was tanned and windbeaten.

The intelligence operative and Al Blake went into a long-lost brother routine for the benefit of the eavesdroppers in the adjoining rooms and the Japanese listening at the other end of the dictograph. The O.N.I. was listening in, too. If the Japanese could plant a "bug" in Blake's room, so could Uncle Sam's agents. Thus, the American counteroperatives could hear the drama put on by Blake and Campbell, judge its effectiveness as it unfolded and make appropriate suggestions to Campbell for those parts of the plot yet to be unfolded.

Campbell asked, "What brings you out here anyway, Al?"

"Something that might be worth a lot of dough to both of us, Jimmie," said Blake.

"How do you mean dough? I could use some."

"Couldn't we all?" countered Blake. "But first of all, Jimmie, how are you getting along in the Navy?"

Campbell uttered an obscenity to express what he thought of the Navy.

"I didn't know you were *that* fed up, Jimmie," said Blake.

"Listen," said Campbell, "here I've been in this damned outfit since the last war—when we were in together, Al—and where the hell am I? I'll tell you where I am: I'm beneath a lot of punks that came in after I did and got shoved ahead of me."

"You don't sound very patriotic, Jimmie," said Blake with a laugh.

"Patriotic, hell!"

"Well, look," said Blake. "This is going to make things easier for me. I came out here with a proposition for you but I figured I might have to sell you on it a little. But now that I see how things are it should be a cinch."

"What's up your sleeve, anyway, Al?" asked the intelligence operative. Up to now the conversation had been carried on in a normal tone, with no effort at privacy should anyone be out in the corridor. Certainly Blake and Campbell both knew that what they had said up to that point had carried through the thin walls to the German and Japanese listeners in the adjoining rooms. But from here on, the only words that would be heard outside the rooms would be those that passed through the dictograph.

Blake took Campbell by the arm and steered him to

a point just under the dictograph—perfectly normal behavior under the circumstances, inasmuch as anyone
who did not wish to be overheard would be likely to
step toward a window rather than toward a wall or a
door. Now Blake began to put the Japanese proposition up to the man whom the listeners thought was a
yeoman on the *Pennsylvania*. The King of the Robots
talked in a low tone that was just loud enough to be
picked up by the delicate dictograph above his head,
and then amplified as much as necessary in the room
where the Japanese Secret Service operatives were stationed.

Blake asked Campbell for precisely what Commander
Tachibana had instructed him to ask for. The details
of this phase of the plot cannot be disclosed until after
the war, if then. Suffice it to say that what the Japanese
wanted—and remember, this was in May, 1941, less than
seven months before Pearl Harbor—would have placed
Japan in a position where, within the space of a few
hours, she would have stood in a fair way of utterly
crippling our Pacific fleet. As bad as Pearl Harbor
turned out to be, it wasn't that bad; and just how the
dangerous game that Blake and Campbell were playing fitted into the Pearl Harbor mosaic we shall see
later.

The strategy was for Blake to request all the information that he sought of Campbell without stating whom
he wanted it for and without being interrupted while
he was talking. It took Blake about ten minutes to
speak his piece. Then Campbell said, "Who you working for, Al—the Japs?"

"Yes."

"How much are they willing to pay for all this dope —really big dough?"

"We could just about write our own ticket, Jimmie."

"You mean five thousand dollars or something like that—enough to start a little business when my enlistment's up?"

"Yeah, dough like that. What do you say?"

Now the strategy called for Campbell to say that while he didn't like the United States Navy he didn't like the Japs either. The O.N.I. had decided that a note of realism and authenticity would be added if the Japs overheard themselves being spoken of in an unfavorable way. Carrying out this idea still further, Blake added, "Well, dough's dough, no matter where you get it. There's a lot of things about the Japs I'm not nuts about either, Jimmie, but what the hell, if you can make a deal with them, well and good."

The strategy now called for some silence, during which Campbell was to pace up and down the room, as if debating with himself. He paced heavily enough for the dictograph to pick up the sounds of his footfalls. Then he rejoined Blake under the dictograph and said, "This stuff I'm supposed to get—codes and so on—what would happen if the big boys on the *Pennsylvania* missed it?"

"You don't understand, Jimmie," said Blake. "You're only supposed to borrow it or copy it. You've got all the chance in the world to do that. It would never be missed. And anyway, suppose the worst happened and it was missed, how could they pin it on you? Why, any one of a *hundred* guys could have taken it."

Campbell did some more pacing, and when he talked again he said, "How do I know the Japs wouldn't doublecross me if I got this stuff? You know they're a bunch of doublecrossing bastards, Al."

Blake assured Campbell that he wouldn't be doublecrossed.

"Why," countered Campbell, "*you* might be doublecrossed yourself, Al. Then where would you be? Why, you couldn't even squeal on the bastards because if you did you'd be slapped in prison for going in on the deal in the first place."

"Everything you say might sound all right to you, Jimmie," said Blake. "But figure this way: The Japs have got lots of money. If we pull this job for them, they'd pay us if it was only because we might be able to do *another* job. They stand to gain by paying and to lose by not paying."

Blake pretended to get a little miffed at his old friend because Campbell had doubted his sagacity. "I'm not exactly a dope, Jimmie," he went on. "I didn't explain to you about a guy named Kono in Los Angeles. I've known Kono for almost twenty-five years." Now Blake added a touch that Lieutenant Stanley of the O.N.I. had thought up for him—another touch that had been originated on the theory that the Japanese would be listening in on conversations between Campbell and Blake. By way of leading the listening Japanese to the conclusion that he was doing his level best to sell his friend, Campbell, on the idea of espionage, Blake began to picture to Campbell a totally fictitious intimate relationship that had long existed between himself and Kono.

Campbell seemed impressed. "Oh," he said, "that makes it a little different. Why didn't you tell me that in the first place? If you know one of the Japs *that* well we won't stand much of a chance of being double-crossed."

When Campbell was about to leave, the arrangement was that he would come to Blake's room again the next night. But here again the O.N.I. resorted to some psychology. They wanted everything to appear perfectly natural. Had things gone too smoothly or too easily for Blake, the Japanese might have become suspicious. So Campbell telephoned to Blake the following night an hour before he was due. He knew that every word he said over the phone would be heard by the Japanese, for the O.N.I. had in the meantime learned that Blake's phone had been tapped. Campbell said that he couldn't get off the ship that night, and that he would make it the following night. Blake, trying to appear as anxious as became anyone on so serious a mission, inquired, "Anything doing on that matter I spoke to you about, Jimmie?"

"So long Al, see you tomorrow night," snapped Campbell, as if he were afraid to talk.

By methods of its own, the O.N.I. was keeping a careful watch on the Germans and the Japanese in the rooms adjoining Blake's. Under instructions, the King of the Robots was spending his time as would any tourist—seeing the sights and hitting the high spots. But wherever Blake went or whatever he did he was under surveillance, either by one or both of the Japanese or one or both of the Messrs. Mueller. A curious feature of the relationship between the two sets of spies was that they never had contact with each other in any way and hadn't since they had left the Japanese Consulate in San Francisco together just in time to get aboard the *President Garfield*.

When Campbell put in his second appearance at Blake's hotel room but one thought seemed uppermost in his mind—the possibility of getting caught. Blake argued the matter under the dictograph for almost half an hour, and finally seemed to persuade Campbell that it would be safe enough for him to go ahead. Up to this time not a word had been said about the ease or difficulty with which Campbell could obtain the desired information, but the inference was that the espionage itself would be quite easy. Now Blake brought up the matter. "Hell," answered Campbell, "it's a lead-pipe cinch. So far as laying my hands on the stuff you want, it's like taking candy from a kid. The only thing that bothers me is that something could go wrong somewhere."

Now Blake began a discussion of certain naval secrets that any yeoman knew, apparently in an attempt to find out just how well-informed Campbell was and how potentially useful he could be. He asked certain questions and Campbell gave quick, detailed answers—answers that had been carefully thought out by the O.N.I. beforehand with inaccuracy in mind. No doubt the Japanese listening in over the dictograph were highly pleased at the way things were going.

Blake sent down for some drinks and presently Campbell began to have misgivings again. Blake tried to get from him precisely what the source of his fear was. Campbell didn't seem to know; he seemed to be only afraid on general principles. Certainly, so far as the listeners would be able to ascertain, Blake was far from through with his difficulties with Campbell. The yeoman seemed reluctant to go all out for espionage. Then Blake asked if Campbell could bring him a sample of what could be possibly obtained. That seemed more agreeable to the yeoman. "I could bring you something next time I come," he said.

"Good enough," said Blake. "When will that be?"

"I'll have to ring you. Maybe I can get away to-morrow night again, and maybe I can't. You know there's a lot of Jap funny business going on here in the Islands and I don't want to come here too often, Al."

The day following Campbell's second visit, the two Germans took up Blake's trail when he hired a car to do a little sightseeing on a pineapple plantation. The Germans in turn were being trailed by O.N.I. agents. The intelligence operative calling himself Campbell was very busy with his duties on the *Pennsylvania,* just in case the Japanese had any way of checking up as to what he was actually doing aboard the big ship. Mr. Horner—the gentleman from the *President Garfield*—was deliberately making a spectacle of himself by his drinking in various Honolulu bars. The two Japanese who had crossed with Blake went off on a trip by them-selves right after the King of the Robots left to visit the pineapple plantation. Other O.N.I. agents trailed the two Japs.

One of the Japanese went into a beauty parlor in downtown Honolulu—a place operated by one Ruth Kuehn, a German girl who had come to Honolulu with her mother and stepfather six years previously. Miss Kuehn's beauty parlor was one of the best in Honolulu and numbered among its clientele the wives of many Navy officers stationed at Pearl Harbor.

The O.N.I. wondered why the Japanese stopped at the beauty parlor. He wasn't in the place long, and when he came out and rejoined his companion in their hired car the two were driven to a pretty little house overlooking the water at Kalama.

It was quickly established that the mother and step-father of Ruth Kuehn, the beauty-shop operator, lived in the Kalama house. The couple—Mr. and Mrs. Bernard Julius Kuehn—had come to Honolulu from Germany in August, 1935, and taken up residence. Kuehn, a coarse-featured man of middle age with wide, intelligent eyes, had apparently made quite a bit of money before landing in Honolulu, because he showed no disposition to engage in any work there after his arrival. Kuehn's wife, Friedel, was a crafty-looking woman of dark complexion who wore rimless eye-glasses. She seemed devoted to her husband; she seldom bothered speaking to anybody else. The fact that the Japanese were visiting the Kuehns naturally made the German couple and their daughter marked persons from then on.

Blake didn't see Campbell for a week. The so-called yeoman called him on the phone night after night, canceling appointments, and making what must have seemed to the Japanese listeners-in like feeble excuses. When he finally did appear, he didn't bring anything with him. Blake asked why. "I've got to see the color of some of that dough first, Al," said Campbell. "I've been thinkin' things over and that's just the way I feel about it."

Blake explained that there probably wouldn't be any money forthcoming until something was actually delivered. "Well, then," said Campbell, "I don't know how interested I'll be." The two men separated not on the best of terms.

Blake was undressing, preparing for bed about half an

hour later, when an envelope was slipped under his door. In it was a one-thousand-dollar bill with a note. The note said,

You are doing good work. Give this to your friend as a down payment. Act quickly.

Campbell had made it a practice to stop at a certain bar in downtown Honolulu after leaving Blake's room. Blake put through a telephone call for the bar and reached the intelligence officer. "I've got good news for you, Jimmie," he said, "if you can come right back. Something immediate."

When Campbell returned and Blake gave him the thousand dollars, the intelligence man promised to get right to work. "For a few more of these, Al," he said, "I'll turn over the whole God damned fleet."

From that point on, the negotiations proceeded smoothly. Bit by bit, Campbell turned over to the King of the Robots one of the most stunning collections of spurious information ever designed by one great world power to mislead another one. A great deal of thought had gone into the information that Blake was to take back with him. From their experiences with Japanese espionage operatives in the Farnsworth and Thompson cases in particular, Naval Intelligence operatives knew that the Japanese were well acquainted with certain supposedly closely kept secrets relating to the United States Navy. It would never have done, then, to have concocted information that was too far from the truth; it would have been spotted for what it was immediately. The problem had been to steer a middle course wherein the information would appear to be accurate but would in reality be dangerously inaccurate.

Blake sailed for San Francisco pretty well loaded down with the spurious data. Just why the Japanese elected to have him return to the mainland with what he was carrying, and run the risk of being detected by customs men in San Francisco, was something of a mystery to the investigators. Perhaps the answer was that there was considerable jealousy among the personnel of the Japanese Secret Service and that information arranged for by one operative—Commander Tachibana, in this case—was not to be turned over to another operative. But certainly it would have been a far simpler matter for Blake to have turned his information over to Japanese Consular officials in Honolulu, who could have routed it to Japan through diplomatic pouches that were immune to search. It is a mistaken idea to suppose that just because one United States government agency is in on an investigation other agencies know about it. In the Blake case, for example, the F.B.I. had not yet been called into the picture. While the F.B.I. and the O.N.I. cooperate to the fullest extent when both agencies are working on the same case, each often operates quite independently for a long period of time. It is usually the practice of the O.N.I., for instance, to build a case up to a certain point before summoning the F.B.I.

For some reason, Blake was not tailed on the return trip to San Francisco. The two Japanese who had shadowed him to Honolulu and who visited the Kuehns during their stay had since gone on to the Orient. So had Mr. Horner and his wife—on the same boat as the two Japanese, singularly enough. The two Mr. Muellers remained in Honolulu, where more was to be found out about them.

Blake got through the customs all right in San Francisco, but when he got on a plane for Los Angeles, where he was to meet Kono and Tachibana and turn over the data, he noticed sitting across the aisle from him an alert-looking young man, still in his twenties. When the plane made a stop at Santa Barbara, the young man arose, leaned over to Blake and whispered, "I am from the F.B.I., Mr. Blake. If you don't mind, I wish you would step off the plane here with me for a few minutes while we have a little talk."

Blake, wanting to be certain that the stranger was in reality an F.B.I. agent, asked the young man to produce his credentials. This the agent did, as any F.B.I. man is required to do when asked to identify himself.

Blake and the agent had a talk in the administration building of the airline at Santa Barbara. The plane, meanwhile, was being held up at the F.B.I.'s request. Blake's baggage was taken off while Hoover's men went through it. The King of the Robots in the meantime was putting into reverse his ability to control his facial muscles, and going all out in his effort to put sincerity into his facial expression as he explained to the F.B.I. agent how he had come into possession of the documents he was carrying. Blake was not to learn until long afterward that he himself had been under suspicion by the F.B.I. in Honolulu simply because he had occupied the room between the two Germans and the two Japanese, who had been under F.B.I. as well as O.N.I. surveillance.

Things had looked even blacker for Blake, from the F.B.I. viewpoint, when he had been seen in such frequent contact with the Naval intelligence operative who was posing as a yeoman and whose pose was so good that it fooled even the F.B.I. The whole situation was grimly ludicrous and began to resemble a rather bad and over-drawn movie melodrama with too much plot and so much counterplot that the whole thing became con-fusing. Even officials of the F.B.I. and the O.N.I. had a good laugh over the crossing of wires after the situa-tion was cleared up following a telephone call from the F.B.I. man from the Santa Barbara airport.

Kono and Commander Tachibana received Blake with open arms upon his return to Hollywood. Tachi-bana was particularly excited about what Blake had brought back. He spoke vaguely of big things for Blake in the future. But he was immediately concerned by something else—a quick return trip by Blake to Hono-lulu.

Blake inquired of Commander Tachibana the rea-son for the return trip to Honolulu since he had just come back loaded down with what the Japanese spy un-questionably regarded as vital information. Tachibana replied that Blake would be secretly instructed by an attaché of the Japanese Consulate in the Hawaiian city upon his return there. While he was talking to Blake, Tachibana glanced at Kono, and there was something in the glance that caused Blake to become apprehensive about his personal safety.

Blake brought up the question of money and Tachi-bana showed a desire to haggle. He said he would have to examine Blake's information more thoroughly before he could determine just how much it was worth to the Japanese government.

The next day Blake left his apartment in Hollywood and took a bus for Los Angeles with the intention of going to the offices of the O.N.I. and reporting to Lieutenant Stanley, the first officer he had seen after Kono and Tachibana had asked him to work for the Japanese. As on the first occasion when Blake had ridden into Los Angeles on the bus en route to the O.N.I. offices, the King of the Robots discovered that he was being followed by two Japanese in a Ford car—apparently the same two Japanese, in the very same Ford, who had trailed him the first time.

Blake had been told what particular motion picture theater to go to in the event that it was ever again necessary for him to attempt to shake the shadows off his trail. It was obviously necessary for him to go to that theater now, for only inside the darkened playhouse would he stand any chance of getting away from the two men who were following him.

After Blake purchased his ticket and walked into the darkened auditorium he turned to see if the Japanese were coming in after him. He cast a quick glance at the two, who were at the ticket window. They would be inside in a matter of seconds.

Just then someone whispered in Blake's ear. Blake turned and in the semi-gloom he was startled to find himself face to face with a man who bore a striking resemblance to him. In a twinkling Blake took further note of the man's appearance. Not only did this person resemble Blake facially, even to the trim little mustache, but he was the same height and build and was dressed precisely like the King of the Robots, with a blue double-breasted suit, the same type of shirt and necktie, the same kind of shoes and even a Leghorn hat that was a duplicate of that worn by the counterespionage man. All this Blake took in at a glance. Not five seconds passed between the time when the man had first whispered in Blake's ear, saying, "Listen carefully, Blake," until he spoke again. This time he said, "O.N.I. I'm taking your place. Beat it quick, out the back way, and I'll stick around here and let those two Japs watch me in here. Be back here in two hours flat, come in the front way and go direct to the men's room. Be waiting there and the minute I come in, you go out. My disguise is good enough for a dark place, but it would never stand up in daylight." The O.N.I. agent glanced out into the lobby. "Beat it quick, Blake," he said. "Here they come."

The scheme worked out perfectly; at least the first part of it. As the Japanese came into the auditorium, Al Blake was well on his way down a side aisle to a rear exit, while the O.N.I. agent who looked so much like him was walking across the rear of the theater as if he had just come out of the men's room. He saw that the Jap agents spotted him immediately and knew that they followed him and took seats two rows behind him as he settled down to watch the picture.

Blake had certain misgivings as to whether the masquerader in the theater was actually an O.N.I. agent or not, since there had been no time for the man to display credentials. Certainly, if the man in the theater was a white member of a Japanese spy ring the cat was out of the bag. It was thus with great relief that Blake learned from Lieutenant Stanley that the double had in fact been one of Stanley's operatives.

There was still a question in Blake's mind as to how the double had managed to be inside of the theater before himself, and dressed exactly like him. Blake was told that the agent possessed a wardrobe that almost exactly duplicated that of Blake. He was always stationed in a room only half a block from the theater, constantly wearing a skillfully contrived theatrical make-up to resemble the King of the Robots. The agent's sole job was to be ready to dress as Blake did on very short notice and hasten to the theater, have his ticket purchased and be inside, ready to switch places with Blake if the counterespionage agent was trailed into the theater by the Japanese.

"But how did he know what I would be wearing?" Blake asked Stanley.

The Lieutenant smiled. "One of our men near your apartment in Hollywood saw you leaving and telephoned ahead. It was really quite simple."

Time was important, for Blake would have to get back to the theater within two hours of the time he had left so as to be in the men's room when his double popped in. It wasn't necessary for Lieutenant Stanley to consume part of that valuable time in speaking to Blake about what had happened in Hawaii. The O.N.I. knew all about that. What interested Stanley was this latest plan of Commander Tachibana to have Blake return to the islands. Stanley thought briefly about the matter when Blake mentioned it to him, then left the room to confer with other intelligence officers. When he returned, his face was grave. "Blake," he said. "I might as well be frank with you. They are asking you to go back to Honolulu for the purpose of killing you there."

CHAPTER 11

A Death Trap for the Robot King

"How do you figure that?" asked the King of the Robots, who was living up to his name, for no suggestion of fear showed in his face.

"Their psychology would be this, Blake. Your usefulness to them is over. As long as you live you will be a potential menace to them. It's the old story of dead men telling no tales. While I am certain that they have not caught on to what you are really doing, they themselves have no assurance that you will not eventually run afoul of our organization or of the F.B.I. And if you were ever picked up, the Japanese would figure that you might talk."

Lieutenant Stanley brought his fingertips together, swung his chair around and gazed thoughtfully out of the window. "That's what the score is, Blake, and we want you to appreciate fully just what your Jap friends are up to. You don't have to go, you know, and so long as you are here on the mainland we can practically guarantee you protection. But out there"—Lieutenant Stanley shrugged—"we can't guarantee you very much. We know for a fact that during the past year in Hawaii no less than three white people who worked for the Japanese have been murdered. Two were men and one was a woman."

"I think as much of my neck as the next man," said Blake, "and naturally I don't want to stick it out for a Japanese axe. But tell me this, Lieutenant: Could I accomplish anything worthwhile for the United States Government if I returned to Hawaii as they want me to?"

Stanley gazed out of the window for what seemed to Blake to be an interminably long time before answering. When he spoke, he said, "That's just the point, Blake. You can render your greatest service on this second trip."

Blake wanted to know how. "You said that Tachibana told you that an attaché of the Japanese Consulate in Honolulu would look after you this time," said Stanley. "All right. We need such a contact but haven't been able to effect one so far. If you were to go out there and establish such a connection it might be possible for you to get hold of some vital information for us." Again Blake asked, "How?"

The details of what Lieutenant Stanley had in mind are still secret, but the general idea can be told. Blake, it appears, was to establish once more a rendezvous with the operative who was posing as Yeoman Jimmie Campbell of the U.S.S. *Pennsylvania,* and Campbell was to stumble across certain new and apparently vital information. Blake was to mention this information to the attaché of the Consulate. The data were to be so arresting that the Japanese would decide to give Blake what amounted to a reprieve until such time as he turned over to them this latest intelligence. However, during his conversations with the Japanese in Hawaii about this newest information, he was to learn just how much the Japanese knew about certain other vital naval and military secrets. This knowledge was to be gained by observing the intensity of Japanese reactions when Blake turned over certain information. "In other words," explained Lieutenant Stanley, "we will be able to learn how much the Japanese know about specific subjects from the amount of interest they express in certain data that you turn over to them. As a matter of fact, for more than a year now we have had the data I speak of all prepared to be tested on the Japanese but we have never succeeded in maneuvering things so that we could get a white man to put it up to them without arousing their suspicions."

Lieutenant Stanley lapsed into silence again. Then he said, "That's how things are, Blake. Understand, there's no guarantee that the Japanese will go for this bait. All we could guarantee, if you return to Hawaii, would be the closest shave you've ever had in your life; that is, if you don't actually get killed. Still want to go?"

The very least that can be said for Al Blake is that he was a patriot. Moreover, he had come to despise the Japanese thoroughly through association with them. Thus he was motivated by personal feelings as well as patriotism. "Sure as hell I want to go," he said.

"Hadn't you better think it over for a day or two, Blake?"

"I've been thinking it over all the time I've been here, Lieutenant," said the King of the Robots. "When I make up my mind, I make it up—and it's made up."

Lieutenant Stanley reached into his desk and handed Blake an envelope. In the envelope, he said, were more than thirty statements of apparent vital facts relating to both naval matters and military matters that were closely linked with naval operations. These were the half truths and three-quarter truths that the O.N.I. had carefully prepared more than a year previously for purposes of one day getting Japanese reactions to them.

Blake was told to memorize thoroughly the statements contained in the envelope, and then to burn the paper on which they were written and flush the charred remains down a toilet. The O.N.I. knew that the Japanese would probably still be going through Blake's apartment while he was not there, and Lieutenant Stanley and other officers were taking no chances on the Japanese going to such lengths as taking the remains of burned papers from a wastebasket in Blake's apartment, substituting other burned remains, and then having what was removed restored in a laboratory. The O.N.I. was not deluding itself into believing that the Japanese were not keeping pretty much abreast of the United States in all phases of intelligence operations. The O.N.I. didn't want Blake to carry the envelope with the statements he was to memorize any farther than from Lieutenant Stanley's office to his Hollywood apartment, by way of the theater, where the masquerader was waiting to switch places with him again.

Blake assumed that his quarters in Honolulu, wherever they would be, would be wired for sound, as they had been on the occasion of his first trip. If that were so, and if he were supposedly to come across the bait data through the medium of the operative who called himself Yeoman Campbell, Blake wondered how he would get the opportunity to observe Japanese reactions if the Japanese first learned of the information over a dictograph. Lieutenant Stanley explained that new strategy had been devised relating to meetings of Blake and Campbell in Honolulu. The two men were to do no talking whatsoever in Blake's quarters on this trip. The excuse for their changed behavior was to be a statement by Blake to Campbell to the effect that he was afraid to discuss anything in a hotel room (where supposedly he would stay) because American agents might be listening.

The O.N.I. subterfuge in the theater worked as well when Blake was on his way home as it had worked while Blake had been en route to see Lieutenant Stanley. Blake slipped into the men's room just five minutes before his double appeared. The moment the latter entered, he whispered to Blake, "Start washing your hands; I think one of them's coming in." Thereupon the masquerader ducked into a pay toilet compartment not five seconds before one of the Japanese came in. Blake appeared to be a man who had just seen the show when he commented on the picture to the Japanese. Then he was tailed back to Hollywood.

The Japanese, it turned out, were just as cheap as the Germans when it came to paying spies—and that was going some, for many a German spy had been paid off with an autographed picture of Der Führer. Commander Tachibana began to find fault with some details of the information that Blake had brought back, quite obviously for the purpose of keeping down expenses. The Japanese officer finally maneuvered the situation around to the point where Blake agreed to wait for payment until he had returned from Honolulu the second time. Blake was given just enough to cover his steamship fare to the islands and for hotel expenses there. On the occasion of his first visit he had been given enough money for return passage; this time he wasn't. Commander Tachibana explained that failure to supply Blake with money to come back with was merely routine. The Japanese Consulate in Honolulu would supply it, he said. Had there been any doubt in Al Blake's mind that Lieutenant Stanley of the O.N.I. had correctly diagnosed the situation, it would have been removed by Tachibana's failure to arrange for Blake's return passage.

Not thirty-six hours after he had received instructions from Lieutenant Stanley, Blake found himself on an overnight limited from Los Angeles to San Francisco, from which point he was, on the day of his arrival, to take a steamer for the islands. Just before his departure on the liner, Blake was approached at the pier by a little Japanese he had never seen before. He was given instructions on what hotel to stay at when he reached Honolulu, and also informed that he was not to leave his hotel room under any circumstances until he had received word of some kind from an attaché of the Japanese Consulate. Blake asked what he was supposed to do about food.

"Order your meals served in your room," was the answer.

Blake was two days at sea when he arrived at the definite conclusion that there were no shadows aboard ship. This was further indication to him, if he needed any, that so far as the Japanese was concerned, he was sailing to his death.

On arrival at Honolulu, when he checked into the hotel—not the same hotel he had previously stopped at —he found that a dictograph was planted in the room.

This time the "bug" was not behind a blind, but was concealed inside a secret compartment of a small writing desk.

The Japanese had not instructed Blake against communicating with Yeoman Campbell, so he called the U.S.S. *Pennsylvania* and got the intelligence operative on the phone. Proceeding on the theory that his telephone had been tapped again, Blake spoke with that in mind, and so did Campbell. The supposed yeoman was all for meeting Blake at once, mentioning, in guarded language, the fact that he was anxious to get the remainder of his pay for the data that he had previously turned over to Blake. The King of the Robots, mindful of the fact that the Japanese had told him not to leave his room until he received a communication from a Consular attaché, stalled Campbell along, explaining that he would give him another ring when it was all right to come to the hotel. "I can explain everything when I see you, Jimmie," said Blake. "In the meantime, you've got to trust me."

Campbell sounded very suspicious about the fact that Blake was in Honolulu again and that there would be a delay in the two of them getting together. The O.N.I. had decided that this reaction on Campbell's part would sound like normal behavior by a person who had turned over valuable confidential data, expecting to be paid for it. Anything that could be done further to convince the Japanese that Al Blake had been absolutely on the level with them was considered of paramount importance. No matter what else happened, it was vital that the Japanese should regard the information that Blake had already turned over as being authentic in every respect. Naturally, in the summer of 1941—almost half a year before

Pearl Harbor—American realists in high places did not know just when, where or how a Japanese attack would come—but they knew it would come. And they were preparing for it so that when the attack was made Japan would be acting on certain false information—the information that had been planted on the Imperial Japanese Government through the medium of Al Blake.

On the second day of Blake's return visit to Honolulu there was a faint tapping on the door of his hotel room in midafternoon. Blake opened the door to find a smiling young Japanese, faultlessly tailored in white linen, at the threshold. "Good afternoon, Mr. Blake," said the visitor, stepping inside without waiting for an invitation.

The man identified himself as a Consular attaché but did not give his name. Without preliminaries, he got right to the business at hand. He told Blake just what would be expected of him during this sojourn on the islands. He would be required to get in touch again with his friend, Yeoman Campbell of the *Pennsylvania,* with the idea of having Campbell arrange things so that Blake could go out to Pearl Harbor and make certain observations at certain locations where men with yellow faces couldn't go without arousing the suspicion of the naval authorities.

When Blake asked for details of what he was to observe, the Japanese brought out a little book and consulted it. He thereupon took some stationery from Blake's desk and drew diagrams of certain locations at Pearl Harbor. Among other things, Blake had been made acquainted with information such as this in order that he would be able to evaluate Japanese moves as he went along. Thus it was that when his visitor told him just what it was he wanted him to observe at Pearl Harbor, Blake had further evidence that the sole motive of the Japanese in getting him to Hawaii for the second time was to kill him.

For, in the first place, the observations that the visitor asked him to make were of the most innocuous sort—the type of thing that would have little or no intelligence value, and certainly hardly the kind of information that would have warranted the Japanese bringing Blake all the way from the mainland to obtain. If the Japanese were not indeed already in possession of the information that the little man in the linen suit was asking Blake to get, it would have been comparatively simple to obtain by more than one means. But in order to get the information, it would be necessary for Blake to go out to Pearl Harbor. Such a trip entailed passing over certain stretches of lonely territory that lay between the hotel and the naval base—territory where it would be ideal for killers to wait in ambush until their victim came along.

Blake inquired when he would be expected to begin his observations. "That depends," said the Japanese, "on certain factors that haven't been decided yet." It didn't require much imagination on Blake's part to conclude what the factors were; they would relate to getting the stage set for a murder somewhere between the hotel and Pearl Harbor.

The Japanese prepared to depart after telling Blake that he would be in touch with him again within a few days. Then Blake brought up the subject of his restricted movements. "I'll go nuts," he said, "if I don't get out of this room." His visitor told him that he could feel free to do whatever he wished. "That is," he concluded, "until it is time for you to begin your work." Blake was to say later that when he heard that remark he felt like a condemned man who was given his choice of food at a last meal.

After his visitor left, Blake telephoned to the intelligence operative on the *Pennsylvania*. The man calling himself Jimmie Campbell arrived at the hotel room early that evening. He wanted to know where his money was, and Blake explained that payment would not be forthcoming until he returned to Los Angeles after his present mission, as the Japanese were trying to arrive at a fair figure for the data. Campbell thereupon went into a tirade against the Japanese, calling them every unprintable name that he could lay his tongue on. This was considered sound psychology, since it would have been normal behavior of a man who considered himself betrayed. Then, when he was through with his tirade, Campbell let loose a remark, "But I was smarter than those bastards were, at that."

"How do you mean, Jimmie?" asked Blake.

"They didn't get one-tenth of what I got my hands on."

Blake pretended not to believe Campbell, and the intelligence operative took up the challenge. "You think I'm bluffing, eh? Well, take a look at this." The operative rustled some sheets of perfectly blank paper on the desk where the dictograph was planted. To those listening at the other end, it must have sounded as if Blake were really looking at some extremely valuable information. "Well, for God's sake!" Blake would say at appropriate intervals.

After the amount of time had passed when he might have glanced through all that Campbell had, Blake said, "Jimmie, look—will you let me have some of this stuff to take back with me? I tell you we're not being double-crossed and if I could only show them this you'd get more money than you would be able to count. In fact, there's only one thing that bothers me—they'll think I'm a prize dope for only going back with what I did go back with, when you had all this stuff right along."

Campbell was adamant. "Nuts to that," he said. "I want to see the color of their dough before I let this stuff go. Hell, I could sell this almost anywhere—to Italy or Germany, to name two places. Why the hell should I let the Japs have it when they owe me dough now?"

When Campbell left late that night, both he and Blake were entitled to feel that they had put on another good act. There was no doubt in the mind of the intelligence operative that what he and the King of the Robots had said and done in the hotel room had been of the most tantalizing nature to anyone listening over the dictograph.

That Campbell's deduction was correct was proved less than an hour after he left, when the attaché of the Embassy called on Blake unexpectedly. He offered as an excuse for his second call the fact that he had neglected to take up certain details that he had intended discussing with Blake during the afternoon. Then, when he had finished with the ostensible reason for this second call of the day, he said to Blake, "I wonder if it would be possible that you could perhaps get some additional information for us while you are here—I mean information such as you obtained from Mr. Campbell on your last visit."

Blake looked steadily at the Japanese for several seconds, then said, "I've tried to play fair with you people, but Campbell doesn't think you've played fair with him. I'll be perfectly honest with you. He was here not an hour ago and asked where his money was for the stuff

I took to Hollywood and gave to Commander Tachi-bana. As you probably know, I have not been paid for that yet, and all Campbell has seen is a thousand bucks down payment."

"Yes?" the Japanese said, eagerly.

"We'll just have to get some dough, or at least some assurance as to what the eventual price is going to be. If that can be arranged, I don't mind telling you that I'll be in a position to get some of the damnedest stuff for you that you've ever even thought of."

As if he didn't know what Blake was driving at, the Japanese asked for details. "I don't know the details, as a matter of fact," said Blake. "I didn't have long enough to study the stuff. Campbell had it with him when he was here and he let me see just enough of it to know that it's practically priceless. I hate to admit it, because it makes me out a sort of a dope, but the guy held out on me when I was here before. I figured I had got everything he had, but he was a little too cagey for that, and I went back with only a fraction of what's available."

The Japanese was obviously in deep thought when he departed. Early the next morning he was back at Blake's room again. He handed the American an envelope. "There's three thousand dollars in there in American cash," he explained. "Give it to your friend, Campbell, and have him turn over to you some of this new information." While Blake was counting the money, the Japanese said, "To use an American expression, that will be but a drop in the bucket compared to what you and Campbell will get if this information turns out as good as it promises to be."

In the ensuing several days, Blake turned over the Campbell information bit by bit. Keeping his face as expressionless as possible, he studied the expression on the face of the Japanese as the information was turned over. Blake was well aware of the fact that the Japanese were similar to him in that one way—they were able to mask their inner feelings, as a rule. However, the intensity of interest that shone from the eyes of the consular attaché as he examined the spurious information was a definite tip-off to Blake that the newest Campbell data were going to be regarded as of paramount importance in Jap quarters.

Now Blake was to begin to feed the yellow men information which, while deliberately off-base and therefore valueless, was nevertheless close enough to the truth to make it appear authentic. The data touched upon subjects with which, the O.N.I. suspected, Japanese espionage experts had long since been familiar. But the O.N.I. couldn't be certain about this until they found out what the Japanese reaction to the information was. It was, of course, of the utmost value to the American operatives to learn just what the Japanese already knew. And certain of the spurious data that Blake was to show to the consular attaché would be the yardstick by which the O.N.I. could measure the extent of Japanese espionage knowledge. Once that measuring was complete, appropriate steps could be taken.

In the meantime, both the O.N.I. and agents of the Honolulu Field Office of the F.B.I. had been looking into Mr. and Mrs. Bernard Julius Kuehn, the German couple who had come to Honolulu more than six years before and settled in a pretty little house at Kalama, overlooking the ocean. Since they had first come under surveillance, following a visit to their home by the two Japanese who had trailed Blake across the Pacific during his first visit to the islands, the Kuehns had become more interesting to the investigators with the passing of each day. For one thing, Kuehn himself had, it was developed, recently purchased the most powerful pair of binoculars in stock in a Honolulu sporting goods store.

Kuehn's stepdaughter, Ruth—the child of his wife Friedel by a previous marriage—was also looming as a figure of increasing importance to the investigators. They learned that when Ruth Kuehn opened her beauty shop in downtown Honolulu more than a year before it had been equipped with all of the very latest gadgets of her trade. By all tokens, Ruth Kuehn should have charged rather fancy prices for the service she gave, but the investigators had learned that her prices were far below what they should have been. In fact, when the F.B.I. made it a point to become thoroughly acquainted with operating costs in beauty parlors, the conclusion was reached that Ruth Kuehn was not even breaking even; she was actually losing money.

Two and two made four when surveillance of Ruth's beauty shop disclosed that the patronage consisted chiefly of Navy wives. Naturally, wives of naval officers, whose incomes are moderate, would have been quick to learn of a new beauty shop where the service was good and the prices remarkably low.

The reports about Mr. and Mrs. Kuehn, and Ruth Kuehn, were sent in routine fashion to J. Edgar Hoover in Washington. None of the reports expressed an opinion of any kind; only the bald facts were set down. Kuehn and his wife had kept very much to themselves since their arrival in Honolulu in 1935. Kuehn had not been observed doing any work of any kind, so it was obvious that he had money from somewhere. The fact that

he hadn't engaged in any occupation could not be as-
cribed to ill health, for the man was apparently in very
good health. His purchase of the binoculars, and the fact
that his stepdaughter Ruth was operating her beauty
shop at a loss just about completed the report to Hoover.

After Hoover considered the known facts, he decided
the chances were very good that Kuehn had been sent to
Honolulu from Germany for the purpose of taking root
in the community against the day when he could secure
for the German or the Japanese government, or both,
confidential information relative to United States naval
matters. The psychology of the Kuehn set-up, Hoover
decided, had been good enough, as far as it went. The
F.B.I. director knew from long official experience that
women became more voluble than usual in two places—
on shipboard and in a beauty shop. With the beauty-
shop angle in mind, Kuehn had obviously been behind
the opening of his stepdaughter's establishment. Once
the business was established, it would be a simple matter
for the daughter to take careful note of chit-chat among
the Navy wives under the dryers and pass along valuable
information to her stepfather.

There was no question in Hoover's mind that an investigation of Kuehn's bank account might explain a
great deal, so he sent instructions to the Honolulu Field
Office that the German's financial status be investigated
on the quiet, and that Kuehn be kept under surveillance
twenty-four hours a day.

Since it was an open secret among American investigators that the Japanese Consulate in Honolulu was the
fountainhead for spy activities on the islands, every consular attaché had long since been carefully watched. As
a matter of fact, F.B.I. agents had more than once crossed

each other's trails through shadowing the Japanese diplomats. Even had Al Blake been what he pretended to the Japanese—a man who was selling out the United States—he would have come within the F.B.I. horizon in Honolulu, for a G-man was on the trail of the particular consular attaché who went to Blake's hotel room.

By the same token, Kuehn would have come under observation in the early part of June, 1941, even had O.N.I. agents not become interested in him earlier when the two Japanese who had trailed Blake from San Francisco called at the house in Kalama. For, not twenty-four hours after the arrival of Hoover's orders to keep the German under constant surveillance, one of the G-Men assigned to shadow a man named Tadasi Morimura, fourth secretary of the Japanese Consulate, found himself following the man late one night to a lonely spot halfway between Honolulu and Kalama. Another F.B.I. agent, trailing Kuehn, followed the German to the very same spot. Now, it so happened that owing to the darkness of the night and the fact that neither agent wanted to get so close to the object of his surveillance that he would uncover himself, both agents returned to the Honolulu Field Office with incomplete but substantially similar stories. The man each had tailed had obviously had an appointment at the spot midway between Honolulu and Kalama. Neither agent, however, had the slightest inkling of the person his subject was meeting. But when both reports were put together, it became quite obvious that Tadasi Morimura, the fourth secretary of the Japanese Consulate, had had an appointment with Bernard Julius Kuehn, the suspect of Kalama.

Although banking transactions, like commercial telegraphic, cable and radio messages, are of a confidential nature, the average financial institution cooperates with government investigators in a probe into a matter of grave suspicion, such as one relating to espionage. Officials of the Honolulu bank where Kuehn did business dug into their records on the German. It transpired that during the years 1936, 1937 and 1938, almost ninety thousand dollars had been deposited to the German's account through drafts from the Rotterdam Bank Association in Holland.

Since war between the United States and Germany had not yet broken out and this country still had diplomatic representatives in Germany and other European countries, it was possible for American consular representatives to do a little digging on the quiet within the Third Reich. In addition to this, both the F.B.I. and the State Department had for a long time been in possession of huge files filled with unrelated information which, it was hoped, would some day be of value.

Included in this unrelated information was the fact, gleaned more than three years before by an attaché of the American Embassy in Berlin, that the German Gestapo used the Rotterdam Bank Association as one of the mediums through which to transfer large sums of money to German agents in all parts of the world. The use of a Dutch bank was a clever enough idea, as the Gestapo no doubt figured that if the source of money to a spy who was unfortunate enough to get caught was ever traced and the Rotterdam Bank Association found to be on the other end, the Gestapo would be in the clear. But, naturally, it wasn't working out that way, since the American grapevine had found out about the plan. Thus a scrap of information in Washington—that relating to the Gestapo's use of the Dutch bank—together with the information forwarded from Honolulu relating to the source of Kuehn's affluence—definitely marked the man as a German spy some six months before the outbreak of hostilities. And now began a check-up inside Germany bearing on Kuehn's past.

Kuehn, it developed, had been born in Berlin in 1895, which made him forty-six in 1941. He had served in the German Navy in the first World War—a rather important fact to the investigators. Most of the German spies the F.B.I. had so far run across had had German army experience if they had fought for Germany in the first World War. A suspect with navy experience was something new. That background would certainly have been of inestimable value to a spy operating in the vicinity of Pearl Harbor.

According to information picked up in Germany by American consular agents, Kuehn, a brilliant man with a college education, had been one of the original Nazis back in Hitler's beer-hall days. When Hitler had come into power in 1932, Kuehn's rise in party circles had been rapid. He had become a member of the Gestapo and had been a great favorite of the Gestapo chief, Heinrich Himmler. Kuehn had exhibited such a talent for treachery that by 1935 he was slated for the post of deputy chief of the Gestapo, right under Himmler. But somehow or other he had incurred the displeasure of a powerful Nazi who was later to take on world infamy as Heydrich the Hangman. After incurring Heydrich's displeasure, Kuehn found another man appointed to the post he cherished.

Kuehn was of such potential value to Hitler, however, that Himmler, according to the information American agents picked up (and they had reason to believe it was fairly accurate), went to Der Führer on Kuehn's behalf. It was decided to send Kuehn to Hawaii, where he would take root and be in a position to gather information of value to Japan and, therefore, of value also to Germany.

Al Blake had been in Honolulu for almost two weeks of his second visit when the man posing as Yeoman Campbell of the U.S.S. *Pennsylvania* called at his room one night and, while greeting Blake in routine fashion for the benefit of the Japanese listening in on the dictograph, held up a note saying:

I am going to suggest that we go out together. Pretend that you don't feel good and don't want to go, but agree with me in the end and come with me.

There now started a conversation along the lines outlined in the note, and in a little while Blake and Campbell left for a Honolulu hot spot. Campbell had mentioned the name of the place that he wanted to take Blake to, so that the Japanese would send shadow men there rather than put tails on the Americans at the hotel. Once beyond the range of the dictograph, however, Campbell advised Blake of his strategy and the two headed for another spot. They found a secluded corner and had their first opportunity for a long talk. "You are in grave danger now, Al," said the intelligence operative. "The Japs have all the information that it would be possible for a man in my position to lay hands on, and they know it. So now you are definitely on the spot."

"You mean that they're going to send me on that Pearl Harbor mission now, and get me along a lonely stretch of road between here and there?"

The intelligence operative nodded. "That's just what they intend to do," he said, "and that's just what we intend to avoid."

"How can you avoid it? How can I start ducking them without their getting suspicious?"

"We haven't figured that out yet, Al. And it's very important that they don't get on to the fact that you know they're out to kill you. For if they do get wise, that'll throw suspicion on every last bit of the negotiations you have had with them since that day last year when Kono walked into your exhibit at Treasure Island."

Blake asked how the over-all strategy had worked out so far. "I'm not allowed to give you details, Al," said the man posing as a yeoman. "It's against regulations for any of us to give information of a highly confidential nature to anyone not in government service. But I can clear you up on the picture as a whole. You have rendered a patriotic service to your country that is valuable beyond measure." The intelligence operative then explained to Blake that the response of the consular attaché to certain information, as passed on by Blake in notes that he wrote and handed to Campbell from time to time when Campbell visited his hotel room, had cleared up for Naval Intelligence, for the first time, just about what the Japs knew and didn't know about all phases of the Pacific fleet.

"The result is," the intelligence operative explained, "that we will be able to take certain precautions. We know that when the Japanese attack comes that it will be sudden, and that it will be perpetrated in the midst of diplomatic negotiations that will be carried on in Washington between Japanese representatives and our State Department."

"And this information that you have gotten through Japanese reactions to the false stuff that I have shown them has enabled you to make plans for this sudden Japanese attack?" asked Blake.

The operative nodded. "We know now just about what the Japanese have in mind," he said. "All we have to do is to be alert twenty-four hours a day." And then the operative made a prophetic remark. "Of course," he said, "it is always possible that there might be a slip-up somewhere. For instance, our information may not be taken as seriously as it should be in certain quarters. That's often so with information of this kind. Certain people doubt it, because a good deal of it is deduction. God help us if any of this is doubted."

At this point Blake inquired how the O.N.I. had come into possession of details about his danger. The F.B.I., it seems, had supplied the information to the Navy. Two Germans—not the same two, however, who had occupied a stateroom next to Blake's during his first trans-Pacific crossing—had checked into the room next to Blake's at the hotel. The German pair had been in Honolulu for about three weeks, or a week longer than Blake, having disembarked from a liner that had stopped at Hawaii en route from Japan to San Francisco. The pair had first checked into another hotel, and the F.B.I., who had immediately put them under surveillance, had gotten the impression that they were just waiting around for something, probably instructions of some sort. Now that they had moved into the room next to Blake's, it became apparent that they were the assassins who had been brought to Honolulu for the express purpose of his execution.

Before the intelligence operative and Blake parted

for the night, the spurious yeoman cautioned Blake, "I'll be over again sometime tomorrow. Whatever you do, don't leave your room until I get there. When I arrive I hope we will have something worked out for your escape. If by any chance you get instructions to go out to Pearl Harbor before I arrive, stall them off, whatever you do. Play sick if you have to."

It was at this point that Blake himself made a suggestion. Playing sick was a good idea, and by way of building up for an illness, he suggested that he pretend that he had had too much to drink when he got back to his hotel room that night. "I'll stumble around and mutter to myself, and knock things over," he said, "and then I'll drink a lot of hot water and make myself vomit. If the vomiting doesn't carry over the dictograph, it'll certainly carry through the wall to where those two Heinies are. How does it sound?"

"Great," said the intelligence man.

Blake put on his act that night. The next morning, about ten, the Japanese consular attaché called at Blake's room. The King of the Robots gave a splendid imitation of a man suffering from a hangover and the jitters. The Japanese was obviously disappointed at Blake's condition.

"I wanted you to start on that Pearl Harbor business this afternoon," he said. "Do you think you'll be able to go?"

Blake looked at the Japanese woefully. "All I want is my bed," he said. "Couldn't we put it off until tomorrow?"

"Yes," said the Japanese, "I suppose so, if we have to. Will you be ready to start tomorrow afternoon at three?"

"I'll be all right by then," said Blake. "I'm sorry this

happened. But it's been a great strain, and I had to relax."

"I trust you didn't relax too much," said the Japanese, "and do a lot of talking."

"I never talk," said Blake, "no matter what condition I'm in."

"Where did you go last night?" asked the attaché. Blake mentioned the spot.

"Oh," said the Japanese, as if a small mystery had been explained to him.

The naval operative called at Blake's at seven that night.

After a preliminary conversation, during which the two men dwelt on the amount of drinking they had done the night before, the operative handed Blake a note. It read as follows:

The two men in the next room are the ones who are to kill you. That's definite.

Blake wrote a note:

How do you know?

The answer was:

They were followed this morning to a lonely spot not far from Pearl Harbor where you would have to pass to get there. F.B.I. men using glasses saw them examine the spot apparently where they are to hide until you come along.

Blake asked in another note:

How do you propose to get me out of here?

The answer was ready:

In a little while now you will get a cablegram saying that your mother in Illinois is not expected to live. A boat leaves tomorrow afternoon for San Francisco and you are openly to make arrangements to get on it. The Japs will figure that you can probably make the trip to Pearl Harbor earlier so that you could do the job there and still catch the boat. But a Clipper leaves at noon and you can just wander into the Clipper office a few minutes before it goes out as a sort of a second thought to get back to the United States as early as possible and just go out on it. But before you go drop a hasty but nice note to the Japanese Consulate, telling them what you did and explaining that you are almost out of your mind through anxiety about your mother and that you will come back.

CHAPTER 12

Denouement in Little Tokyo

THE FAKE CABLEGRAM announcing his mother's serious illness arrived for Blake not an hour after Campbell returned to the U.S.S. *Pennsylvania*. Blake smiled grimly as he examined the envelope before opening it. The envelope had been opened, perhaps right in the hotel, before being delivered to him. He opened the cable at the desk where the dictograph was planted so that the listeners could hear what he was doing. As he read the spurious message he gave a deep sigh, muttering the words, "My God—poor mother!" And then he began to sob. Blake did some of his best acting to date in the ten minutes that followed his opening of the message.

The Japanese attaché put in another of his unexpected appearances not half an hour afterward. "I just stopped by to see how you were feeling," he said. Blake handed him the cable. "This is too bad," said the Japanese when he read the message that he had no doubt been acquainted with before entering the room. "What do you intend to do, Mr. Blake?"

"When's the next boat out of here?" asked Blake. "I want to be on it. Something tells me I'll never see my mother again, and I'll come back and do that Pearl Harbor business then."

The Japanese was pacing up and down the floor, deep

in thought. "The next boat leaves tomorrow afternoon," he said, "and you can be on it and do the Pearl Harbor business too."

"How? If I don't leave for Pearl Harbor until three o'clock, how can I manage to be back in time to get the boat?"

The answer to that, the Japanese explained, was that Blake could leave for Pearl Harbor at noon, do his snooping, and return in time to get the liner.

"But," said Blake, "that's not a small job you've given me to do at Pearl Harbor."

The Japanese seemed impatient. "Do whatever you can," he said, "and we'll talk about the rest of the work later."

The attaché left Blake a disconsolate figure. The King of the Robots gave every appearance of a man who had lost interest in his espionage work because of his grief.

Blake was up early in the morning. He went down to the bar for a drink, assuming the behavior of a man seeking solace in alcohol to lighten a personal tragedy. It was his first visit to the hotel bar since his arrival. Inasmuch as he was leaving for Pearl Harbor not later than noon, so far as the Japanese knew, he was somewhat surprised to find two men of Teutonic aspect entering the bar immediately after him. Blake had not seen the two Germans who had checked into the room next to his, but he supposed that these two were the pair. He noticed something else. Both men bulged suspiciously at the hips, as if they were carrying guns in their rear trousers' pockets.

Blake had several drinks, and then took a walk around the hotel grounds. Psychologically, a man in his mental state could be expected to do the unexpected without arousing suspicion. Blake took advantage of this situation by making several sudden changes in his course as he went from one point on the hotel grounds to another. Whenever he backtracked on his own steps he saw one or both of the Germans.

Shortly before ten o'clock he went over to a steamship office to pick up passage for the liner that afternoon, which he had ordered the night before through the hotel desk.

When he was returning to the hotel from the steamship office he noticed that the two Germans were following him.

Back at the hotel, Blake went up to his room—more than an hour before he had arranged to leave for his mission at Pearl Harbor. As he sat in his room reading a newspaper, and looking over the top of it at the partly open door, he saw that the two Germans were softly walking up and down the corridor, taking a look into Blake's room each time they passed.

Blake went downstairs again and walked around the hotel grounds once more. Whenever he turned he saw one or both of the Nazis although he showed no evidence of it. The assassins, who no doubt were being paid a good price by the Japanese government for killing Blake, were carrying out their mission with typical Teutonic thoroughness. They were being rather crude about it, but Germans frequently are none too subtle. These two, as they fastened themselves to Blake's trail like leeches, resembled Peter Lorre and Sidney Greenstreet up to some skulduggery in a movie melodrama. In fact, the thought had crossed Blake's mind many a time that were the experiences he was going through, and all the other ramifications, made into a fiction story or a movie, the tale would seem unreal because it was so overdrawn. He hardly needed to remind himself, however, that it was all a matter of the grimmest reality.

Blake was to leave his hotel at high noon in a chauffeur-driven automobile that the Japanese were to supply. Final instructions were to be given him just before he left. Perhaps the attaché would call again, or perhaps the chauffeur of the automobile would have the last-minute orders.

Blake knew that the Clipper left at noon, and that he would have to be on it if he were to avoid death or the casting of suspicion on his entire negotiations with the Japanese. He was wondering just how he would shake off the two Germans and get down to the Clipper airport before the big plane left. It was now about half-past eleven, and Blake, who had returned to his room, realized he would have to set forth if he wanted to catch the Clipper. He had decided to shake off the Germans between his room and the entrance of the hotel, where he would get a taxi. The two Nazi killers were in the next room, he knew, for he had heard them enter just after he had himself returned.

Blake was leaving his baggage. He didn't want it to look as if the Clipper trip had been planned without the knowledge of his Japanese employers. His departure should have the appearance of a sudden impulse. He put on his hat and was just about to open the door and steal silently downstairs, when suddenly there was a faint rapping on the door.

Opening it, he found a smiling Japanese in a chauffeur's livery. The man obviously was much above his station, however, for there was no deference in his manner. He walked into Blake's room without being invited, closed the door behind him, and said, "I'm a little early; we aren't supposed to start until twelve o'clock."

"Suppose," said Blake, "we go down and sit in your car. I need some air." Blake was certain that the Germans in the next room were listening in, and now that the Japanese chauffeur had arrived they would perhaps leave for the death rendezvous so that they could be well settled before Blake came along. The more Blake thought about the early arrival of the chauffeur, the more he became convinced that the timing was part of the plot.

He stalled for a couple of minutes, going into the bathroom to bathe his face in cold water; he wanted to see whether the Germans would leave in advance of him. They did, for Blake heard the door of their room slamming.

It was twenty-five minutes to noon when Blake and the chauffeur left the room and went down to the car. "What about my last-minute instructions?" Blake asked the chauffeur.

"I am not to give you those until we are nearly to Pearl Harbor, where you are to get out of the car and go on foot." Blake realized that there were to be no more instructions, because the point at which he was to leave the car was well beyond the place where the F.B.I. had observed the Germans rehearsing for murder.

"Say," said Blake, "I've just thought of something: the man I work with mentioned something to me night before last about the Pan-American Clipper base. I think we've just got time enough to ride out there." Blake had a certain hypnotic quality in his eyes, and now he called that quality into play for the first time since he had been dealing with the Japanese. He fastened his gaze on the chauffeur, and the chauffeur nodded and said, "Why not?"

Blake could hardly believe it himself when he realized that the Germans were no longer on his trail and that the Japanese chauffeur was driving him to the very spot where he wanted to get in a hurry.

On the way, Blake took to brooding over the news he had received in the cablegram. The King of the Robots was never a better actor than when he brought tears to his eyes as he showed the Japanese the cablegram he had received the night before. Blake, in fact, put on such a good act that the Japanese seemed to become somewhat apprehensive about the man's mental balance; that was apparent from the way he stole furtive glances at Blake through the rear vision mirror. Al Blake was playing his greatest role, and playing it to the hilt.

The car reached the Clipper base only two minutes before the departure of the big ship. Blake rushed in and got the reservation that the Navy had made for him—the last space on the plane. He waited until it was almost time for the departure. Then he rushed outside and handed the chauffeur a note. "Give this to the man in the Consulate that I have been dealing with," he instructed the chauffeur. "He never did tell me his name, but I guess you know who he is."

Almost mechanically, the chauffeur took the envelope from Blake and put it in his pocket. "What's going on?" he asked.

Blake, still acting like a man who was almost off-balance mentally, sputtered something about an act of God. The Japanese didn't know what that meant. "Somebody cancelled a Clipper reservation," said the King of the Robots, "and I got it. It would never happen like this in a month of Sundays. Why, I didn't even *try* to get a Clipper reservation. Now I can probably see mother before she dies."

The chauffeur was nonplussed. Emotions of surprise, anger and disappointment flickered across his face. "But the job you have to do," he said; "what about that?"

Blake answered that the sooner he arrived in the United States the sooner he could return to pick up where he had left off. "I've explained everything to the consular attaché in this letter," he said. "I've also just run into something here"—he jerked his head toward the Clipper base—"that will beat anything I've found out yet. It's perfectly amazing. It will make the other information seem unimportant by comparison." Blake appeared to force a smile of courtesy through his excitement and sorrow. Then he extended his hand to the chauffeur. "Well," he said, "good-bye until we meet again."

All the way across to California on the Clipper, Blake wondered if the nature of his departure had caused the Japanese to become suspicious. It was just before the Clipper arrived in San Francisco that he received a wireless message which set his mind at rest. The coded dispatch stated that the act he had put on at his departure had been most successful. The O.N.I. did not say just how they had found this out, but he did learn that Naval Intelligence operatives had planted a sound-detection apparatus in the hotel room occupied by the two Germans.

When the Clipper was three hours out and the Germans had returned to the hotel, wondering why Blake had never appeared at the scene of the projected murder, Blake's Japanese chauffeur called on them. A conversation had taken place among the three men, in German. One of the O.N.I. operatives listening in understood German well. The German assassins questioned the chauffeur about the events of the day. The Jap told them of Blake's erratic behavior. The Germans, too, had noticed that he had behaved erratically during the hours before his departure, but had never doubted Blake's motives any more than had the chauffeur.

What pleased the Navy listeners-in more than anything else was the conclusion of the conversation between the Germans and the Japanese. "You men can have a nice vacation here," the Japanese told the Germans, "until Blake comes back. Even in his grief he picked up some information at the Clipper base just before he left and is so excited about it—whatever it is—that he will probably hurry back after his mother dies."

Once more Al Blake was received cordially by Mr. Kono and Commander Tachibana when he returned to Hollywood and met them at Kono's apartment on Bronson Street. Not that these men were pleased to see Blake at all, for they weren't. The King of the Robots divined that the two were just pretending.

Blake said he would have to leave immediately for Illinois, but would return to Hollywood, en route back to the Orient, after he had seen his mother. "I don't know what your people must think of me in Honolulu," said Blake to Commander Tachibana, "because of the way I left. But I just wasn't thinking straight, and won't be until I have seen mother."

Tachibana asked the nature of the information that Blake had picked up at the Clipper base. Blake revealed certain spurious data that the O.N.I. had thought up for him. Mr. Kono and Commander Tachi-

bana looked at each other. "Perhaps," said Tachibana
to Kono, "Mr. Blake will be of further great value to
us."

Blake pretended to be unable to get plane connections for Illinois until the following morning, so he
and Tachibana and Kono made an appointment to
meet that night in a Japanese restaurant on San Pedro
Street in Los Angeles. The three of them had a fine
sukiyaki dinner and there was a considerable amount of
talk during the meal about further espionage work
that could be done in Hawaii by, as Commander Tachibana put it, "any smart American."

Before, during and after the meal both Kono and
Tachibana drank large quantities of saké—the potent
Japanese rice wine that Blake had never seen either
of them touch before. Tachibana began to grow voluble about negotiations he had opened whereby he
could, within the borders of the United States, lay hands
on certain naval data which, he said, he felt certain
would prove of greater value to Japan than anything
yet picked up by any Japanese operative. This was an
unusual thing for Tachibana, who was a close-mouthed
official, to do. Perhaps subconsciously he felt that he
was now safe in relaxing and talking in front of Al
Blake, because Blake was as good as a dead man. He
was only on a reprieve, so to speak, through the accident of his mother's sudden illness and the cancellation at the last minute of a Clipper reservation. Blake,
though still pretending to be griefstricken, nevertheless displayed such enthusiasm about the latest information he had run across in Hawaii that both Mr. Kono
and Commander Tachibana no doubt figured that nothing would stop him from going back.

It was late in the evening when Blake, Kono and Tachibana left the restaurant. The three were walking along a dark part of the street not far from the restaurant, with Blake on the outside, silent, and Tachibana and Kono jabbering away in Japanese. Suddenly they heard Blake exclaim, "Hey! What the hell is this—a hold-up?"

"No," were the next words the two Japanese heard, "this is not a hold-up. You three men are under arrest." Someone had seized Blake and pinned his arms behind him, and two other men had done the same to Kono and Tachibana. Two or three other men hovered near by in the darkness.

Blake became the spokesman for Kono and Tachibana. "Under arrest for *what?*" he demanded.

"You'll find out soon enough."

Blake, Kono and Tachibana were led to a waiting automobile. Their captors, after searching them for weapons—and finding one on Blake—shoved them into the car and got in after them. Not long afterward the three found themselves in the offices of Lieutenant Stanley of the O.N.I.

Kono and Tachibana were practically speechless. Blake put on an act of belligerence. He demanded to know what the O.N.I. had on him. He was told that he had been arrested on suspicion of espionage. "Suspicion, hell!" roared Blake. "What have you got on me that's *definite?*"

Lieutenant Stanley, and other O.N.I. officers, were putting on a good show. They "admitted" that they didn't have anything definite on Blake and the two Japanese. Kono and Tachibana smiled at each other.

Nevertheless the three men were held in custody, and

the story was released to the newspapers that Al Blake, as well as Mr. Kono and Commander Tachibana had been arrested on espionage charges. The O.N.I. hadn't figured out yet just how much evidence it would choose to release when the two Japanese were indicted and brought to trial. The whole business was ticklish in the extreme, particularly since the State Department, hoping against hope that peace with Japan could be preserved, didn't want such a man as Commander Tachibana "offended." The fact that the King of the Robots also was arrested would meanwhile serve as a smoke screen to cover Blake's real role in the dangerous espionage game.

The O.N.I. had moved against Tachibana more quickly than they wanted to. It had originally been the plan of the O.N.I. to leave Tachibana out on the hook as far as the line would stretch. But the O.N.I. had learned of his connections in certain high places within the United States and of his being in possession of the very information that he had referred to during dinner with Blake that night. The investigators had reason to believe that no other Japanese had this information and that Tachibana was not going to let his superiors know about it until he himself returned to Japan. They had information, too, that Tachibana was about to lay hands on physical amplification of the information he had that, as a way of getting this physical evidence safely past customs inspectors, he had arranged with the Japanese government to be appointed, prior to his departure for the Orient, to the diplomatic corps. Thus his baggage would not be subject to search.

Certainly the O.N.I. had, in Tachibana, a big fish in the net. The investigators of that organization and the

F.B.I. were convinced that by the arrest of the Commander they had struck a telling blow against Japan. The underground from Hawaii was to the effect that Japanese officials in Honolulu were unperturbed over Tachibana's arrest, since a good deal of the information that Blake had dug up on his second visit was already in their possession. Moreover, when the Federal officials in Honolulu made no move to arrest Yeoman Campbell, it probably seemed apparent to the Japanese that the Federal officials hadn't known about Campbell. All of which would have left undisturbed the status of information planted on the Japanese through Blake.

Then something shameful happened. The State Department, instead of coming out and letting the American people know what was what, hushed up the Kono and Tachibana affair after the first flurry of excitement in the newspapers. The soft pedal was put on the whole thing when the State Department decided that it could not risk offending a "friendly" power. And, believe it or not, Commander Tachibana's punishment was banishment to the Orient! Mr. Kono was permitted his liberty, and wasn't snared again until after Pearl Harbor.

Al Blake's true role in the whole affair did not come out until after Pearl Harbor. The King of the Robots today can well regard himself as a patriot who has done much for his country. Had it not been for his intelligent appraisal of the reactions of the Japanese to the spurious information handed them, the tragedy of Pearl Harbor, as bad as it was, would have been considerably worse.

The courageous operations of Al Blake had given the Federal investigators several new leads. One of these had put them on the trail of Bernard Julius Kuehn, the mystery German of Hawaii. Kuehn was later found to have close contact with the Japanese Consulate in Honolulu, and when that fact was established, the German was given the same treatment as spies for Japan on the Pacific Coast. He was kept under constant surveillance and, after Pearl Harbor, he and his family were nailed. His wife and stepdaughter—Ruth, the girl who ran the Honolulu beauty parlor patronized by Navy wives—were interned. Kuehn himself was tried before a military commission in Honolulu and sentenced to be shot. On October 26, 1942, however, his sentence was commuted to fifty years imprisonment at hard labor.

The Congressional Committee on Un-American Activities, headed by Representative Martin Dies of Texas, was busy on the Pacific Coast in the months immediately preceding Pearl Harbor. The so-called Dies Committee has from time to time been the subject of unfavorable comment in the press, usually because certain Communist elements that have infiltrated into American newspaperdom have naturally been opposed to what the Dies body has unearthed about Communism. A careful examination, however, of the facts developed at hearings conducted by the Dies Committee over a period of years discloses that the Committee had, more than any other organization or individual—with the single exception of Walter Winchell—warned the American public as to what was going on below the surface before Pearl Harbor. Maybe certain statements that were given to the Committee by witnesses are open to question, here and there; but documents and photographs don't lie. The Dies Committee dug up such documents and photographs by the hundreds—yes, by the thousands.

For example, it was the Dies Committee that dug up photographs of the correspondence whereby the Chancellor of the Japanese Consulate in Los Angeles requested, in 1934, details on the water supply system of Los Angeles. It remained for the Dies Committee first to make public the sequel to that correspondence. When the Chancellor of the Consulate had failed to get the information he sought, he took other steps. He succeeded in infiltrating Japanese-Americans into the Los Angeles Department of Water and Power. Perhaps it was only a coincidence that a Japanese-American—Kiyoshi P. Okura, the son of Momota Okura, an alien Japanese and a Japanese war veteran—was an examiner of the Los Angeles Civil Service Commission. At any rate, the personnel of the Department of Water and Power had some curiously interesting additions after the Chancellor had failed to get through correspondence the information he wanted about details of the water supply system. Prior to the time the Chancellor wrote his letter, there was only one Japanese-American in the Department of Water and Power. But between April 23, 1938 and April 18, 1941, twelve more Japanese-Americans were appointed through Civil Service to jobs in the Department. One man was in the water distribution system at 410 Ducummon Street, and others were in such key spots as the test laboratories at 1630 North Main Street, and the power drafting department on Second Street. They held such posts as junior civil engineer, structural draftsman, electrical draftsman and junior mechanical engineer.

In the late summer of 1941, two of the Dies Committee's ace investigators—Steedman and Dunstan—sent the following self-explanatory telegram from the Pacific Coast to Washington:

SA 17 402 COLLECT GOVT NT 1/180—TDS HOLLYWOOD CALIF 8 ROBERT E STRIPLING SECRETARY SPECIAL COMMITTEE ON UN-AMERICAN ACTIVITIES 531 OLD HOUSE OFFICE BLDG. WASH D C

APPROXIMATELY TWO HUNDRED FIFTY JAPANESE OPERATED FISHING BOATS IN LOS ANGELES HARBOR. NO DEFINITE RELIABLE STATISTICS. ANY VESSEL CONVERTIBLE TO NAVAL CRAFT AND IN HANDS OF UNFRIENDLY ALIEN WITH ACCESS TO OUR HARBOR AND UNDER AMERICAN REGISTRY WOULD MENACE HARBOR SECURITY. NAVY RECENTLY PURCHASED THIRTY-TWO SUCH SHIPS LOCALLY FOR USE AS PATROL CRAFT, MINE SWEEPERS AND TENDERS. FURTHER DANGER LIES IN FACT THAT APPROXIMATELY ONE THOUSAND JAPANESE ARE TRAINED PILOTS AND FAMILIAR WITH HARBOR AND COASTLINE. NUMEROUS ALIEN JAP SEAMEN ON COAST AS ALIEN SEAMEN. NO EFFORT BEING MADE TO ROUND THEM UP. CAN FURNISH WITNESS ON THESE FACTS. VAN CAMP PACKING COMPANY AND CALIFORNIA PACKING COMPANY HAVE FINANCIAL INTERESTS IN CONTINUANCE OF JAPANESE FISHING FLEETS AND HAVE FOUGHT ALL LEGISLATION WHICH HAD FOR ITS PURPOSE THE ELIMINATION OF THE JAPANESE FISHING BOAT MENACE. SUBJECT: TERMINAL ISLAND AND IN LOS ANGELES HARBOR. THIRTY-FIVE HUNDRED TO FIVE THOUSAND JAPANESE BOTH ALIENS AND CITIZENS LIVE ON ISLAND WHICH IS ADJACENT TO REEVES FIELD NAVAL AIRBASE, BETHLEHEM SHIPBUILDING CORPORATION, UNION OIL AND REFINING COMPANY AND DRY DOCKS, AND ALSO OIL AND BUTANE STORAGE TANKS. ALSO APPROXIMATELY FIVE HUNDRED MILLION DOLLARS IN DEFENSE PROJECTS LOCATED ON THE ISLAND. HAVE BEEN INFORMED BY RELIABLE PERSONS THAT ARMY AND NAVY ARE NOT CONCERNED OVER THIS CONDITION. JAPANESE PREFECTURAL SOCIETIES CALLED KENS: FIFTY-SEVEN IN NUMBER IN LOS ANGELES. ALL JAPANESE ALIENS ARE MEMBERS OF SOME KEN. HEADQUARTERS OF EACH KEN IN JAPAN. HEAD MAN OF ALL LOS ANGELES KENS KATSUMA MUKAEDA. IMMIGRATION RECORDS REVEAL MUKAEDA HAS MADE FOUR TRIPS TO JAPAN. KENS ARE PRESSURE GROUPS OP-

ERATED ON SAME BASIS AS OTHER FASCIST GROUPS. SUBJECT: SHINTO CULTS. SIXTEEN SHINTO TEMPLES IN LOS ANGELES. THIS IS NOT A RELIGION BUT WORSHIP OF THE JAPANESE RACE PERSONIFIED IN THE EMPEROR. SUBJECT: SOUTHERN CALIFORNIA IMPERIAL MILITARY VETERANS ASSOCIATION 1291/2 EAST FIRST STREET. COMMANDANT DOCTOR RIKITA HONDA . . . THIS ORGANIZATION COMPOSED OF ALIEN JAPANESE WHO HAVE FOUGHT IN JAPANESE ARMY AND NAVY. MEMBERS NOT ADMISSIBLE TO AMERICAN CITIZENSHIP DUE TO EXCLUSION ACT.

STEEDMAN AND DUNSTAN

By the first week of September, 1941—three months before Pearl Harbor—the Dies Committee was in possession of a remarkable map, copies of which had been widely distributed among Japanese aliens and Japanese-Americans on the Pacific Coast. This map went into extensive detail relating to fleet positions and battle formations of the United States Navy in the vicinity of Pearl Harbor, and it also contained vital military information on the Panama Canal. Incorporated in the data on the map were vulnerable spots of the Panama Canal and Pearl Harbor.

The Committee had also talked with a former attaché of the Japanese Consulate in Honolulu who told members that there was an organized fifth column in Honolulu that had for some time been conducting secret drills for the express purpose of collaborating with the armed forces of Japan when Pearl Harbor was attacked.

Investigators Steedman and Dunstan and their assistants had thoroughly probed the fishing-boat situation, particularly at Terminal Island. They had definite information, backed up by photographs, to the effect that some of these boats carried huge stores of dynamite and guns. Dunstan and Steedman had looked on from secret vantage points while Japanese naval reservists in California held torpedo drills, complete with Rising Sun flags, just outside of the three-mile limit off San Pedro. They had information, too, that most of the fishing boats, which numbered about a thousand, were easily convertible into torpedo boats which could blow up defense installations on the West Coast.

Thus it was that three months before Pearl Harbor the Dies Committee made arrangements for fifty-two witnesses to go from the West Coast to Washington for public hearings. Among the witnesses were American fishermen who had observed Japanese fishing-boat activities in Pacific waters from Mexico to Alaska; Terminal Island officers of the Los Angeles Police Department; a Federal Judge who had made a complete study of the Japanese situation on the West Coast; and the afore-mentioned erstwhile attaché of the Japanese Consulate in Honolulu. And so Congressman Dies wrote, in the last week of August, 1941, to the Attorney General of the United States. Dies said that if the Attorney General had no objection, he would like to conduct a hearing in Washington which would acquaint the American public with some real facts relating to the Japanese menace, particularly in California. Dies received the following reply to his letter:

OFFICE OF THE ATTORNEY GENERAL
Washington, D.C.

September 8, 1941.

Hon. Martin Dies,
House of Representatives
Washington, D.C.

My dear Mr. Congressman:

In your letter of August 27, 1941, addressed to the Attorney General, you stated that if the Attorney General had no objection, you would suggest to your committee the advisability of conducting public hearings to receive evidence regarding Japanese activities in the United States.

The Attorney General has discussed the situation with the President and the Secretary of State, both of whom feel quite strongly that hearings such as you contemplate would be inadvisable. The Attorney General is of the same opinion, and accordingly, is unable to approve the course which you have in mind.

Sincerely yours,

(Signed) Matthew F. McGuire,
Acting Attorney General.

That's all, Brother!

CHAPTER 13

Mr. Matheson Takes a Trip

WHEN, IN JUNE, 1938, one of America's venerable and most respected monthly magazines, *The Living Age,* changed hands, the Federal Bureau of Investigation gave the transaction a little more than passing thought. Although it is not generally known, the F.B.I. keeps very close tabs on what is published in magazines, newspapers and books. Sometimes, buried in type, there might be a very meaningful message of some sort, designed to make sense only for espionage operatives. And in the few years immediately preceding Pearl Harbor, the F.B.I. was very vigilant when it came to propaganda of any kind. While propaganda, not being of the violent and sensational nature of sabotage, seldom makes the headlines, it is every bit as important to the security of the country. It is realized now, at this late and sad day, that German and Japanese propaganda paved the hellish road that led to Pearl Harbor.

When *The Living Age,* which had been tottering for some time, changed hands in 1938, the three new owners hardly seemed to the F.B.I. to be the type of men who would normally be interested in such a publication. The magazine had been founded in 1844 as a high-brow publication dealing almost exclusively with international affairs and opinions. Among the contributors to the very first issue were Charles Dickens and William Makepeace Thackeray.

The three men who were down on the transaction records as the new proprietors of the respected old publication were Joseph Hilton Smyth, Irvine Harvey Williams, and Walker Grey Matheson. Matheson—a hard-faced, hard-drinking little man who walked with a limp —had been employed not long before by the Japanese Chamber of Commerce in New York City. He had spent some time in Japan, the F.B.I. already knew, since it had made it its business to jot down any existing facts about anyone associated with the Japanese in an official or semi-official capacity.

Irvine Harvey Williams was a British subject. An interesting fact, to the F.B.I. at least, was that he had been born in Japan and spent considerable time there. Just as interesting was the fact that Williams apparently had no literary background. A man without a literary background becoming associated with a magazine like *The Living Age* would be something like a bricklayer buying into an antique shop.

The third of the new proprietors—Joseph Hilton Smyth—seemed to fit into *The Living Age* picture more normally than the other two. Smyth, who had come from an old Puritan family in Plymouth, Massachusetts, had been a writer most of his adult life. He had done fact and fiction for most of the big magazines and had at one time been paid as much as two thousand dollars for a short story for the *Saturday Evening Post*. He was now, in his late thirties, a tall, emaciated-looking man with sunken eyes and a big nose.

The F.B.I. didn't have to investigate Smyth by the usual procedure of talking with people who had known him at various stages of his career. His life was an open book—his own autobiography, *To Nowhere and Return,* published in 1938. In this frank book Smyth told that he had run away from a military academy in Texas at the age of thirteen to become a bellboy in a San Antonio hotel. His parents prevailed upon him to return to his studies, and eventually he entered Harvard. Kicked out of Harvard, he did newspaper work for the Boston *Globe,* the New Orleans *Times-Picayune* and the Paris edition of the Chicago *Tribune.* Following his newspaper career, he began writing for the magazines, and was a success in that field until the bottle caught up with him and, according to his own admission in his autobiography, he was for several years a dipsomaniac. Not much more than a year before becoming one of the proprietors of *The Living Age,* he had been a hopeless drunkard, not far from the end.

Then, early in 1937, a German-Jewish doctor in New York, once physician to the American Embassy in Berlin but recently escaped from that country, got hold of Smyth and performed what amounted to a miracle. The treatment that resulted in Smyth's recovery from his dipsomania was so remarkable that it became a case history in a medical book.

In 1938 Smyth and Matheson shared a house together at Third Avenue and Thirty-eighth Street. This place was soon under surveillance by the F.B.I. The watchers were hardly surprised to see Japanese in attendance at some of the parties that Smyth and Matheson gave. The magazine offices were now located on Madison Avenue, less than two blocks from the Japanese Consulate on Fifth Avenue. G-Men covering both places saw Smyth and Matheson go from *The Living*

Age to the Consulate the very first day of the surveillance. They stayed about an hour. On the second day of the surveillance, Shintaro Fukushima, the Japanese Vice Consul in New York, was seen walking from the Consulate to *The Living Age.*

Fukushima was in *The Living Age* offices for more than an hour, and when he left the Madison Avenue address to walk back to the Consulate, he was carrying proofs in his hands. He was so interested in peering at the proofs through his thick-lensed glasses that he bumped into passers-by on more than one occasion, and grinningly apologized. While the watchers were unable to learn just what the proofs related to, it was suspected that they were proofs of a forthcoming article in *The Living Age,* and that the Japanese Consulate was vitally interested in the article in question.

Sure enough, when the next issue of *The Living Age* came out there was an article in it filled with sly Japanese propaganda of the type intended to lull America to sleep while the Japs perfected their machinations behind the scenes.

Digging into the financial aspects of *The Living Age,* the investigators found that it had been losing approximately $2,000 a month since Smyth, Matheson and Williams took it over. Under the previous ownership, the magazine had been losing about $4,000 annually. This didn't add up. A good part of the increased expenses were due to a bigger overhead. The first move the new owners had made upon taking over the magazine had been to take sumptuous quarters on Madison Avenue—a totally unnecessary move, unless proximity to the Japanese Consulate was desired. No attempt had been made to increase the public appeal of the magazine or to change its physical appearance in any way, which was also significant. The transaction papers disclosed that the sum of fifteen thousand dollars had been paid for *The Living Age* and it would have been only normal for the new owners to make some attempt to start getting this money back. Where the purchase money had come from wasn't at all clear. Bank records disclosed that the three new owners, who had never carried more than a few hundred dollars in their accounts, had each made a deposit of five thousand dollars *in cash* shortly before buying the magazine.

Continuing to keep a close eye on each issue of the magazine, the F.B.I. saw that whatever was being done was carried out in a sly, careful way. While certain articles unquestionably contained statements favorable to Japan, no statements were strong enough to be labeled out-and-out propaganda. Propaganda is one thing, and expression of opinion is something else.

Continued check-up of the bank accounts of Smyth, Williams and Matheson failed to produce any evidence. There were inferences to be drawn from the figures in the bank accounts—but no evidence. Each had for some time—since, in fact, the date of the purchase of *The Living Age*—deposited five hundred dollars monthly in his checking account, always in cash. If Fukushima, the Japanese Vice Consul in New York, who was still making frequent visits to the Madison Avenue editorial offices, was the paymaster of Smyth, Matheson and Williams, he wasn't drawing the money out of the Vice Consul's bank account in Manhattan. No, if he were the paymaster, the Japanese would be too cunning for that. The money must have been coming from somewhere else—perhaps the Embassy in Washington. The Embassy frequently drew huge sums in cash for purposes that were not marked down on any of the checks.

Considerable time passed. When war broke out in Europe in September, 1939, there was considerable scurrying back and forth between the editorial rooms on Madison Avenue and the Japanese Consulate on Fifth Avenue. Frequently, Vice Consul Fukushima couldn't wait until he got back to the Consulate to read proofs but read them on the street. In the meantime, Smyth began to make frequent trips to Washington. His destination there was always the same place—the Japanese Embassy. Once, after a prolonged stay in the Embassy, Smyth was seen coming out with none other than Ambassador Kichisaburo Nomura himself. The two took a walk for more than a mile before they slowed up, and as they walked F.B.I. agents shadowing them noticed that they chatted like two men who had known each other well for some time.

It was at this stage of the investigation that little Matheson, who was showing signs of becoming as bad an alcoholic as Smyth had been, was followed one afternoon from his place of business to his home. When he came out he was carrying baggage, and he was trailed to Grand Central Station where he caught the Twentieth Century Limited for Chicago. In Chicago he caught the Chief for the Pacific Coast. Even before Matheson's eventual destination was known, his trans-continental trip on fast and expensive extra-fare trains was significant to the F.B.I., whose agents stuck with him right across the continent. Matheson had been on the borderline of insolvency, if not right in it, for most of his adult years, and the affluence that would enable him to travel in style certainly wasn't explained by the proprietorship of *The Living Age.* The magazine was still losing money. The F.B.I. had ascertained that by checking up on production costs and subscription and news-stand sales.

Matheson took a steamer for Japan, and arrangements were made to have an American agent in the Orient pick up his trail there and see what he did and where he went. This information was to be cabled to Washington and placed in the hands of the F.B.I., so that it could be ascertained how it fitted into the situation under investigation in New York.

Smyth, meanwhile, was branching out into other activities. He bought into two other magazines—the *North American Review* and the *Saturday Review of Literature*—publications with good reputations. The F.B.I. decided that he had bought into these magazines merely to cover up his activities in *The Living Age.* Meantime, too, he had purchased a big stucco mansion overlooking Long Island Sound at Mamaroneck, and he was driving two custom-built automobiles. Inasmuch as all of his activities were taken up by editorial work on *The Living Age,* the wherewithal of Smyth's funds became more of a mystery than ever. Certainly he was getting far in excess of the five hundred dollars monthly that showed up in his bank account, probably funds paid over during his visits to Washington.

In the meantime, Smyth had also organized a Negro news syndicate to service Negro papers throughout the country. This came to light when the F.B.I. received complaints from Negro newspaper editors that Smyth's service contained Japanese propaganda. When the F.B.I. looked into some of the columns that had been emanating from Smyth's service they saw something far more dangerous than had yet appeared in the columns of *The Living Age*. The material that Smyth was writing would have, had the astute editors not seen through it and refused to publish it, sown the seeds of discord among Negro readers and probably produced race riots like those in Detroit in June, 1943. Smyth's columns openly praised Japan and stated that the Negroes were getting a raw deal from the United States. It was further indicated, if one read between the lines, that the only hope the Negro had was to look for the day when Japan would rule the world.

In Tokyo, Matheson, being carefully followed, was seen going to the hotel apartment of Foreign Minister Matsuoka. The Foreign Minister and the American publisher spent many a long hour together, drinking whiskey-and-soda and talking in such low tones than an investigator in an adjoining room could hear nothing through the almost paper-thin walls.

When Matheson returned to the United States, after a four-month absence, his bank account revealed a deposit of two thousand dollars—in cash. That would have been at the rate of five hundred dollars a month—if it was pay.

It was late in 1940 that Smyth and Matheson began really to go to town with propaganda in *The Living Age*. Williams, it had by this time developed, had little to do with the editorial end of the magazine. He confined himself to the business end. Articles began to appear in which the Japanese were painted in nothing short of glowing colors. Month after month *The Living Age* informed its readers that if there was ever any trouble between Japan and the United States it would be the fault of "Mr. Roosevelt and other such alarmists."

The articles were signed under a variety of names. The F.B.I. checked into the names and found them to be *noms de plume*—no doubt those of Smyth and Matheson. In fact, some of the articles voiced opinions which acquaintances of Smyth and Matheson from away back had heard both of those men utter on numerous occasions.

Despite the fact that the articles were loaded with propaganda, they didn't appear to be what they actually were. The poison had been so skilfully concocted and so slyly introduced that it was hardly noticeable for what it was. Yet it had its effect. Readers of *The Living Age,* followed from newsstands where they were seen to purchase the magazines, found themselves conversing with pleasant strangers whom they met in subways, street cars, buses and trains in different parts of the country. These strangers were investigators who wanted to find out just what kind of effect Smyth's and Matheson's propaganda was having. They learned that the propaganda was going over in the way it was meant to go over. Some readers told the investigators that they had long held to the opinion that Japan had designs on the United States—until they had learned otherwise from these "intelligent" and "forthright" articles in *The Living Age.* Yes, the propaganda was hitting where it was meant to hit.

In 1941, in the July issue, was an article by Matheson entitled, *War in the Pacific Unlikely.* This was less than six months before Pearl Harbor. In the August issue, Matheson signed his own name to an article called, *When Japan Missed the Bus.* In this piece he made quite a case for Japan along the line that the Japanese were a nation of naive, guileless people who had been schemed against by the "rascals in Washington."

Then, in the fall of 1941, just a few months before Pearl Harbor, *The Living Age* suddenly suspended publication. Williams, Smyth and Matheson joined the ranks of the unemployed. The F.B.I. decided that the magazine had been suspended because the Japanese had probably become suspicious that the real motive behind the ownership of *The Living Age* had perhaps become apparent.

The F.B.I. waited to find out what the trio would do next. Smyth and Williams didn't do much of anything, but Matheson got a job—right in Nelson Rockefeller's Inter-American Co-ordinator's Office. He was hired as a news analyst and specialized in the writing of short-wave radio broadcasts for Latin America.

The F.B.I. arranged to examine all of Matheson's broadcasts before they were sent, just to make certain that they did not embody any secret code that would be listened for in Axis spy strongholds. But Matheson was being cagey. He wasn't—not yet, at least—attempting to use his position to further any Japanese machinations. It became obvious that the Japanese, finding Smyth, Matheson and Williams no longer useful, had dropped them just as they had dropped John S. Farnsworth, the traitorous cashiered naval officer.

Then Matheson began to drink very heavily. F.B.I. men made it a point to be in the Washington bars that he frequented after he had done his day's work for Mr. Rockefeller's office. When, one night, he was overheard to make a very pro-Japanese remark while in his cups, J. Edgar Hoover decided that the time had come to move.

Matheson, Williams and Smyth were obviously not going to lead the agents to any further contacts, for they had none. So, in 1942, they were arrested. The only technical charge that could be applied against them, despite the heinous nature of their work, was that they had failed to register as paid agents of a foreign power. For this little piece of neglect they were each sentenced, on November 12, 1942, to seven years in prison.

CHAPTER 14

The Tip-Off in Winchell's Column

CHUZO HAGIWARA—otherwise Sleepy Joe—the fleshy and alcoholic chief of the New York bureau of Domei News Agency, Japan's number one news-gathering organization, was not popular with his colleagues in the Foreign Press Association. Sleepy Joe not only couldn't hold this liquor, but in the poker room, he somehow gave the impression that the only reason he didn't carry a couple of spare aces in his shirt cuffs was because he realized he couldn't get away with it.

Hagiwara's working quarters were in the offices of the Associated Press, then located at 383 Madison Avenue. His desk was handy to teletypewriters which, twenty-four hours a day, clicked out news from Washington. Some of the news that came over the machines near Sleepy Joe's desk was not for publication; it was of a highly confidential nature and purely for background information of newspaper editors whose papers were serviced by the AP. For example, when the President is away from Washington—on a nation-wide tour of the war industries, or out of the country—the Associated Press, together with other news agencies, gets permission of the White House to send the news to its member newspapers and labels it confidential and not for pub-

256

lication. It can be seen, then, that Sleepy Joe, whose heart belonged to Hirohito, was, because of the location of his desk, in a most favorable spot for getting sub rosa intelligence and sending it on to Tokyo in code.

The election, in 1938, of a young man named Guenther Reinhardt as membership secretary of the Foreign Press Association seemed none too popular with Sleepy Joe Hagiwara, and he mumbled as much in the green-room bar one night. Reinhardt, an American, was—and is—the ranking U.S. correspondent of the big Swiss newspapers; he has always had a nose for intrigue as well as for news, and he simply couldn't convince himself that Sleepy Joe, or any of the other fifteen Japanese who belonged to the Association, were up to any good. In fact, through means of his own, Reinhardt had ascertained beyond reasonable doubt that various Japanese in the United States—such as the sly and sinister Roy Akagi, manager of the New York offices of the South Manchuria Railway—were masquerading under false though apparently legitimate fronts and were nothing more or less than propagandists and espionage operatives sent here by Tokyo.

Reinhardt learned, early in 1938, that David A. Smart, the publisher of *Esquire* and *Coronet,* and Arnold Gingrich, the editor of those two magazines, were planning to bring out a new monthly called *Ken.* The new magazine, he further learned, was going to pull no punches in articles that were in the public interest, no matter whose feelings suffered contusions—a policy that the Messrs. Smart and Gingrich still adhere to today in *Esquire* and *Coronet.*

The thought came to Reinhardt that *Ken* just might go for an article that would, among other things, awaken the American public and a lethargic Congress to the Japanese menace. And so he prepared an article, to be signed "Anonymous," entitled *A Label for Propaganda,* which included an exposé of how American laborers in the Tokyo vineyard were slyly lulling America into a false sense of security by planting pro-Japanese articles in leading newspapers and magazines.

Naturally, Reinhardt didn't want such people as Sleepy Joe Hagiwara to know that he was the author of the *Ken* article, so the precaution was taken of having a prominent businessman—a friend of Reinhardt and of Smart and Gingrich—act as go-between in the negotiations for the sale of the exposé. The writer had no direct contact whatever with either the publisher or the editor, or anyone else in the Esquire-Coronet organization. Even the check that was drawn in payment for the piece on the City National Bank and Trust Company in Chicago, where the principal editorial offices of the Esquire-Coronet publications are located, was made out, not to Reinhardt, but to the businessman. The latter cashed the check personally and turned the proceeds over to the author.

The article, which appeared in the first issue of *Ken,* in April, 1938, caused a national sensation. It was, in fact, directly responsible for the passage in Congress of a bill that had for a long time taken a severe kicking around—a bill that required agents of foreign powers to register with the State Department. Two weeks after the article appeared, Reinhardt was attending a dinner to the press given aboard the Dutch luxury liner *Nieuw Amsterdam,* which was in the port of New York after her maiden voyage across the Atlantic. A Japanese photographer was present, and he snapped a picture of Reinhardt, sitting at the table.

After taking the picture, the photographer smiled and said to the correspondent, "So glad to obtain a photo of Mr. Reinhardt, who writes about Japan—in *Ken* magazine." The photographer vanished from the banquet room before Reinhardt could catch up with him. Reinhardt asked other Japanese present who the photographer was, but they just smiled, shrugged and said they were so sorry, but they didn't know.

All of which gives you an idea of the Japanese talent for finding out the details of supposedly air-tight secrets.

Not long after the *Ken* article appeared, a newspaperman named James E. Edmonds, who had worked both in the United States and in foreign countries, was approached by Sleepy Joe Hagiwara and asked to write an article for Domei News Agency on Russian activities in the United States and in the Far East—a subject on which Edmonds was an authority.

After the first article was turned in, Sleepy Joe told Edmonds that Domei was so impressed by the piece that it wished to have Edmonds do more along similar lines. Edmonds said that would be fine, for Domei had paid him well for the first job, and asked Sleepy Joe what the next assignment was. "Our Mr. Sato," said Sleepy Joe, "will take that up with you."

"Mr. Sato?" repeated Edmonds. "Who is Mr. Sato? I thought you were the New York chief of Domei."

Sleepy Joe smiled and shrugged, and took another sip of whiskey. The conference was taking place in a midtown restaurant. "Mr. Sato is my boss in Domei. I am not really the New York chief; he is."

Sleepy Joe made an appointment for Edmonds to

meet Mr. Sato. This was, it later turned out, the same Mr. Sato who had four years before in Washington approached John S. Farnsworth, the cashiered Lieutenant Commander in the United States Navy, to sell naval secrets to the Naval Attachés of the Japanese Embassy in Washington.

The first meeting between Mr. Sato and Edmonds took place in a restaurant. The thought occurred to Edmonds that it was odd that Mr. Sato didn't transact business at the offices of Domei, at the Associated Press, or in the New York Times Building, where Domei also had men quartered, particularly in the syndicate room on the third floor, where world news, both confidential and for publication, poured in around the clock.

Edmonds covered several assignments for Mr. Sato, and Mr. Sato seemed quite pleased with them, and paid well. But by the fall of 1938 Edmonds had become suspicious of Sato's behavior. Sato never met him anywhere except in a hotel lobby or in a restaurant—usually a quiet, homelike restaurant such as Joe Romano's famous Italian eating place at 142 West Fifty-fourth Street. When Edmonds delivered a story to Sato, the Japanese, instead of glancing through it, quickly stuck it in his pocket, as if afraid to be seen with it, and remarked, "I'll read this at home; I can concentrate better there." When payment was made, it was never by check; always in cash. And the cash was always passed over to Edmonds in a surreptitious manner.

Since his first association with Sato, Edmonds had had his telephone number. He had called it frequently, in the daytime or evening, and a girl had always answered first, after which Sato got on the phone. Edmonds had always assumed that the girl was a maid in Sato's home, wherever it was. The thought now dawned on him that he did not know where Sato lived, and that Sato had never mentioned that little matter.

Edmonds began putting two and two together. He decided that perhaps Mr. Sato wasn't connected with Domei News Agency at all, but was an official representative of some kind of the Japanese government. He sought out Sleepy Joe Hagiwara, who had first put him in touch with Sato, and sounded him out. But trying to get information from Sleepy Joe was, Edmonds soon learned, rather like attempting to get blood out of a turnip, and approximately as successful.

When Edmonds looked up the telephone number of the Japanese Consulate on Fifth Avenue, he was struck with the fact that the Consulate number was only two digits removed from the number through which he always reached Sato. He concluded that the Consulate had one or more private numbers not listed in the telephone directory, and that the number Sato had given him was one of them. So he called the Consulate number one day in September, 1938, and asked for Mr. Sato. The girl who answered at the Consulate switchboard sounded suspiciously like the girl who had always answered Sato's number, and whom the reporter had taken to be a maid.

"There is no Mr. Sato at this number," said the girl. "This is the Japanese Consulate."

"But there *is* a Mr. Sato at this number," Edmonds insisted. "He told me I could reach him here."

"Just a moment," said the girl. Presently, Edmonds heard Sato's voice saying, "Hello. Sato speaking." Edmonds hung up; he had found out all he wanted to know.

Edmonds went to the F.B.I. in the Federal Building on Foley Square and told the Agent in Charge of his dealings, first with Sleepy Joe Hagiwara and then with Sato. The F.B.I. knew all about Sato from the case of Farnsworth, the renegade naval officer, and they told Edmonds to maintain the status quo with Mr. Sato, and report what was happening.

After Edmonds' telephone call to the Consulate, Sato became somewhat cagey, and while he gave no evidence of suspecting Edmonds of having made the call, he nevertheless did not broach any espionage plans to him, which, Edmonds felt certain, he had been on the verge of doing. Instead, he introduced Edmonds to a German spy named Doctor Ferdinand A. Kertess, a chemist leasing offices in the Fred F. French Building on Fifth Avenue.

Dr. Kertess, who had taken out his second citizenship papers in June, 1938, put Edmonds to work at getting information on explosives, and sent him to Halifax to dig up data on the sailing of Canadian convoys. As a result of information on Dr. Kertess turned over to the F.B.I. by Edmonds, the doctor was nailed in good time —but that is another story.

The Dies Committee got hold of Edmonds in October, 1940, and he told his story. Even before publication of the fact that Edmonds had spoken to investigators, Sleepy Joe knew that he faced exposure. One night in the green room of the Foreign Press Association he announced that he was so sorry, but he was leaving for Japan next day.

Guenther Reinhardt, the membership secretary, soon met Sleepy Joe's successor, Nagahura Yasuo, a smiling little man with ways far more winning than Sleepy Joe's, but underneath he was just as sinister, Reinhardt felt certain.

In the meantime, white colleagues at the Associated Press, which was now located in Rockefeller Center, and at the *New York Times,* where a total of fifteen Japanese newspapermen were spotted, began to tighten up on their conversations when the Jap scribes were within earshot. And when anything confidential came over the tickers, a white man would make certain to get it before Yasuo, Sleepy Joe's successor, or any of the other Japanese could see it.

By the fall of 1941, some of the Japanese and some of the other correspondents at the Foreign Press Association were barely exchanging the time of day. On October 1, when the bills for the annual dues were sent out, an English correspondent remarked, "Wouldn't it be fine if the Japanese failed to pay their dues so they could be dropped."

The remark was a grim sort of jest. Membership in the Foreign Press Association was of vital importance to the Japanese. The Association was accredited to the State Department and had enjoyed a semi-official status since the days of Woodrow Wilson. All sorts of privileges were accorded to members in good standing, and official channels barred to ordinary foreign correspondents in this country were open to F.P.A. men. The Japanese might have been denied continued membership in October, 1940, when the testimony of Edmonds before the Dies Committee involved, at least by inference, Sleepy Joe Hagiwara, but had they been kicked out, retribution would have descended on American correspondents in Japan. Yes, the joking hope of the Englishman that the Japanese would not pay their dues and would therefore be automatically dropped from membership for a reason that even Tokyo could not complain about was only a jest.

For twenty years, the Japanese had been sickeningly prompt when it came to paying dues in the F.P.A. There was, in fact, another joke around the Association to the effect that the only things certain were death, taxes—and the checks for annual dues of the Japs.

It is important, in the light of what was to come, that we consider the routine by which the Association collected its annual dues. On October 1, bills were sent out. On November 1, gentle reminders were sent out to those who had ignored the October 1 notice. If by December 1 a member had still not opened his check book, another reminder, not quite so gentle as the previous one, was sent to him. If by January 1 he had still not paid, he was automatically dropped.

For two decades, the Japanese had been the first to send in their checks after the first notice of October 1— in fact, the records showed that not a single Japanese member had ever paid his annual dues later than the eighth day of October.

When Guenther Reinhardt learned, on October 15, 1941—less than two months before Pearl Harbor—that not a single Japanese check had come in, he became curious. When, a week after the reminder of November 1 had been sent out, and still not a single Japanese check had come in, Reinhardt became suspicious. He waited until the fifteenth of November, then dropped over to the AP and had a chat with Yasuo, successor to Sleepy Joe. "None of you Japanese has paid his annual dues this year," said Reinhardt. "Do you want to be dropped from the Association the first of the year?"

Yasuo just smiled, and resumed work at his typewriter.

Reinhardt talked this Japanese matter over with another officer of the Association—an Englishman. "Guenther," said the Englishman, "you're too suspicious; you think there's a spy under every bed."

"But I tell you," said Reinhardt, "I know these Jap bastards; they're up to something. *They know something.*"

Reinhardt waited for another week—until November 22. Still not a Japanese check had come in. Then Reinhardt went to Washington, and told his story to officials of the State and Justice Departments. They listened to him solemnly, and then told him, in effect, the same thing his English colleague at the Association had told him. "Why, Reinhardt," said one official, "this is just a coincidence, this business of the Japanese being late with their checks. Those checks will come in in good time. The negotiations between the President and Mr. Hull and the Japanese Ambassador and the Special Envoy from Tokyo are progressing *splendidly.*"

Reinhardt, determined, brought out records of the Association. Membership cards each year were numbered consecutively, from number one on up, and given out in relation to the order in which checks were received. For more than ten years, no white correspondent had ever held as low-numbered a card as any Japanese— black-and-white proof that every one of the Japanese members had always paid up before the first white member shelled out. Yet the Washington officials saw no significance in this unexplained reversal of long-standing Japanese behavior.

Back in New York, at the Stork Club (where many

an event of international significance is planned) Reinhardt ran into a slim man with prematurely gray hair—
Walter Winchell—just after returning from his futile
trip to Washington. "Say, Guenther," said Winchell,
"what's this I hear about the Japs at the Foreign Press
Association being behind in their dues?" Where Winchell had received the tip Reinhardt didn't know, and
he didn't ask.

Winchell and Reinhardt drank coffee until early
morning. Winchell was busy jotting down notes. He
could hardly believe what Reinhardt was telling him.
"You're sure of your facts, Guenther?" he kept repeat-
ing. "You're absolutely sure of your facts?" When Winchell had the whole story, he said to Reinhardt, "If I
didn't know your reputation, I wouldn't believe this."

Even after he had the whole story, Winchell was
undecided what to do with it. The Flash Man, more
than any single American, had been warning the American public for years of the dangers within. For his
trouble, he had been called a warmonger and other
names by stuffed shirts and by men in Congress who
should have had the welfare of their country at heart.
These men should have been behind Winchell instead
of against him; these were the men whose duties Winchell
was performing when they had fallen down on the job
to the point of criminal negligence.

Winchell mentally walked around Reinhardt's story
twice. As a patriot who put his country before a scoop—
a fact that anyone who is acquainted with the man will
bear out—he actually considered not printing anything
about the tip-off at the F.P.A. He didn't want to print
a single line that would adversely affect the negotiations being carried on in Washington. But when he con-

sidered all aspects of the situation, and concluded that the peace protestations of the Japanese diplomats were strictly phony, he decided that it was his patriotic duty to break the story. And so, in his column of November 24, 1941, he wrote the following:

> For twenty years the Japs were promptest at paying their dues in the Foreign Press Association . . . This year they are two months overdue. What's the lowdown . . . got some inside news on something happening before January first?

There it was, in black and white, for millions to read. There it was, for the State Department. There it was—the tip-off to Pearl Harbor—for the whole world to know about, *thirteen days before December 7.*

On Pearl Harbor Day, when agents of the New York Field Office of the F.B.I. began rounding up the Japanese correspondents at their homes and offices immediately following receipt of the news from Hawaii, most of the Jap scribes were packed, all ready to leave for wherever they were to be taken. Not packing, mind you —but *packed.* From the amount of packing that most of them had already done, it was a simple matter to deduce that they had begun to pack well *before* the first Japanese plane had appeared over Pearl Harbor.

The files of the Japanese correspondents were seized. Unquestionably those files had normally contained propaganda and espionage dynamite dating back to the days of Sleepy Joe Hagiwara. But nothing except of the most innocent sort was found in the files—if you would call one of the filthiest collections of pornographic photographs this side of pre-war Paris innocent. The Japanese correspondents had prepared well in advance, for everything.

If there weren't any red faces in the State Department when Winchell's item of thirteen days before was pondered in retrospect, there should have been. The man who had been called a warmonger and an hysterical alarmist had given a clear warning of danger. It must have seemed almost incredible to the Japanese that we could be so accommodatingly stupid.

Even red faces could not make up now for the treachery of Pearl Harbor, and for the lives lost there. Shame and sorrow—not merely a loud indignation—should have been felt by several in responsible places, including Congress; but shame and sorrow are feelings of real men, not of stuffed shirts.

CHAPTER 15

The Japanese Sabotage
Menace of 1943

IN VARIOUS PARTS of the United States today there are thousands of Japanese—both aliens and American-born —who have been released from relocation centers, where they were sent after Pearl Harbor, and *who have not been checked up on, in any manner, by the F.B.I.* This appalling situation is due to the simple reason that the War Relocation Authority, a Federal bureau with a singular lack of personnel experienced for the job of dealing with the relocation problem, has adopted the policy of releasing alien and American-born Japanese in wholesale lots without even informing the F.B.I.

What does all this add up to? Simply this: There are at large today men of Japanese ancestry who are awaiting only the propitious time and the opportunity to commit acts of sabotage which, if successful, will be of hideous enormity. It is no secret in Washington that J. Edgar Hoover has his fingers crossed because of the "liberal," not to say stupid, policy of the War Relocation Authority. Officials of the W.R.A. do not know the slightest details about the backgrounds of some of the Japanese they are turning loose, and are making no attempt whatsoever to ascertain whether those being released are among the thirteen hundred alien and American-born

Japanese who were known to the F.B.I. to be up to their necks in espionage and prospective sabotage guilt before Pearl Harbor.

Considerable misguided sentiment has been directed toward the Nisei (American-born Japanese). Some of the Nisei are dangerous enemies who would stop at nothing, as witness the fact that one notorious American-born Japanese by the name of Kibei made the statement, on March 23, 1942, aboard a train to the relocation center at Manzanar, California: "We ought to have guts enough to kill Roosevelt!"

Liberty magazine, on page 54 of its issue of August 7, 1943, printed the following:

In a moving, revealing article in next week's Liberty, a Japanese-American girl tells what a Relocation Center actually looks and feels like to those who have been compelled to leave their homes and live in one.

And so, in the August 14 issue of *Liberty*, there began on page 11 an article by one Mary Oyama entitled, *My Only Crime Is My Face*. The face of Mrs. Oyama was reproduced in the upper right-hand corner of page 11, and it was a quite attractive face, not at all the type of physiognomy that Federal agents have usually encountered at the end of an espionage or sabotage trail.

Mrs. Oyama and her husband, Fred, are Nisei. They spent some time in a relocation center after Pearl Harbor, and were later released when they were found to be loyal American citizens. It was of her experiences in the relocation center that Mrs. Oyama wrote.

Now, there can be no question about the loyalty to the United States of a certain percentage of Nisei. Just what that percentage is, there is naturally no way of determining. Mrs. Oyama, however, seemed to arrive at a figure, at least by implication. Anyone reading her story in *Liberty* who wasn't acquainted with certain facts in the files of the Federal Bureau of Investigation might well have concluded that the Nisei were one hundred per cent loyal. Mrs. Oyama didn't mention at all the Nisei who, the F.B.I., the O.N.I. and G-2 had long known, had been members of Pacific Coast branches of an organization called Butoku-kai, which was the youth section of the nefarious Black Dragon Society.

Mrs. Oyama's article, which certainly gave Uncle Sam a sharp crack in the teeth, was written in the best sob-sister tradition. It dripped with hokum that would have convinced any grade-A moron that Uncle Sam had dealt out injustice on a wholesale scale to thousands of poor, innocent Nisei. But Mrs. Oyama, bless her kind soul, was concerned with nothing but sweetness and light. Her selectivity of facts showed her to be a great humanitarian. She recorded a simply heartbreaking incident about the relocation center where she had been. Here it is (and see if you can keep from crying as you read it):

In the thick dust and sticky summer heat, above the dinning babel of voices, old friends, jammed up tightly against the wire fence, shocked to see their Nisei friends "caged in." There was the day when some one brought a dog which had formerly belonged to a Nisei couple with a small baby girl. The dog wagged his tail violently upon recognizing his former owners. The Nisei mother pushed the perambulator closer, right up against the fence . . . The child stuck a chubby fist through the fence. The dog licked the little hand affectionately and he kissed the tops of her tiny shoes. Some people took out their handkerchiefs and blew their noses hard. . . .

Mrs. Oyama, her husband Fred and their two small children—Rickey and Eddie—had occupied, prior to going to the relocation center, a "brand-new 'dream house' which had sat on top of a hill, a little white six-roomed cottage with sky-blue shutters and gay tinkly door chimes." Presumably Mrs. Oyama is en route back there now, by easy stages, and will one day again answer the door at the sound of the gay tinkly chimes. But there was a night when she seemed somewhat envious of anyone who lived in comfort. She wrote:

But the crowning bit of irony came on the last night of the trip. After a sweltering, nerve-racking day of desert summer heat and bawling babies, our crowded car stopped momentarily alongside another train headed in the opposite direction. Our day-coach windows evened up alongside of windows which showed the cool, dim-lit, spacious interior of a de luxe dining car. A dozen well-dressed people were sitting comfortably at table eating what seemed to us a royal feast. The soft glow of shaded lamps was reflected by the white tablecloths. The contrast was so painful that every mother in our car groaned. For the rest of the evening we were glumly homesick.

By way of buttressing her remarks about what she called the injustice and the illegality of placing Nisei in relocation centers until they were given clean bills of health, Mrs. Oyama quoted an alien Japanese as follows:

An elderly Japanese doctor remarked, "I feel sorry enough for us, the Issei [alien Japanese], but at least we have a country. I feel sorrier still for you Nisei [American-born citizens of Japanese descent], because it looks as if your own country, the United States, has repudiated you."

Nor was Mrs. Oyama one to overlook drama. "Once," she wrote, "after a long hot afternoon, I heard an Issei father singing an old Japanese song in a plaintive minor key."

In another part of her remarkable article—remarkable because it was printed at all—Mrs. Oyama said, "But, whatever we were, we stared in unbelief at the camp's sentry watchtowers and the barbed wire (looking for all the world like the pictures of Nazi concentration camps in Poland)."

The singular editorial policy that brought about the publication of Mrs. Oyama's article caused raised eyebrows in high official circles in Washington—circles that are deeply concerned with the problem of the Japanese, both American-born and alien, in ten relocation centers in Arizona, California, Idaho, Utah, Wyoming, Colorado and Arkansas. Articles like the one in *Liberty* do nothing except add fuel to the flames of an already dangerous controversial fire.

Let us look into the relocation problem. Residents of the Pacific Coast were understandably fear-ridden after the Japanese attack on Pearl Harbor on December 7, 1941, because approximately one hundred and twenty thousand citizens of Japanese ancestry and Japanese nationals were concentrated in California, Oregon and Washington. Early in 1942 the Commanding General of the Western Defense Command ordered the evacuation from certain areas of the West Coast of persons of Japanese ancestry, United States citizens and aliens alike.

At first the evacuation was on a voluntary basis, but only eight thousand persons of Japanese ancestry removed themselves to the interior of the United States. As a result, the Western Defense Command issued a freezing order which had the effect of holding both Nisei and Issei Japanese in the affected areas until a plan could be worked out whereby all such persons could be removed in orderly fashion from the military area of the West Coast.

The War Relocation Authority was established in March, 1942, by order of President Roosevelt, and the agency thereupon proceeded to establish ten relocation centers at various inland points. More than one hundred thousand Japanese, both American citizens and aliens, were thereupon evacuated to those centers.

Now, all that was all right as far as it went—but it didn't go far enough. There was no attempt to segregate aliens from American-born Japanese in the relocation centers.

In the latter part of 1942, members of the Special Committee on Un-American Activities of the House of Representatives began to receive complaints from residents of the West Coast to the effect that subversive activities were rife in the war relocation centers and that there was a strong possibility that some of the Japanese released to return to civilian life after supposedly establishing themselves as loyal to the United States were in actuality dangerous espionage agents.

In May, 1943, a member of the Committee on Un-American Activities—Congressman J. Parnell Thomas of New Jersey, a conservative veteran legislator with strong humanitarian leanings—became exercised at the policy of the War Relocation Authority in releasing approximately one thousand evacuees a week for resettlement in various parts of the country. As a result, Congressman Thomas went to California and conferred with individual citizens, groups of citizens and state authorities. The up-shot of the visit of Congressman Thomas to the Pacific Coast was that the Congressional Committee of which he was a member ordered an intensive investigation into conditions in relocation centers. Briefly, this is what the investigators found:

1—About twenty-five hundred persons made up the administrative personnel of the War Relocation Authority, but only a small percentage of these people seemed to be qualified by experience for their jobs. The Director of the War Relocation Authority, for example, Dillon S. Myer, had a background of almost thirty years as an expert in agriculture.

2—Certain Japanese were being released before the F.B.I. could check up on them.

3—Certain Nisei in the relocation centers had been "converted" by alien Japanese so that their allegiance was to Hirohito and not to the United States (a little matter that Mrs. Oyama had neglected to mention in her *Liberty* article).

4—Evacuees in the relocation centers were being supplied with food through the Quartermaster Corps of the United States Army in greater variety and quantity than was available to the average American consumer.

5—Discipline in relocation centers was lax in the extreme. Some of the personnel in authority were so lacking in training for the jobs they held that subversive activities were being carried on right under their noses without their knowing it.

On June 11, 1943, investigators obtained by subpoena, records and files of the Washington office of the Japanese American Citizens League, located at 1324 Fourteenth Street, N.W. This League, the headquarters of which are in Salt Lake City, is an organization devoted to working for the welfare of Nisei, and is composed of American citizens of Japanese ancestry. The Committee on Un-American Activities held hearings in Washington in July, 1943, for the purpose of questioning two executives of the League—Mike Masaoka, national secretary and field executive; and Joe Kanazawa, eastern representative. It was established that Masaoka and Kanazawa helped to plan the policy of the War Relocation Authority and that, in fact, these two gentlemen of Japanese ancestry consistently received copies of official administrative instructions of the W.R.A. before these instructions were passed on to the officials at the relocation centers.

At hearings held by the Committee on Un-American Activities in Los Angeles in June of 1943, Tokutaro Slocum, a Japanese-American who had been evacuated to the relocation center at Manzanar, California, had some interesting things to say about conditions at Manzanar. Let us take a look at excerpts from some of Slocum's testimony:

... with more leisure time, dormant forces are beginning to create disturbances. What has seemingly appeared to most Caucasian administrators as a placid community life, in reality covered a cauldron in which differing ideologies, unmixable as oil and water, seethed and boiled. The surface indications of this internal strife have appeared from time to time. However, center officials have usually dismissed these symptoms with academic leniency.

The real threat to peace and order within the centers will not come from individual lawlessness. The bomb shell that will shatter these communities will be the blow-off of (1) accumulated resentments, (2) harbored injustices, (3) racial discriminations, (4) pro-Japan convictions, and (5) real and fancied grievances. As time goes on, rather than a settling process, mob outbreaks, massed demonstrations, gang atrocities and acts of terrorism will recur frequently.

W.R.A. administrators must realize the dynamite they are dealing with; they must be realistic; they must not encourage the mushrooming of small incidents by condoning with official laxity; individuals advocating constructive attitudes and activities must be shielded from vengeful harm; deleterious elements in each camp must be recognized, and intelligent yet stern methods must be instituted to curb them.

Numerically, this pro-Japan element is small, but the damage their insidious propaganda can do to the peace and order of the community should not be too lightly regarded.

Internal security should be exactly what its title connotes. Reports issuing from some centers indicate that security of life and limb for those bespeaking constructive attitudes does not exist. On the other hand, malefactors have been so condoned that their nefarious beatings of decent citizens continues not only unabated but with increasing frequency.

Tokutaro Slocum told the Committee that a Japanese organization calling itself the Blood Brothers Corps was leading an underground movement, political in nature, at the relocation center at Manzanar. On November 6, 1942, the Manzanar Commission on Self-Government, composed of evacuees at the center, received the following communication:

Think of the shame the American Government has put us into. Think of the disruption of properties, and the imprisonment of the Niseis.

To start a self-government system now is nothing but a dirty selfish scheme. As the Army put us in here without regard to our own will, we should leave everything up to the Army, whether they want to kill us or eat us.

Because this is the only way the American government can think of as a means of absolving itself from the blame of mis-conducting its affairs, the government thought of a bad scheme, that is, this formation of the self-government system.

The hairy beasts (white) are out actually to run the government, while using you people who can be used. It is evident if you read Article I of the Charter and can be proved by the facts of the past. You fellows who are acting blindly are big fools.

If you do such things as those, which tighten the noose around the necks of your fellow people, some day you will receive punishment from Heaven, so beware.

BLOOD BROTHERS CORPS WHICH WORRY FOR THEIR FELLOW PEOPLE.

On the following day—November 7—the members of the Manzanar Commission on Self-Government received another letter from the Blood Brothers, this one reading as follows:

Calling you fools who are running around trying to set up a self-government system:

Think back! The fact that the positions, the properties, and the honor with which our fellow Japanese built up and won by blood and sweat during the past fifty years have all been stamped and sacrificed by the arrogant and insulting American government after we have been put into this isolated spot.

For what are you beating around? What use is there for establishing self-government? Especially with such a Charter so full of contradictions? Although we are ignorant people, we can foresee the tragic results which will come out of this self-government.

Remember that the majority of our people are absolutely against the self-government system. What do you think of the fact that six months ago, in Santa Anita, the same attempt which you are now trying, was made, to organize a self-government. But it broke down before it materialized.

Leave everything completely as the Army pleases. If you nincompoops realize the fact that you are Japanese, why don't you assume the honorable attitude which is typical of Japanese? What a shameful sight you are about to present by being fooled by the sweet words of the government. By so doing, you are inviting suffering to your fellow Japanese.

We fellow Japanese are all like fish laid on the cutting board, about to be sliced. To jump around at this stage is a cowardly thing to do. Better lay down and let the government do as it pleases, either cook us or fry us.

You should remain calm and conduct yourselves like nationals of a first-class power. Give more thoughts and deep reflections as to your attitude.

In her *Liberty* article, Mrs. Oyama skipped blithely over the number of Nisei who refused to declare their loyalty to the United States when they were asked the following question in the relocation centers:

Will you swear unqualified allegiance to the United States of America and faithfully defend the United States from any or all attack by foreign or domestic foes, and forswear any form of allegiance to the Japanese emperor, or any other foreign government, power or organization?

The editor of *Liberty* fell for this statement of Mrs. Oyama's: "It did us no good to argue that we had sons and brothers in the Army. . . . Nobody would listen." Members of the Committee on Un-American Activities listened to almost twenty thousand of the Nisei in the relocation camps—the very people that Mrs. Oyama spoke so highly of. These twenty thousand were all males between the ages of seventeen and thirty-eight. The following figures speak for themselves, showing as they do that about one out of four Nisei in the relocation centers admitted their disloyalty to the United

States, and that only six out of every one hundred of them volunteered for service in the United States Army:

Relocation Center	Number Registered	Number Answering "no" to loyalty question	Number Volunteers
Central Utah	2,420	806	116
Colorado River	3,356	671	238
Gila River	2,488	547	119
Granada	1,117	117	121
Heart Mountain	1,881	451	47
Jerome	1,341	110	33
Manzanar	1,826	913	101
Minidoka	1,607	32	310
Rohwer	1,585	300	37
Tule Lake	2,342	836	59
TOTAL	19,963	4,783	1,181
Average (per cent)		24%	6%

In numerous instances, the War Relocation Authority has released for resettlement into civilian life American-born Japanese who were known to the F.B.I., the O.N.I. and G-2 as members of the Butoku-kai, the youth organization of the Black Dragon Society.

The Black Dragon Society need not be commented on at length here. It is enough to say that many members of this dread secret organization functioned up and down the Pacific Coast prior to Pearl Harbor—men whom the Federal investigators linked to the more desperate sabotage plans when war came. The Black Dragons vowed allegiance to the Emperor of Japan and to nobody else, and it was hardly reasonable to suppose that they attempted to inculcate into the American-born members of their youth branch loyalty to the United States of America.

In order to appreciate the significance of a member of the Butoku-kai being at large in the United States today, let us examine the background of the Butoku-kai, taking as the basis of the examination facts that have come direct from the dossiers of various Federal intelligence services.

On September 27, 1929, a Japanese named Tekichi Nakamura arrived in Los Angeles from Hawaii. He posed as a Korean. Intelligence operatives became suspicious of him, however, when he fraternized exclusively with Japanese. A check-up disclosed that he had once been a bandit leader in Manchuria and that he was on very friendly terms in Japan with men high in the councils of the Black Dragons.

Nakamura returned to Japan in 1930, but came back to California the following year. He went once again to Japan, but this time intelligence operatives noticed that he was accompanied by fourteen Nisei—the same Nisei who were praised so highly in *Liberty*. Consular attachés of the American Government in the Orient kept an eye on the movements of Nakamura and his fourteen American friends and observed that, among other things, the Nisei worshiped at the Imperial Palace in Tokyo.

Two years later, in 1933, Nakamura visited the United States again, and took another party of fourteen American citizens of Japanese ancestry to Tokyo. This time an American consular agent who understood the Japanese language heard one of Nakamura's California friends saying, during a public speech in Tokyo: "We, in whose veins flow the blood of the valiant Japanese people, must throw off the American atmosphere and learn the spirit of Japan's Way of the Warrior."

During his visits to the United States, Nakamura collected funds for the establishment of an institution that began functioning in Tokyo in 1938. The name conferred on it was the North American College of the Imperial Way, and its prime objective was the instruction of Japanese-Americans sent from the United States.

As a result of Nakamura's work, branches of the Butoku-kai were established up and down the Pacific Coast. From time to time, intelligence observers saw the Japanese-Americans about whom Mrs. Oyama spoke so glowingly at secret meetings from Oregon to San Diego. Japanese flags were always much in evidence at these gatherings. A pamphlet was handed out one day in 1938 by the leader of the Seattle branch of the Butoku-kai, a copy of which was finally obtained by an F.B.I. man. The pamphlet said in part:

Your problem is much more intricate than it appears to be because you have as your parents subjects of our Japanese Empire which is struggling for the top rank amongst the great powers of the world. The causes of Japan's foreign wars are unavoidable but America's wars are based on her own ambition so that there is a great difference between them.

When it was learned that the sponsors of the North American College of the Imperial Way in Tokyo included such people as Mitsura Toyama, head of the Black Dragon Society, ten admirals in the Japanese Navy, twenty-one generals in the Japanese Army and almost one hundred prominent Japanese political figures, the true character of Butoku-kai was not to be questioned. There was a constant scurrying back and forth between the Pacific Coast and the Orient of some of the most prominent Nisei born in California. Many of these supposedly loyal Americans were actually seen by American agents in the Orient in personal contact with Toyama, the head of the Black Dragons.

While the Butoku-kai was primarily a Nisei organization, some of its officers were alien Japanese. In 1935, for example, Tomokazu Hori, the Japanese Consul in Los Angeles at the time, became the president of the Los Angeles branches of the organization. What sort of ideas Consul Hori inculcated at Nisei meetings can best be judged by what was learned about him after Pearl Harbor, at which time he had long since been back in Japan. Hori now broadcasts propaganda from Tokyo for domestic consumption. On April 23, 1943, American listening posts that picked him up on short-wave noticed that he was in high humor. His broadcast on that day was devoted to gloating over the execution of the American flyers who were captured after the Doolittle raid on Tokyo. This was the same man who was looked up to by Los Angeles Nisei, and some of these Nisei have been discharged from relocation centers and are among us today.

There is no need to speculate about Japanese who have been released from relocation centers. The bare facts are alarming enough. In June, 1943, after quite a number of Japanese had been released from the relocation center at Poston, Arizona, Ralph F. Stringfellow, a special agent guarding Parker Dam, which is near the Poston center, discovered that three hundred and fifty pounds of dynamite and more than one hundred fulminite of mercury caps had vanished from a government warehouse at the dam. These sticks of dynamite were too large even for ordinary mining purposes, but ideal for sabotage. When the theft of the dynamite was discovered it was recalled that a few months prior to the outbreak of war between the United States and Japan, not one but two groups of Japanese engineers had received official permission to visit and inspect the dam. Parker Dam diverts water into the Colorado River aqueduct, which supplies more than one-half of the water for Los Angeles and other Southern California communities; the dam is in addition an important source of electric power. The stolen dynamite has never been located, and it is only reasonable to suppose that whoever stole it is awaiting only the chance to slip through the ring of vigilance around the dam and commit a major act of sabotage.

The theft of the dynamite from the strategic point in Arizona is by no means the only case of its kind; rather, it is illustrative of similar incidents by the score which cannot be commented on at this time.

There are three different kinds of leaves that the W.R.A. has been giving to Japanese. The first is the indefinite leave, which carries no limitations except that the released person must remain outside of military areas. Second, there is the short-term leave, by which an evacuee is permitted to leave a relocation area for a limited period, not to exceed thirty days. The third type of leave is the one relating to seasonal work. Sabotage could easily be perpetrated during any one of the three kinds of leaves.

As of July 6, 1943, there were almost ten thousand Japanese out of relocation centers on indefinite leaves, and another five thousand on seasonal leaves. At that time approximately one thousand Japanese were being released each week. According to the admission of Director Myer himself, of the W.R.A., *fifteen out of every hundred Japanese being released were aliens.*

You may be sure that among those who were not moved to tears by Mrs. Oyama's article in *Liberty* was J. Edgar Hoover. A large portion of the American public is under the impression that the F.B.I. gets a chance to make a thorough check-up on the Japanese who are released from the relocation centers. *This impression is distinctly false.* It was brought about by an erroneous statement made by a W.R.A. official, and later denied by both the W.R.A. and the F.B.I. The most that has ever been done to get the benefit of the F.B.I.'s slant on an evacuee about to be released is that the W.R.A. has inquired whether the F.B.I. has a criminal record on the evacuee. In April, 1943, the W.R.A. "liberalized" its program for releasing evacuees by ceasing to consult the F.B.I. at all in regard to most of the Japanese who were released.

Certainly the W.R.A. must be acquainted with certain discoveries that were made after Pearl Harbor. For example, there was the tunnel that ran underneath a Japanese florist shop on Wilshire Boulevard in Los Angeles to a point three quarters of a mile away. The tunnel was stocked with hundreds of thousands of dollars' worth of weapons and ammunition for the Japanese Fifth Column in Los Angeles. Inasmuch as it must have taken years to secretly excavate that tunnel (it was about six feet in height and four in width) and inasmuch as the tunnel wasn't discovered until after Pearl Harbor, it is only reasonable to suppose that there may be some others like it, undiscovered and still stocked.

What do you suppose would happen if enough Japs released by the W.R.A. got together and succeeded in reaching such a place?

When Pearl Harbor Day arrived, the various intelligence services had a total of thirteen hundred dangerous Japanese under surveillance. These people were picked off very quickly. But there were other Japanese, unquestionably just as dangerous, in the tens of thousands who were automatically taken out of circulation. These men have proved, time and time again, how dangerous they really are by starting riots in relocation centres. As late as the summer of 1943 some of these bad ones were virtually in control of the relocation centre at Poston, Arizona—and the Army had to move in.

Isn't it only logical that some of the Japanese who are now being released—particularly the aliens—are just as dangerous, but smart enough not to show their feelings until they can make an expression of feeling really count, by, for instance, an act of sabotage? These men wouldn't think twice about getting caught. That wouldn't mean a thing to them so long as their sabotage had been committed. Their supreme pleasure would be to die for their country.

This book does not attempt a solution of the difficult problem posed in this last chapter—that is not its province. It presents a picture—by facts. It is a picture of a situation definitely dangerous, now, to the American public, to all of us. And, incredibly, a situation *allowed* to be dangerous.

Sentimentality will not help at all—more than that, it is itself a part of the menace, for sentimentality toward a terrible potential evil may be as vicious in its results as the active treachery at work against us. And, oddly enough, those whose way of handling a situation is by sentimentality seem to have such small minds that the only alternative seems to them to be cruelty. They must be "kind"—and blind—to all Nisei indiscriminately, and to Issei too.

We have no use for cruel treatment; we have no use for sentimental treatment. Instead, there is such a thing as clear-headedness, as being alive to the truth and the danger, as being willing to see evil, to face it, and to act against it.

We are far more truthful in our picture of the Nisei situation if, recognizing the loyalty and goodness of *some* Nisei and being eternally glad for it, we are also willing to expose the evil that is among them. In fact, it isn't at all clear how Nisei really loyal to America can wish otherwise than to have that evil exposed, and acted on. And as for Americans who are really loyal—who would rather help their country than harm it—well, stupidity can bring as terrible results as disloyalty.

We have in this book told some of the reasons why Pearl Harbor happened—and why it need not have happened. We have set forth in this last chapter why another catastrophe may be ahead. What will the excuse be then?

Before the last shot of the war has been fired, there may be a slogan to supplant "Remember Pearl Harbor!" If certain arch-fiends at large in the United States this very minute—at large by the grace of men in government jobs who have displayed criminal stupidity—get the chance to carry out what they have long planned, the new slogan may well be: "Remember the W.R.A.!"